Human Rights in the
Post-9/11 World

Human Rights in the Post-9/11 World

Bethany Barratt, editor

International Debate Education Association

New York, London & Amsterdam

Published by
The International Debate Education Association
105 East 22nd Street
New York, NY 10010

Library of Congress Cataloging-in-Publication Data
Human rights in the post-9/11 world/Bethany Barratt, editor.
    pages cm
    ISBN 978-1-61770-072-9
    1. Human rights. 2. International relations. 3. Terrorism—
Prevention. I. Barratt, Bethany.
    JC571.H769545 2013
    323—dc23   2012045495

Composition by Brad Walrod/Kenoza Type, Inc.
Printed in the USA

 IDEBATE Press

Contents

ACKNOWLEDGMENTS

In 2010, the human rights sections of the American Political Science Association, the International Studies Association, and the International Political Science Association, collaborated for the first time on an international conference. Held at Roosevelt University in Chicago, Illinois, the theme was Human Rights Nine Years After 9/11. The rich exchange of ideas that resulted led to the regular scheduling of such conferences biennially. These ideas and insights did not, however, immediately lend themselves to being organized into a single volume. I was grateful, therefore, when two years later I was approached by Eleanora von Dehsen of the Open Society Foundations about editing a sourcebook on the impact of 9/11 and its aftermath on international human rights. This was an opportunity to revisit some of the arguments made by conference participants and to survey the terrain of the international human rights regime in a way that was accessible to a more general audience.

Boundless thanks go to the many authors and editors who so generously agreed to the reprinting of work in this volume and displayed great forbearance in allowing me to substantially edit down their work. Alison Swety and Bruce Lockwood at Johns Hopkins, the publisher of *Human Rights Quarterly*, as well as the publishers of the *Journal of Politics and the Behavioral Sciences* and the *Denver Journal of International Law*, were especially kind in granting permissions gratis. Eleanora von Dehsen and Martin Greenwald of the Open Society Foundations were wonderfully patient with me when, already a couple of weeks behind schedule, I had to take several weeks off the project. Anthony Guerrerro, my former graduate assistant, was instrumental in the review of original literature; his successor, Nela Taskovska, not only wrote the introduction to Part 4 and compiled the appendix, but also formatted the entire work and double-checked my edits against the original texts, often working late into the night. Finally, I am grateful for the support of the Joseph Loundy Human Rights Center at Roosevelt University, which was the host of the 2010 conference, the State of Human Rights Nine Years After 9/11, that was the starting point for this work.

Introduction

When hijackers working for the international terrorist organization known as Al Qaeda flew passenger planes into the World Trade Center and Pentagon, and attempted to fly another into a second Washington target, the world witnessed an event that was in many ways unprecedented. Not only was this by far the deadliest terrorist attack to date on U.S. soil, but the methods used by the terrorists, which had largely been unanticipated by the U.S. national security community, seemed to call for a response that was unprecedented as well.

Because so many elements of the events of 9/11 were unexpected—the use of passenger planes as weapons of mass destruction, the ability of the terrorists to carry out a lengthy and detailed planning process on U.S. soil undetected, the terrorists' overwhelming success in penetrating the heart of the U.S. financial and political infrastructure—policymakers believed it prudent to revisit many long-standing assumptions about the way the world worked. Because the hijackers had lived for months in the United States, much closer monitoring of immigrant communities was deemed appropriate. Because they had succeeded in wresting control of the planes with very primitive weaponry, all commercial airline passengers now needed to be screened in greater detail than ever before. Because Osama bin Laden had succeeded in directing an operation of this scope from a remote and mysterious location in Afghanistan, the Bush administration deemed it appropriate not only to attempt to penetrate arguably impenetrable terrain abroad but also to cut off the financial support bin Laden enjoyed from state sponsors of terrorism (those who provide covert financial support to terrorist organizations). When all else failed, those state sponsors would be held responsible for failing to stop those who operated on their soil or with their tacit—or active—support. And, because the War on Terror was a new kind of war, with a new kind of enemy, a less visible enemy, it was hard to know when victory had been achieved. Therefore, suspected "enemy combatants"—those who were arrested on suspicion of aiding terrorist organizations either within the United States or abroad—would be held for an indeterminate time and subjected to treatment from which those captured in wartime are usually protected.

The Bush administration also successfully sought to establish new legal powers that it argued were necessary to fight a new kind of war—one against a non-state actor rather than a traditional nation-state (the kind of conflict that most existing laws of war deal with). The most comprehensive of these attempts was the lengthy USA-PATRIOT Act, hastily passed by Congress on October 26, 2001. While many of the act's provisions have either expired or been declared unconstitutional, some are still in force and, in fact, have been renewed by Pres. Barack Obama. Almost all of the act's most controversial provisions affect, or potentially affect, important human rights.

For example, one section of the act allowed access to individuals' library records and online search and purchase histories—access that was argued by some to be at odds with the implied right to privacy protected by the Constitution of the United States and in the constitutions of many other nations. Another provision affected privacy: the wiretapping of individuals with no criminal records or known links to terrorist organizations. Another controversial section allowed for the indefinite detention of enemy combatants. The indefinite detention provision can violate an individual's right to habeas corpus (literally "I have the body"; it mandates that when a suspect is arrested, evidence of the alleged crime must be produced in a reasonable amount of time). So, too, did the related Military Commissions Act of 2005, which allowed such suspects to be denied access to the evidence that formed the basis for their arrest and detention. Perhaps most dramatic of all was the secret authorization by the Bush administration Justice Department of the practice known as "waterboarding" and other coercive interrogation techniques that many observers argue are forms of torture and therefore infringe upon an individual's right to bodily integrity.

The Bush administration justified many of these actions by arguing that terror had heretofore been understood in an incomplete way. Early antiterror laws, especially those developed during the Clinton administration, were modeled on laws to combat organized crime. To an extent, then, terror was treated as a special sort of organized crime, and it was combatted using methods that were conventionally accepted for crime fighting. The Bush administration argued that this understanding was partly to blame for the country's unpreparedness for the 9/11 attacks. What the Bush administration argued was that we needed to understand terror as *war*. The phrase "War on Terror" was not merely semantic construct— terrorist organizations were now going to be approached as military targets.

To be sure, this was a new kind of war. Throughout human history, war has been fought between nation-states or similar political entities. Terrorist organizations (defined in Section 22 of U.S. Code [of Laws] as organizations that operate outside the officially constituted military of a state and that pursues political means through violence aimed at civilians) were a slipperier target than nation-states—they may not have the same reliable sources of manpower or money, but they also lacked the vulnerabilities of nation-states: identifiable territory and a civilian population. But the administration and its supporters argued that new technologies, especially virtual communications and access to weapons of mass destruction, have enabled terrorist organizations to credibly threaten nation-states. This is "asymmetrical warfare" (in which opposing groups have unequal military resources), they argue, but warfare nonetheless.

The legal significance of reclassifying the current terrorist threat as a "war" is that it provided justification for the United States to suspend or at least curtail certain individual rights when it could argue this action enhanced collective or national security. This is a recognized principle that is incorporated in even the most capacious international human rights laws.

THE CONCEPT HUMAN RIGHTS

The U.S. response to the 9/11 attacks raised crucial questions throughout the international community about core values that had been emerging and becoming institutionalized over the course of the last several centuries. These values have ancient roots, but their terminology, and the international structures and processes that support them, are primarily the products of the twentieth century. While the term "human rights" had been used before World War II, it was the horrors of that war that gave it real traction. The international community, particularly in the context of the nascent UN system, was determined to do all it could to institutionalize prohibitions on the worst extremes of suffering—the kind produced by the Nazi concentration camps, the atomic bomb, and the fire-bombings of cities such as Tokyo and Dresden.

With the approval of the entire UN, a select committee, headed by Eleanor Roosevelt, worked over the course of several months and many rounds of revisions to draft an exhaustive list of rights that, according to Article 2 of the resulting document, the Universal Declaration of Human Rights, "Everyone is entitled to ... without distinction of any kind, such as race, color, sex, language, religion, political or other opinion, national or social origin, property, birth or other status. Furthermore, no distinction shall be made on the basis of the ... country or territory to which a person belongs." These rights, therefore, were to be protected for all persons, not by virtue of their citizenship of a given country, but by virtue of their membership in the human race. They were, to use the word that would come to capture this quality, "universal."

The list, which has become the touchstone for much of the international human rights advocacy movement, includes individual liberties like those enshrined in the U.S. Constitution, the English Bill of Rights, and the French Declaration of the Rights of Man and the Citizen. These include guarantees of individual liberties that cannot be infringed on by government, such as freedom of speech, religion, press, and assembly, and access to due process of law. But the Declaration also includes rights that go far further, implying substantial obligation on the part of states to provide for certain basic needs of their peoples. These include, for instance, the rights to education, basic health care, shelter, employment, a decent wage, and leisure. The Declaration's drafters included these rights on the premise that, without them, the kind of individual liberties described above could not be fully realized.

While the international community has not been in complete concert about the interpretation of some of these economic and social rights, individual liberties along with what have been called "personal integrity rights" (right not to be tortured or extrajudicially killed or imprisoned; right to physical safety) have enjoyed nearly universal assent in the international community, at least in word (if not, often, in deed). Therefore, these are the kind of rights that, when violated, tend to provoke the most widespread outcry in the international community.

One of the reasons that the Bush administration wanted to be clear that terrorism was a form of warfare is that both written and customary (informal) international laws allow states to suspend some of these rights *temporarily* in moments of national crisis. The administration not only argued that terror suspects' rights could be abridged up to a point because of the exigencies of war, but also that such suspects did not necessarily enjoy the protection of the Geneva Conventions (discussed below), which guarantee certain rights of individuals in wartime. These two positions, many critics argued, were mutually contradictory. Additionally, the United States was in a particularly vulnerable position as a target of accusations of human right violations because it had made such accusations against its rivals so frequently in the latter half of the twentieth century (not always without merit).

THE CONCEPT AND PRACTICE OF HUMAN RIGHTS
IN HISTORICAL PERSPECTIVE

Although the language of human rights is modern, the potential conflict between security and liberty is not new.

A review of U.S. history might suggest that security and rights have always been assumed to be in tension. Many of the earliest writings by American political philosophers demonstrate widespread acceptance of at least some restraints on personal liberty in the name of order. Thomas Jefferson, Thomas Paine, and

Benjamin Franklin all were heavily influenced by the English political philosopher John Locke, whose *Second Treatise on Government* (1690) explicitly contrasts the purpose of government with the state of nature—government can only protect and promote natural rights (life, liberty, property) by restricting individuals' ability to interfere with one anothers' natural rights. Having passed the Alien and Sedition Acts of 1798, following mounting tensions with France, the U.S. Congress sought to use those laws to ascertain the origin of immigrants into the new United States with the ultimate goal of identifying possible sympathizers and monitoring distribution of libelous or treasonous material. The Alien and Sedition Acts made explicit that the very rights and liberties that impelled revolution against England were, in fact, suspendable when the survival of the new country was at stake. Similarly, many have called Abraham Lincoln a hypocrite because of his broad suspension of basic rights and liberties, including habeas corpus. During a period of pronounced labor unrest during the late 1910s and early 1920s, the "Red scares" saw a widespread rise in fear of leftist tendencies and culminated in raids (the Palmer Raids) on groups that were often doing nothing more than exercising their right to free speech.

One of the most concrete and indiscriminate policies that suspended basic human rights in the name of security was Executive Order 9066, issued in 1942 by Pres. Franklin Roosevelt. Order 9066 ordered the removal to isolated camps of Americans of Japanese ancestry from large areas of the United States, depriving them of their rights to freedom of movement, of assembly, and to property, among others. These episodes, the witch hunts of McCarthyism during the Cold War, and countless other examples all illustrate that perceived national peril has often led policymakers to suggest and implement undemocratic, and sometimes inhumane, policies that fly in the face of the very democratic values that they also claim to defend. In the U.S.-led offensive against "terrorism," we can see similar processes at work.

The Emergence of a Global Recognition of Human Rights

The War on Terror has played out against an international context in which the idea of human rights institutionalized after World War II has grown in breadth of acceptance and degree of implementation. The concept of human rights has matured into what scholars of international politics refer to as a "regime"—core values about a particular issue wedded to norms (unwritten rules of behavior), structures, and laws. Most of the cases in the foregoing section date from well before the consolidation of the international human rights regime. In contrast, this volume's contributors are responding explicitly to the effects of the War on

Terror on the set of institutions and norms that have been established over the course of the last several decades.

The spread of this regime has been encouraged by the more general process of globalization. In an increasingly interconnected world, many theorists and policymakers argue that global problems can only be solved by global solutions. The only way to reach global solutions is through an understanding of the common interests shared by all people, regardless of religion, race, nationality, or culture. It is this sense of commonality and equality that is the bedrock of the modern concept of human rights, as well as being the driving force behind the creation of the laws and organizations that monitor and promote states' protections of these rights.

The international organizations and treaties that support human rights—most notably the UN and the documents, treaties, and bodies that have emerged from it, but including nongovernmental organizations (NGOs—whose members are individuals, rather than states) as well—have also been facilitated by technological improvements in communication and transportation. We live in an era in which the citizens of most nations have more direct access to information about the actions of their government than ever before. They also have more direct means of expressing their opinions about these actions. Therefore, inconsistencies and atrocities arguably have greater *potential* to be exposed than at any time in the past.

Of importance, one need not be an altruist to believe in protecting and preserving human rights both at home and abroad. Observers such as Kenneth Roth (president of the NGO Human Rights Watch) have argued that promoting human rights around the world makes other nations less prone to go to war, better trading partners, and more likely to respect democratic ideals—and therefore to cooperate in a global system that supports these kinds of values.

Over time, the tendency is for regimes to become further institutionalized and for what were once aspirations to become expectations, sometimes tied to clear material incentives. However, in times of crisis, regimes can erode. Since 9/11, many observers have watched anxiously for signs of erosion or resilience in the young human rights regime.

HUMAN RIGHTS AND WAR IN INTERNATIONAL LAW

While the current elucidation of "human rights" may be new, the understanding of the need to curb the excesses of war is not—in fact, quite the opposite. The very oldest international laws are the laws of war. The code of Hammurabi, for instance, dating to the first large-scale state of which we have a record (18th c.

BCE), forbids certain kinds of actions by soldiers in wartime, including gratuitous violence that would lead to a more difficult peace process later. It was only sensible that nations engaged in as costly and dangerous an endeavor as war would want to minimize physical and economic damage to themselves. In addition, utterly destroying an enemy is often self-defeating, leaving less to plunder or otherwise exploit in the future. Therefore, increasing predictability and minimizing needless destruction were goals all nations had a stake in promoting. While the best known laws of war today are likely the Geneva Conventions—protecting noncombatants and guaranteeing shelter, sustenance, medical care, and access to religious counsel for prisoners of war, the wounded and sick on the battlefield and the wounded, sick, or shipwrecked at sea—there are many others.[1] Together, they formalize many of the "customary laws" of war that have existed for generations. (Again, customary laws are those that are generally but informally agreed upon by most nations and by which nations are considered to be bound).

The most important of the principles of customary law may be classed as either *jus ad bellum,* or *jus in bello* (just causes of war and just conduct of war, respectively). Just reasons for declaration of war are commonly understood to include self-defense and the establishment of a longer-term peace. A war that is justly declared should also be a last resort (other means of settling the dispute should be tried first) and must be declared by a legitimate authority (in most cases, the duly chosen leadership of a nation-state). The principles of just conduct are, naturally, a bit more complicated. One is the humane treatment of civilians, prisoners of war, and the wounded or sick on the battlefield or at sea. A second is the sincere attempt to discriminate between combatants and noncombatants. A third is proportionality: an action should be met only with a proportional response, and, in addition, only proportionate force should be used in an attempt to gain a given target.

For even this brief sketch, we can see that these principles were developed around a definition of warfare that may not be met by the global War on Terror. The Bush administration's redefinition of war to include non-state actors like terrorist organizations was (though not without debate) accepted and adopted in other parts of the international community as well, especially by powerful U.S. allies like the United Kingdom. Most international organizations, however, have eschewed a formal stance.

VOLUME OVERVIEW

Part 1: 9/11 and Warfare presents perspectives on the significance of this definitional shift, and of the U.S. dominance of the dialogue around terror in the immediate post-9/11 era. In "Human Rights and Changing Definitions of Warfare," Veena Das argues that Bush administration rhetoric after 9/11 "privileged the experience of North Americans as unique,"[2] existing outside of the context in which many other countries had functioned for decades. Das argues that the response of the Bush administration and its allies has threatened to make counterterrorism the single guiding principle in foreign policy and to recast the human rights dialogue as simply another form of domestic security.

If the War on Terror is war, then logically we might expect the laws of war to apply. In what human rights theorist Michael Goodhart (2010) has described as the most recent incarnation of American exceptionalism, the Bush regime parted ways with the international community and with several millennia of history when it argued that the Geneva Conventions (which, again, codify customary international law) did not apply to accused terrorists because, rather than combatants in the service of a regularly constituted national military, they were "enemy combatants" that lacked the sanction of an official state apparatus. Therefore, argued the Bush administration Justice Department, the safeguards guaranteed by the Geneva Conventions did not apply to suspected terrorists.

What rights, then, did these suspects have? Administration rhetoric challenged the concept that any rights were universal. For the first time, the United States had captured and was preparing to try persons whose status was entirely unclear under international law. In the reasoning of the Bush administration, this necessitated the development of a new set of rules. More important for international law, what had been created was a set of persons who lacked both the protections states afford their own citizens and the protections international law accords combatants in war. According to John Ellis van Courtland Moon in "The Death of Distinctions: From 9/11 to Abu Ghraib," conceptualizing our adversaries as undeserving of basic human protections is in large part the consequence of humankind's evolving ability to inflict destruction remotely. We no longer have to consider the fact that the enemy is in many ways like us, let alone imagine the destruction and pain we might be inflicting on them. Moon argues that the War on Terror and its semantic shifts have further served to end two important distinctions. The first delineation that has been removed is that between prevention (responding to an imminent threat) and preemption (acting to remove future potential threats). The second distinction that has been discarded is even more essential from a human rights standpoint: the line between interrogation and torture. Such distinctions, he argues, have thus far been crucial to mitigating some of the worst horrors that humankind has wrought against itself, thus their "death" must thus be taken seriously.

It is in this breach—this lack of any clear law protecting "enemy combatants"—that the crucial need for international human rights laws becomes clear. For this reason, and because of the Bush administration's treatment of human rights as highly contingent, many have felt compelled to weigh in on the status of the still-young human rights regime and the principles it embodies.

Therefore, Part 2: 9/11's Impact on International Law addresses the larger effect of the responses to 9/11 on international law. At home, the U.S. Supreme Court declared many components of the counterterror response to be unlawful on the basis of their violation of basic rights and freedoms. In *Hamdan vs. Rumsfeld*, the Court declared that several key sections of the 2006 Military Commissions Act were unconstitutional, violating habeas corpus and other due process protections, including the right to speedy trial and protection against unlawful detention. In so doing, the Court effectively declared persons accused under the act to have rights regardless of citizenship or combatant status. This has two possible implications, both of which support the legitimacy and applicability of the international laws of war. First, if the accused have been detained as combatants during wartime, they are accorded all rights and protections of the Geneva Conventions. Second, outside of the laws of war, some rights and freedoms are retained by all persons, regardless of their national, or combatant, status. This is commensurate with the crucial principle of universality. However, as Adrian Jones and Rhoda Howard-Hassman ably document in "Under Strain: Human Rights and International Law in the Post 9/11 Era," the Bush Administration was quite willing to disregard many informal principles of international jurisprudence as well as very specific laws. Besides the Geneva Conventions, these included the right of habeus corpus, the (imputed) right to privacy, the right to bodily integrity, and the protected status of noncombatants.

As the full content and implications of the Bush Administration approach became clear, first shock and then outcry began to come from all sectors of the international community—from both official and unofficial sources within allied states (even while they were, in some cases, secretly cooperating with US rendition plans), from international legal venues, and from civil society. Over time, as it became clear that ignoring the principles of international relations left it isolated internationally, the Administration eventually resorted to reinterpreting international law and redefining some of its most essential terms to suit the Administration's own ends. Many of the most experienced observers of human rights in foreign policy, including Jones and Howard-Hassman, have watched with growing alarm the US willingness to sacrifice for short-term vengeance the principles that protect not only Americans, but innocent people the world over.

In "International Human Rights Law and the War on Terrorism," Derek Jinks contributes to the mounting evidence that 9/11 created significant and long-term change in the perceived (and therefore actual) effectiveness of the international legal system protecting human rights and liberties. "Freedom of movement" and "right to privacy" were treated by the Administration and its allies as though their connotations were necessarily negative. Based on the these questionable redefinitions, the Administration's War on Terror wrought several changes to both domestic and international law whose full implications are only becoming fully clear over a decade later.

These changes revealed that the Administration was not treating this new war like other wars, for it was neither invoking nor applying the laws of war, but neither was it affording suspects the protections that citizens would enjoy against excessive use of force by domestic security forces. So what kind of law governs this new kind of war? A hybrid of the two legal systems? Neither? Jinks believes that there is an obvious body of law that would provide guidance to make certain that short term reactiveness did not jeopardise long term safety: human rights law. This would "establish conclusively . . . that all persons subject to the jurisdiction of the United States . . . are entitled to certain basic rights"[3]—almost all of which have been violated by the Bush administration.

A contrasting perspective is provided by David Forsythe, who (in "The United States and International Humanitarian Law") argues that events since 9/11 have simply represented a continuation of longstanding U.S. ambivalence toward both human rights and international law since at least the mid-20th century. The Bush Administration's cavalier attitude toward violating universally recognized laws and principles is the logical outgrowth of an American exceptionalism that has increasingly looked like hubris. Although the United States was the driving force behind the creation of the current international human rights regime, rather than lead by example it has increasingly portrayed itself as outside or above that regime. Forsythe also cautions that the foreign policy making apparatus should not be treated as a single entity, but that there may be potential for more just and rational approaches to gain primacy if we pay attention to dissenting voices in, for instance, the military and the intelligence community.

Part 3: Freedom from Terror: Should It Trump Other Rights and Freedoms? attempts to deconstruct the Bush administration's claim that "Freedom from Terror" is a right that can be ranked in importance alongside other fundamental rights and freedoms. In "Human Rights and Terrorism," Paul Hoffman, chair of the International Executive Committee of Amnesty International, constructs a detailed litany of the (almost entirely negative) impacts that the

War on Terror has had on other rights and freedoms. Miroslav Nincic and Jennifer Ramos (in "Torture in the Public Mind") demonstrate that the extreme measures embraced by the Bush administration fly in the face of long-standing public support for rights in the United States, and that most people are firmly opposed to the most extreme forms of the administration's disregard for rights. In "'The Empire Strikes Back': The US Assault on the International Human Rights Regime," Rhonda Callaway and Julie Harrelson-Stephens argue that, in contrast, it is the ideological coherence of the human rights regime that has made it resilient both in the face of flagging support of powerful actors like the United States and to the real threats posed around the globe by international terrorist organizations.

Finally, Part 4: Human Rights and International Organizations examines responses to post-9/11 challenges to human rights by international organizations, both organizations of states and organizations of individuals. Rosemary Foot ("The United Nations, Counter Terrorism, and Human Rights: Institutional Adaptation and Embedded Ideas") takes us behind the doors of the UN Security Council Counter-Terrorism Committee and reveals a troubling double standard at work—most counterterror measures are ultimately justified by their contribution to national security, but we must increasingly wonder whether that security should be preserved if it simply serves to secure an undemocratic state. For it is this kind of state that ultimately some counterterror measures risk creating. Finally, Hans Peter Schmitz ("Transnational NGOs and Human Rights in a Post-9/11 World") traces the geneology of the modern human rights movement to give us a more complete context for understanding how and why 9/11 and its aftermath have affected the human rights movement as a whole, and specific NGOs, in very distinct ways. Both authors emphasize that, despite all the incursions to human rights and freedoms since the declaration of the War on Terror, their effects would have been far worse and far more persistent were it not for the work of global civil society.

This volume, then, explores the net impact on the international human rights regime of not only the attacks of 9/11 but also the new era of which they are symbolic. This era is characterized by the truly global reach of international terrorist organizations and also by decisions faced by both states and international organizations: How likely is it that eroding human rights standards will defeat international terrorism, and how far should any such erosion go? They must also decide what respect to accord international law, particularly when the interests of immediate national security appear to conflict with those of long-term international justice.

NOTES

1. For instance, the Hague Conventions, the Chemical Weapons Convention, the Biological Weapons Convention, the Torture Convention, and the Treaty to Ban Landmines.

2. Veena Das, "Human Rights And Changing Definitions Of Warfare," *Journal Of Human Rights* 4, no.1 (2005): 113.

3. Derek Jinks, "International Human Rights Law and the War on Terrorism." *Denver Journal of International Law and Policy* 31, no.1 (2002): 58.

Part 1:
9/11 and Warfare

The oldest international laws—which date from almost the dawn of recorded history—aim to mitigate the impact of warfare on human welfare. These laws aim to:

1. Distinguish combatants from noncombatants, and protect the latter
2. Ensure that military, not civilian, structures and institutions are the primary targets of military exercises
3. Ensure that disproportionate force is not used
4. Protect the sick, wounded, and shipwrecked
5. Protect the basic rights of prisoners of war

Despite the increasing institutionalization of these principles (through the Geneva Conventions and similar international laws), civilians and civilian structures have, over time, become more likely, not less likely, to be casualties of war.

Why this paradoxical result? As warfare has steadily become deadlier, the proportion of civilian casualties (often referred to as "collateral damage") to military casualties has climbed. Technological developments over the last several centuries, such as increasingly accurate and long-range remote targeting capabilities, and greater availability and reach of weapons of mass destruction, have tended to make it more, not less, difficult to distinguish combatants from noncombatants—whether because of the sheer scope of the damage or the remoteness of the target from the initiator. Unconventional warfare, as well as the actions commonly considered "terrorism," rely in part on nonidentification of combatants—the initiators aim to remain difficult to identify, and sometimes also purposely target civilians to send a political message. John Ellis van Courtland Moon ("The Death of Distinctions") documents these trajectories that have led to inherently more unjust war and warns of dangerous future scenarios. Veena Das ("Human Rights and Changing Definitions of Warfare") demonstrates that the United States has exacerbated all of these problems by claiming that only a global war is an adequate response to the 9/11 attacks. She fears the term "human rights" is being reconstrued in a much narrower way that gives precedence not to the security of people but to the security of states.

As you read the articles in this section, consider the following:

1. Das spends some time considering the risk assessment the U.S. government undertook after 9/11. Was this assessment undertaken with due diligence? What should the criteria be for determining when such an assessment has been adequately performed?

2. What other human rights might be negatively affected by armed conflict outside of the basic risks to human life?

3. Why is it important to distinguish civilian from military targets (both for the offensive party and the defensive party)? What are the most important ways, historically, this distinction has been made?

4. Does remote targeting, including drone strikes, change the way that combatants using these techniques think about war? As an analogy, you might imagine the difference between stabbing a potential assailant and shooting her at a distance of 20 or 30 yards. Would one be easier than the other?

5. What is the difference between preemption and prevention, and why is this distinction important—for both the offensive and defensive parties?

The Death of Distinctions: From 9/11 to Abu Ghraib

*by John Ellis van Courtland Moon**

On 11 September 2001, "9/11," *al Qaeda* suicide skyjackers attacked the American homeland, crashing two airliners into the Twin Towers of New York City's World Trade Center and one airliner into the Pentagon. The Twin Towers collapsed; a wing of the Pentagon was heavily damaged. Over three thousand people were killed. Shortly afterwards, a series of anthrax-laden letters was addressed to news-media centers and political leaders, causing five collateral fatalities and a degree of panic. Walls of security that Americans imagined protected them from overseas adversaries—an illusion reinforced by the end of the Cold War—crumpled into the dust of destroyed buildings. America was under attack by invisible enemies.

The destruction of the Twin Towers led to massive demonstrations of patriotism. The psychological mobilization of the nation was spontaneous, cutting across ethnic groups and sweeping from its retaliatory path all but ideologically confirmed pacifists. Mobilization brought overwhelming support for the President of the United States, George W. Bush. In the eyes of his fellow citizens, President Bush became the heroic protector-avenger.

In this article, I follow the road that led from 9/11 to Abu Ghraib: how "the Bush Doctrine" blurred the difference between just and unjust wars, how it eroded the distinction between preemptive and preventive war, how it dehumanized enemy combatants, thereby leading to torture at Iraq's Abu Ghraib prison and other detention centers. Finally, I propose that 9/11 evoked atavistic echoes— fears and loyalties that led to unforeseen consequences blighting the idealism and unity of the immediate aftermath—and, more generally, that such echoes speak to us of survival challenges that long ago shaped our ancestors' environment of evolutionary adaptation.

THE BUSH DOCTRINE

On 20 September 2001, President Bush challenged all terrorist networks, proclaimed a new and putatively universal war against them, and initiated a military doctrine that would lead—or allow—the United States to initiate a "preventive" war in Iraq:

Americans should not expect one battle but a lengthy campaign...We will starve terrorists of funding, turn them against one another, drive them from place to place, until there is no refuge or no rest. And we will pursue nations that provide aid or safe haven to terrorism. Every nation in every region, now has a decision to make. Either you are with us, or you are with the terrorists[1].

The first act of this counteroffensive was an attack against the Taliban and *al Qaeda* in Afghanistan, an attack for which the President won strong support throughout the nation and the world. The second act, the invasion of Iraq in March 2003, divided the nation and was opposed by some of America's long-standing allies. Several consequences of this invasion were unexpected. One was an insurgency throughout nearly all occupied territory. One year later, the President, under electoral pressure, had to reaffirm his vision of the "war against terror."

At a press conference on 13 April 2004, President Bush envisioned the war on Iraq as merely one act in a wider conflict. "We're at war. Iraq is a part of the war on terror. It is not the war on terror; it is a theater in the war on terror." The President depicted this conflict in absolute terms: a crusade fought in the name of freedom, which is "the Almighty's gift to every man and woman in this world"[2]. As the original justifications for the 2003 Iraq war unraveled, he wove his new narrative. The war was no longer justified on the grounds that Saddam Hussein had weapons of mass destruction and that a link had ever existed between *al Qaeda* and the Iraqi regime. Iraq did not pose a present danger to the United States; it posed a *future* danger. Distinctions between present and future dangers were discounted—even denied.

The 9/11 attacks and the wars that followed strengthened the powers of the presidency. All military actions reinforce the role of the President by invoking the Commander-in-Chief clause of the United States Constitution. Shortly after 9/11, the Deputy Assistant Attorney General of the Justice Department, John C. Yoo, stressed the scope of this power: "the Constitution vests the President with the power to strike terrorist groups or organizations that cannot be demonstrably linked to the September 11 incidents"[3].

According to memoranda issued by the Justice Department in the months that followed the 9/11 attacks, the President as Commander-in-Chief had plenary powers not only over the conduct of military operations but also over matters not closely connected with the direct management of the war. Treaties were no hindrance. As Jay S. Bybee, Assistant Attorney General, declared to Alberto R. Gonzales, Counsel to the President: "Under Article II of the Constitution, the President possesses the power to interpret treaties on behalf of the Nation"[4].

Earlier, Yoo had dismissed the imperatives of international customary law, recognized by most nations as binding governments to the observance of restraints in the conduct of war: "We conclude that customary international law...does not bind the President or restrict the actions of the United States military, because it does not constitute federal law recognized under the Supremacy Clause of the Constitution"[5, 6]. As I detail below, this assertion that powers of the President as Commander-in-Chief were almost unlimited had unforeseen and grievous consequences.

The death of distinctions kills truth. In the 2004 US election, the Republican campaign wove its narrative around the theme of the single enemy, terrorism, elevating George W. Bush as the leader capable of defeating it. War, the great simplifier, had once again created false distinctions while obliterating established ones, dismissing as universalist fantasy a reasonably functional reality: customary international law. As Karl von Clausewitz perceived, war gravitates towards *absolute* war, incrementally losing restrictions on the use of force, blurring the just war and the justification of means, the preemptive strike and the preventive war, the aggressor and the victim, the individual human and the dehumanized individual, the individual conscience and the imperatives of the state. War erodes distinctions for hawks and doves alike.

The current War on Terrorism, encompassing different conflicts under a single rubric, thereby eroding the subtleties of decision-making into a simplified stream of response, will stand as a case history of this phenomenon. In an amalgamation tenuously justified by 9/11, *al Qaeda*, Afghanistan, and Iraq—and others, named and unnamed—became *one* enemy. However, each conflict is basically different from all others. President Bush has centered on the image of one enemy and one war, but even the terrorist organizations among his adversaries are multinational and often disparate, activated by different motives, pursuing different goals. Fusing them into a single foe was a feat; splicing them together with regimes intent on self-preservation—the maintenance of their own power over their own subjects—was an astounding achievement, one that negated political distinctions among a multitude of foes. Making Iraq merely the immediate front in a general war has been quite a stunt.

A closer look reveals a more complex reality. According to Christian justification standards, dating from Augustine and particularly Aquinas, and international law, the war against *al Qaeda* is a just war. Osama bin Laden twice "declared war" against the United States by *fatwah*. Before 9/11, when American airspace was violated in a horrific terrorist strike, Americans and US property and interests were attacked repeatedly: in Somalia, at the World Trade Center in 1993, and at the US embassies in Kenya and Tanzania. In 1999, an American destroyer, the *Cole*, was struck off the coast of Yemen, killing 17 sailors. Before 9/11, though, bin Laden's declaration was dismissed as grandiose bluster.

ATTITUDES TOWARDS THE USE OF FORCE:
DOVES, HAWKS, AND REALISTS

The war against *al Qaeda* is a just war. Nonetheless, however just, war raises conflicting attitudes towards the use of force, attitudes reflected in the beliefs of doves (peace activists), hawks (warriors), and realists.

Doves, or at least the more fervent peace activists among them, make no distinctions between just and unjust wars. They also fail to note the distinction between just or necessary wars and the conduct of those wars. Focusing on the indisputable horror of the bombings which kill soldiers and civilians alike, they center their argument not on the causes of war but on the effects, such as the accidental killing of the innocent, which they see as unjustifiable. Although morally admirable, this position is politically and militarily indefensible. Governments must not pursue illusions of moral perfectionism. The prime responsibility of any government is the defense of its citizens. Moral forbearance and forgiveness are excellent qualities in an individual, but they are risky qualities in a government. If the nation it governs is attacked, a government must respond or endanger the existence of the nation itself. A conscientious government cannot forego retaliation, but a wise government will resist tendencies towards absolutist categorizations of its cause and its enemy, and it will exercise whatever restraints are possible in combat and victory. Governments can and *must* make distinctions between imminent threats and hypothetical threats, between real and imagined insecurity[7], and they must act on those distinctions.

In contrast, hawks resist any restriction of violence when used to counter violence. Once attacked, they argue any means, any weapon, is legitimate. The more force used, the sooner victory is achieved and suffering ended. Extreme hawks dismiss the laws of war as contradictions in terms.

Between these extremes, realists argue that violence limiting norms are functional if respected and that they should be respected almost always in almost any conflict. Based originally in medieval Christian just war theory and codified in international law, these norms have established restraints on the use of force: for example, certain weapons are prohibited even in retaliation. The codifiers of international law know that future wars are likely but are committed to restraining their effects by banning or limiting certain destructive means at combatants' disposal.

Nation-states recognize norms of war as desirable although not always observable due to the immense pressures and imperatives of combat. The use of nuclear weapons, not specifically prohibited by treaty, is condemned by customary law and by world public opinion. Chemical and biological weapons are condemned by treaty law as well. The targeting of innocent civilians, attacks on cultural or religious sites, and the killing of those who surrender are almost universally prohibited, although sometimes these moral restraints cannot rigidly be maintained against the imperatives of military action: a fortified city contains trapped civilians; a church or monastery may be used as a center of enemy resistance. Finally, in combat, a commander's prime military responsibility, fulfilling his mission while minimizing the sacrifice of his subordinates, makes other ethical responsibilities secondary. And even well disciplined troops occasionally violate the laws of war, as evidenced by the My Lai Massacre.

Some combatants, of course, do not recognize norms or laws or do not adhere to them. A prolonged conflict in particular weakens moral restraints and encourages a slide into the spiraling violence of overkill. At the beginning of World War II in Europe, the belligerents pledged themselves to spare civilian centers from strategic bombing. These moral restraints eroded as combat intensified. Moreover, opponents spin out justifications to defend actions previously thought indefensible. Rationalization subverts *jus in bello*. Finally, moral restraint typically has an *inverted* meaning for terrorists, since intimidation of the many by the few may most efficiently be accomplished by attacking randomly, cruelly, and, in a cynically calculated way, "senselessly."

International law holds that certain acts are so abhorrent that they cannot be justified even under combat pressure. It holds also that certain weapons—such as chemical and biological weapons but not, ironically, nuclear weapons—are so indiscriminate in their effects that using them makes any conflict unjust, no matter the cause, no matter the intention.

PREEMPTIVE VERSUS PREVENTIVE WAR

Against this historical and legal background, we can evaluate the policies of the George W. Bush Administration. The declaration of a "war against terrorism," a rhetorically exciting phrase, has had the unfortunate effect of blurring the distinction between the war in Afghanistan and the war in Iraq, between military operations and counter-criminal operations, between legitimate interrogation and torture.

The war in Afghanistan began as a justified operation against a then-current—and, unfortunately, still current—threat; the war in Iraq began as a preventive attack against a hypothetical danger. The war against the Taliban and *al Qaeda* forces in Afghanistan was a military campaign; the subsequent pursuit of *al Qaeda* became largely a counter-criminal operation. The campaign in Iraq was a military operation; the subsequent effort against terrorist attacks in Iraq has consisted of counter-insurgency operations. Unlike the war in Afghanistan, which was begun to uproot an identified terrorist sanctuary, the war against Iraq was based on an intelligence mirage. No connection has been made between the events of 9/11 and agents of the Hussein government.

The war against Iraq challenged state sovereignty and departed from an American tradition of striking only when struck first or when threatened directly[8]. The Bush administration found another argument to justify the launching of offensive operations: the need to disarm a state that had previously violated its international obligations by failing to give up its weapons of mass destruction. In its call for war, the Administration masked preventive war as a preemptive strike against a mounting threat. President Bush brushed aside the distinction between current and future threats, between a capability to build weapons of mass destruction and the possession of such weapons.

In a December 2003 interview, Diane Sawyer pressed Bush about the failure to uncover weapons of mass destruction in Iraq. He refused to see any distinction between possession and possible development: "What's the difference?" He elaborated: "The possibility that he could acquire weapons. If he were to acquire weapons, he would be the danger"[9]. One is reminded of the observation of the writer Elias Canetti: "It is always the enemy who started it. Even if he was not the first to speak out, he was certainly planning it; and if he was not actually planning it, he was thinking of it; and, if he was not thinking of it, he would have thought of it"[10].

In many modern conflicts, aggressors have claimed they were fighting "defensive" wars, and, absent an immediate threat, some aggressors have staged provocations against themselves to support future claims. Lost here is the distinction between preemptive attack and preventive war, the latter waged to avoid a hypothetical danger. In 1967, Israel attacked an Arab coalition that was itself poised to attack: a preemptive attack. In 1981, Israel destroyed the Osiraq light-water nuclear-materials testing reactor in Iraq: an act of preventive war. In 2003, the United States and "a coalition of the willing" invaded Iraq. The Administration claimed preemption; but, as it presumably knows now and should have known then, Iraq in 2003 posed no clear-and-present or future foreseeable danger to the United States or its allies. As for American claims, the *prior* was preemption and the *posterior* prevention, but the reality was probably neither.

DEHUMANIZATION OF THE ENEMY

Fighting sharpens distinctions between an in-group and an out-group; it can even create those distinctions[11]. Outsiders are readily demonized. The Puritans cast the Indians as devils deserving extermination. Nazis saw, or successfully portrayed, Jews as the Elders of Zion, designers of world conquest. Fanatical Islamists perceive the United States as "the Great Satan," luxuriating in world domination. Nor are democracies immune: General Philip Sheridan, US Army, consciously pursued an arguably genocidal pacification policy towards the Indians of the Great Plains. During World War II, American propagandists depicted the Japanese as racial primitives, almost as subhumans. The outbreak of hatred against Muslims in the US after 9/11 led in extreme cases to proposals for their mass deportation. The dominant common dehumanizing feature here is failure to see or refusal to acknowledge individual distinctions within an out-group.

Dehumanization is reinforced by military technology that distances attackers from targets. The armies of the world have moved increasingly from man-to-man combat with sword, dagger, and spear, to killing with bombs and missiles. The horrors of war are disguised in euphemisms and generalities. The killing of civilians becomes "collateral damage"; the bombing of civilian sites is justified as the destruction of enemy positions. As Orwell emphasized, words transform, turning opposites into one another. Statistics dehumanize as well: dead bodies are sanitized into numbers that neutralize death.

The news media have helped counter this tendency by showing victims at close range, but the argument that long-distance weapons spares the lives of attackers- killing the enemy and protecting one's own—regularly trumps humanitarian concerns. In Iraq, US forces used high-altitude bombing in the opening "shock-and-awe" campaign and continue to use tactical bombing against the insurgency. Despite efforts to use air power in a discriminating fashion and despite improvements in targeting accuracy, "surgical" strikes are largely impossible, given the distance between target and attacker, which distance compounds failings in intelligence.

TORTURE

Dehumanization and blurred distinctions promote a culture that, under the pressures of war, may promote torture. Law and practice have long distinguished legitimate interrogation from torture, but the distinction between them erodes if torture is justified as saving lives. In the war against terrorism, the euphemism that sanitized abuse was "enhanced interrogation techniques," a phrase that converted torture into non-torture. Despite numerous international and federal enactments forbidding torture, prohibitions were general enough to make legalistic manipulation practicable.

Besides customary international law, the strongest firebreaks against the abuse of detainees were the Third and Fourth Geneva Conventions, ratified by the United States in 1955, and the Convention Against Torture (CAT), ratified by the United States in 1994 and incorporated in Title 18 of the United States Criminal Code[12]. Two specific statutes also dealt with the prohibition against torture: The Torture Victims Protection Act of 1991 and The War Crimes Act of 1997. But these received little attention from the President's lawyers.

On 1 August 2002, Bybee argued that even the federal statute prohibiting torture embodied in Section 2340A of the US code could not bind the President in the exercise of his control over detainees: "The demands of the Commander-in-Chief's power are especially pronounced in the middle of a war in which the nation has already suffered a direct attack. In such a case, the information gained from interrogations may prevent future attacks by foreign enemies." Bybee went on to assert that Congress lacked authority to control the President's power over the questioning of detainees: "Congress may no more regulate the President's ability to detain and interrogate enemy combatants than it may regulate his ability to direct troop movements on the battlefield"[13].

On 25 January 2002, Alberto Gonzales, in a draft memorandum designed for George W. Bush, argued that the war against terror demanded a new approach towards interrogation:

As you have said, the war against terrorism is a new kind of war. It is not the traditional clash between nations adhering to the laws of war that formed the backdrop for GPW [Geneva POW Convention], The nature of the new war places a high premium on other factors, such as the ability to quickly obtain information from captured terrorists and their sponsors in order to avoid further atrocities against American civilians, and the need to try terrorists for war crimes such as wantonly killing civilians. In my judgment, this new paradigm renders obsolete Geneva's strict limitations on questioning of enemy prisoners and renders quaint some of its provisions[14].

Gonzales detailed the case against adherence to the Geneva Conventions: the laws of war were not applicable to the conflict in Afghanistan. The Taliban and al Qaeda were unlawful combatants. The Taliban government was "a failed State"[15]. CAT was federal law, but the President's lawyers challenged its constitutionality, arguing that it hindered the President's powers as Commander-in-Chief. CAT's full title—the Convention Against Torture and Other Cruel, Inhuman and Degrading Treatment—indicated the scope of its prohibition. When considered apart from its further prohibitions, CAT's definition of torture, Article 1, was restrictive:

> [T]orture means any act by which severe pain or suffering, whether physical or mental, is intentionally inflicted on a person for such purposes as obtaining from him or a third person information or a confession, punishing him for an act he or a third person has committed or is suspected of having committed, or intimidating or coercing him or a third person[16].

An abbreviated version, which did not significantly differ from the above definition, was embodied in the US code[17]. But the prohibition was weakened by understandings tagged on to the Convention by the United States Senate as a condition of ratification; these restricted the meaning of "cruel, inhuman or degrading treatment or punishment" to domestic judicial interpretations of the Fifth, Eighth, and Fourteenth Amendments to the US Constitution.

In arrogating plenary powers to the President as Commander-in-Chief, President Bush's lawyers had extended his control over military operations to cover the handling of detainees, sweeping aside the protective safeguards in federal and international law. Customary international law was merely dismissed by the Justice Department. The process that led to the prison abuses went through stages, gradually eliminating the safeguards designed to protect prisoners against abusive treatment.

The first stage centered on President Bush's definition of the global War on Terrorism as a new kind of war, although the struggle against terror and insurrection are as old as recorded history. On 7 February 2002, the President issued an executive memorandum officially formalizing this distinction. Taliban and *al Qaeda* fighters were not regular combatants; therefore, provisions regarding the treatment of prisoners-of-war under the Third and Fourth Geneva Conventions did not apply[18]. However, captives were still to be treated humanely "and, to the extent appropriate and consistent with military necessity, in a manner consistent with the principles of Geneva"[19]. This decision promoted a culture of ambiguity that was to mold the interrogation policy of the United States in subsequent months: treat prisoners humanely but procure the intelligence necessary to prevent further attacks. The President's responsibility for this policy, established despite warnings from the State Department,[20, 21] is inescapable.

The second stage saw a redefinition of torture by the Justice Department's Office of Legal Counsel. Bybee parsed the applicability of CAT's implementation in the US Code[22]. In his 1 August 2002 memorandum to Gonzales, Bybee concluded

... that torture as defined in and proscribed by Sections 2340–2340A, covers only extreme acts. Severe pain is generally of the kind difficult for the victim to endure. Where the pain is physical, it must be of an intensity akin to that which accompanies serious physical injury such as death or organ failure ... Because the acts inflicting torture are extreme, there is significant range of acts that though they might constitute cruel, inhuman, or degrading treatment or punishment fail to rise to the level of torture[23, 24].

In the third stage, the path to Abu Ghraib passed through the chain of command. The emphasis on interrogation practices aggressive enough to forestall future terrorist attacks and to defeat the insurgency in Iraq became intense. General Geoffrey Miller's September 2003 report stressed that "the detention operations function must act as an enabler for interrogation," where what was sought was "actionable intelligence"[25].

The pressure from Washington to get interrogation results traveled down the command ladder from the Secretary of Defense Donald Rumsfeld to the local commander in Iraq, Lieutenant General Ricardo Sanchez, then through the military services to military intelligence and military police[26, 27, 28, 29]. On 11 October 2002, Lieutenant Diane E. Beaver, Staff Judge Advocate of Joint Task Force 170, wrote to her commander, outlining three categories of interrogation techniques that could be used to elicit information. There was no legal problem regarding Category I techniques. Category II techniques had to be used with care but were "legally permissible so long as no severe physical pain is inflicted and prolonged mental harm intended." Even the removal of religious items was legal. In dealing with Category III techniques, Lieutenant Beaver was more ambiguous:

> With respect to Category III advanced counterresistance strategies, the use of scenarios designed to convince the detainee that death or severely painful consequences are imminent is not illegal for the same aforementioned reasons that there is a compelling governmental interest and it is not done intentionally to cause prolonged pain[30].

In April 2003, while stressing that detainees must be treated humanely, Defense Secretary Rumsfeld listed a number of legitimate techniques, emphasizing that the following should be used with caution: "Pride and Ego Down"; "Mutt and Jeff," where a two-interrogator team alternated harsh and friendly techniques; and "Isolation." The Secretary's cautions were well advised. These three techniques could easily degenerate into torture depending on how they were applied. But some of the other techniques approved by the Secretary were Trojan horses through whose opened hatches torture could enter the interrogation room: "Change of Scenery Down," which would place a detainee in an uncomfortable environment; "Dietary Manipulation"; "Environmental Manipulation," including the adjustment of temperature and the blaring of loud music; "Sleep Adjustment," a euphemism which could turn into sleep deprivation; and "False Flag," persuading the detainee that he was being interrogated by someone from another country, one presumably rougher in its methods than was the United States[31]. Curiously, a number of harsh interrogation techniques not contained in the Secretary's instructions appeared in a memorandum sent by General Sanchez to the Commander of US Central Command. In this memorandum, General Sanchez added the following: "Presence of Military Working Dogs" and "Stress position," However, neither item was included in his subsequent 12 October instructions[32, 33].

From the Secretary of Defense down to General Sanchez, the cautions regarding interrogation techniques were repeated. But were they heard? It is unknown how far down the ladder the contradictory messages and humanitarian warnings echoed. Almost inevitably, the balance between concern for humanity and the imperatives of military operations shifted as decision-making traveled downward. Moreover, the horror of 9/11 and the President's proclamation of a Manichaean conflict accelerated this plunge into the pit of abuse.

The fourth stage was "Operation Iraqi Freedom," the military campaign in Iraq. The assumptions that encouraged intervention in Iraq—resistance would be swept away, the US forces would be welcomed by grateful Iraqis, the occupation would be short-lived—vanished in a mirage. Chaos turned liberation into occupation and illusion into insurgency, for which eventuality American forces were poorly prepared numerically, materially, logistically, culturally, and psychologically. In this new and unexpected ordeal, as in Vietnam, sorting friend from foe and the innocent from the guilty was perplexing and perilous.

The final stage was set by failure to achieve rapid success in the war against the insurgency. Unexpectedly brutal combat conditions confronted US soldiers fighting against a ruthless, often unseen, foe in unconventional battle. Close combat sharpens survival skills and focuses loyalties on fellow soldiers caught in the same extremity. As reported by a *New York Times* columnist, soldiers began using derogatory terms to characterize the Iraqis: "raghead" and "Hajji," terms comparable to "Gook," used in Vietnam[34]. Tactics used in random arrests and prolonged detentions fostered brutality and dehumanization. In detention prisons, efforts to distinguish between unlawful combatants and innocent civilians diminished.

Then came the erosion of the distinction between legitimate interrogation and torture, foreshadowed by the Orwellian language of the Bybee memorandum: what was demanded in interrogation was the "mitigation of technique." The guilty and the innocent among the prisoners blended into one another as symbolized in the grotesque pyramid of naked detainees captured on camera. This moral deterioration was furthered by the belief of the abusers that moderate forms of torture had been sanctioned. Implicitly, and perhaps explicitly, top officials had helped create a culture in which "mitigated" torture had become acceptable- even honorable if sufficiently purposeful and laudable if productive.

Consequently, the demonization process, especially common when fighting an invisible enemy, overrode moral distinctions and the differentiations set by the President. Arrests, incarceration, and torture wiped out the distinctions between different types of prisoners: Taliban, al Qaeda, and Iraqi. The first two were denied coverage under the Geneva Conventions; the Iraqis were designated as covered by the Conventions. But treatment of incarcerated Iraqis was little better—and in some sites evidently worse. The precedents for dealing with Taliban and al Qaeda captives established at Bagram Air Force base, Afghanistan, and Guantanamo Bay, Cuba, migrated to the prisons in Iraq. The Hooded Man and the Leashed Man turned dehumanized captives into images of humiliation. Inevitably, fanatical insurgents used the images from Abu Ghraib to strengthen their cause, to gain recruits, and to extend their insurrection. In turn, US forces, the vast majority of whom behaved with decency in exceptionally difficult circumstances, were now branded with a single demonic image.

THE MISSION: DEFENSE OF FREEDOM

With his reelection, President Bush claimed to have passed "the accountability test," his version of events justified despite evidence mounting against it. President Bush had interpreted 9/11 as an attack on freedom. Then, when no weapons of mass destruction could be found anywhere in Iraq, the war was transformed by a syllogism: Saddam Hussein was a tyrant who hated freedom. Therefore, he was a terrorist. This reasoning wiped out distinctions between tyrants and terrorists while ignoring the dictatorial nature of governance in many of America's allies against terrorism.

In the eloquent rhetoric of his second inaugural address, Bush subsumed the war against terrorism into a war to spread democracy: "The best hope for peace in our world is the expansion of freedom in all the world... So it is the policy of the United States to seek and support the growth of democratic movements and institutions in every nation and culture, with the ultimate goal of ending tyranny in our world." The nations of the world are put on alert that there is only one choice: "The moral choice is between oppression which is always wrong, and freedom, which is eternally right." The theme was admirable, the subtext disturbing. How would the United States promote freedom throughout the world?

Would it spread freedom by diplomacy or by force? Interestingly, the President's image for the universal desire for freedom and for its spread around the globe was "untamed fire"[35].

THE HUMAN PARADOX: EVOLUTIONARY
AMBIGUITIES AND IDEOLOGICAL DOMINANCE

How do we explain this paradox of soaring Wilsonian idealism and sordid descent from liberation rhetoric into torture? Is there a deeper explanation than the immediate pressures of combat, the inadequate training of the interrogators, the inadequate prison facilities, the breakdown of the firebreaks engraved in the Geneva Conventions and ratified federal treaties? All of these factors certainly played a role. But were these cumulative pressures determinant?

The violence of war is often described as a regression into savagery. It raises the question: has man evolved since primordial times and what is meant by evolution? In the nineteenth century, during a long period of relative peace, many intellectual and political leaders prophesied that man would triumph over poverty and war. Evolution was synonymous with progress and the course of progress was irresistible. The slaughters of the twentieth century called that prophecy into doubt. Actually, the term "evolution" covers several levels of development: individual, social, national, international, transnational.

On the most basic level, individuals struggle for survival, and those who *do* survive, through adaptive endowment or other forms of good luck, can pass their traits into an uncertain future. However, even before the earliest civilization, individuals improved their prospects for survival, on the whole, by binding together into groups. Societies formed; they grew in scale, complexity, and resource dependency, and so did warfare[36]. Territoriality became formalized and aggrandized as the nation-state, an entity a population could understand and with which it could identify in major ways. Ultimately, people's capacity for identification beyond their groups, societies, and nation-states was enhanced by recognition of transnational identities and sympathies, many circumstantial, such as class. In peaceful periods, men and women could dream of global harmony; in times of war, human sympathy tended to shrink, war and nationalism mobilizing each other interactively.

War calls forth various survival capacities from our evolutionary inheritance; among these is *memory*. War creates public memory clustering around specific events, memory preserved with each generation and ingrained in national culture. Public memory instructs a nation's citizenry to remember the past in a highly selective manner. Memory as organized is self-interested and utilitarian. It builds myths that serve nations in justifying their political aims and conduct, creating comforting and heroic versions of the past. Because these myths are simplifying, they obliterate subtleties and distinctions. Unlike history, which is subject to constant reexamination and revision, public memory tends to rigidify the past into iconic forms. 9/11 became an instant memory: the sights and sounds of burning and crashing buildings and the last words of United Flight 93 haunt the country. Subsequent events, from the war in Afghanistan to the war in Iraq, echoed the horror of that day. National survival—and revenge—moved to the center, reinforced by fear of recurrence.

Nationalism is a concept defining political identity as self-determination within a specific territory, whether possessed or claimed, contiguous or not, accompanied by sovereignty over that territory and its inhabitants- or, in democracies, citizen-sovereignty within that territory. In times of crisis, nationalism demands loyalty from all citizens, whose services can be organized to support the nation, and it demands that scientists and other professionals place their expertise at the exclusive use of the nation. In state-to-state dealings, nationalism presses for the demand that sovereign rights, including political autonomy, be recognized.

But nationalism also carries a moralistic emphasis, one heard when national leaders define a war in moral terms, as the President does the current war. National leaders can use any general emergency to justify extraordinary measures, even ones precluded by custom or treaty, arguing that such measures are necessary for the defense or survival of the state[37, 38]. The persuasiveness of their argument is based on what I term "the nationalization of ethics." Acts that are reprehensible if carried out by private citizens within a society become excusable if executed in the name of state security. Assassination is condemned as murder if it is a private act; but states have justified it as necessary to eliminate dangerous foes, as Israel has done.

In Europe, the nationalization of ethics followed the development of states in the eighteenth and nineteenth centuries, a development challenging the concept of a universal Christian order. Religion and morality were evoked in the service of *national* causes rather than as universal norms limiting individual will. Countless memorials on battlefields sanctify the sacrifice of soldiers to these causes. With the nationalization of ethics, morality was harnessed to state will. The nation became an object of veneration, the national interest a gauge of what was permissible or not in war. Loyalty was unconditional. The army became the "nation in arms." Serving an enemy state, switching sides, becoming a mercenary for a hostile state- all these once commonplace behaviors became treasonous acts punishable by death. In time of war, all citizens were liable to be called up for service.

The nationalization of ethics reached its ultimate stage in the decades before World War I, when Social Darwinism flourished throughout Europe and the United States. As Jonathan Glover concludes, "Nationalism was reinforced by the belief in a Darwinian struggle, with the race or nation being the unit taking part in the struggle. Nations unwilling to fight would go under"[39]. Social Darwinism encouraged other beliefs and doctrines that harmonized with each other: a belief in the inevitability of war between nations, a justification for preventive war, an exaltation of the martial spirit. A fervent belief in national honor elevated the duelist code to state level, obedience to its call obligatory regardless of the consequences[40]. Despite the growth of international treaty law and continuous contemporary attempts to strengthen norms against unrestrained and indiscriminate violence, mankind continues to live within an anarchic world of sovereign states, whose conduct in security matters remains almost wholly determined by the nationalization of ethics.

What will be the direction of war in the twenty-first century? The development of unconventional weapons has given nations a capability for violence that threatens to sweep away restraint and values. Paradoxically, a war fought in the name of national security may explode into a conflagration that destroys all nations. Nationalistic fervor can have extremely dangerous consequences, and it remains "the most widespread excuse for war in our time"[41].

Nevertheless, for an ethnically diverse nation like the United States, with its democratic ideals, war cannot be justified merely in the terms of self-interest or the need to command resources. United States foreign policy in the twentieth and the first decade of the twenty-first century has blended self-interest with an ideological vision. The two World Wars and the Cold War were justified in idealistic language, and now the War on Terrorism is being justified in similar tones, with even grander rhetoric emerging in neoconservative circles: a transformation of the Islamic countries into nations ruled in accordance with western values. The freeing of Iraq would open the Middle East to democracy[42].

Universalist ideology can become a force for domination over others. In the case of Iraq, we have a case of ideological imperialism, reinforced by economic considerations: safeguarding access to oil. In the neoconservative vision, the US seeks through ideological imperialism to create a safe global political and economic environment, a "Garden of Democracy." This vision is frankly universalist, not internationalist. Security-through-conversion- political-ideological, not religious conversion—is envisioned as the means to protect basic loyalties while avoiding xenophobic and ethnic bias.

However, the shock of 9/11 also spawned primitive reactions that tragically undercut the idealistic vision of a world transformed. What many of those the US seeks to convert will remember from this war are the images that have emerged from Abu Ghraib and the stories of abuse that have been told of Guantanamo, Bagram, and Baghdad International Airport. Paradoxically, the dominant face may be one not seen: the ghost detainee, the hooded man, whose identity was his invisibility.

NOTES

1. Address before a Joint Session of the Congress of the United States: Response to the Terrorist Attacks of September 11, 20 September 2001, Public Papers of the Presidents of the United States: George W. Bush: 2001, 2 volumes, Book II: July 1 to December 31, 2001 (Washington, D.C.: United States Government Printing Office, 2003), p. 1142.

2. President George W. Bush, Press Conference, 13 April 2004, http://www.whitehouse.gov.

3. Memorandum: John C. Yoo, Deputy Assistant Attorney General, Office of Legal Counsel to Timothy Flanigan, The Deputy Counsel to the President, Subject: The President's Constitutional Authority to Conduct Military Operations Against Terrorists and Nations Supporting Them, 25 September 2001, in *The Torture Papers: The Road to Abu Ghraib* (New York: Cambridge University Press, 2005), pp. 23–24.

4. Memorandum: Jay S. Bybee, Assistant Attorney General, to Alberto R. Gonzales, Counsel to the President, Subject: Status of Taliban Forces under Article 4 of the Third Geneva Convention, 7 February 2002, in *The Torture Papers*, p. 142.

5. Draft Memorandum, John Yoo, Deputy Attorney General, to William J. Haynes II, General Counsel of the Department of Defense, Subject: Application of Treaties and Laws to al Qaeda and Taliban Detainees, 9 January 2002, in *The Torture Papers*, p. 39.

6. Memorandum, Jay S. Bybee to Alberto R. Gonzales, Counsel to the President, and William J. Haynes, General Counsel of the Department of Defense, Subject: Application of Treaties and Laws to al Qaeda and Taliban Detainees, 22 January 2002 printed in *The Torture Papers*, p. 111.

7. Stephen Van Evera, *The Causes of War: Power and the Roots of Conflict* (Ithaca, N.Y.: Cornell University Press, 1999), pp. 191–192.

8. Van Evera, pp. 182–183.

9. President Bush's Interview with Diane Sawyer, 16 December 2003, http://www.abc.org.

10. Elias Canetti, *Crowds and Power* (New York: Farrar, Straus and Giroux, 1984), p. 73.

11. Bradley A. Thayer, *Darwin and International Relations: On the Evolutionary Origins of War and Ethnic Conflict* (Lexington: The University Press of Kentucky, 2004), pp. 77–78, 243–274.

12. Title 18, Sections 1340–1340A, http://uscode.house.gov/download/pls/18Cl 13C.txt

13. Memorandum, Jay S. Bybee, Assistant Attorney General to Alberto R. Gonzales, Subject: Standards of Conduct for Interrogation under 18 U.S.C. 2340–2340A, 1 August 2002, in *The Torture Papers*, pp. 172–217, at pp. 200, 203.

14. Draft Memorandum, Albert R. Gonzales to the President, Subject: Decision re Application of the Geneva Convention on Prisoners of War to the Conflict with al Qaeda and the Taliban, 25 January 2002, printed in: *The Torture Papers*, p. 118–121.

15. Draft Memorandum, Albert R. Gonzales to the President, Subject: Decision re Application of the Geneva Convention on Prisoners of War to the Conflict with al Qaeda and the Taliban, 25 January 2002, in *The Torture Papers*, p. 118–121.

16. Convention Against Torture and Other Cruel, Inhuman and Degrading Treatment (CAT), http://www.hrweb.org/legal/cat.

17. Title 18, Sections 1340–1340A.

18. Geneva Convention III, Convention Relative to the Treatment of Prisoners of War, and Geneva Convention IV, Convention Relative to the Protection of Civilian Persons in Time of War, 12 August 1949, in *The Law of War: A Documentary History*, 2 volumes, Leon Friedman, editor (New York: Random House, 1972), Volume I, pp. 589–691.

19. Memorandum, President George W. Bush to the Vice President, the Secretary of State, the Secretary of Defense, the Attorney General, the Chief of Staff to the President, the Director of Central Intelligence, the Assistant to the President for National Security Affairs, the Chairman of the Joint Chiefs of Staff, Subject: Humane Treatment of al Qaeda and Taliban Detainees, 7 February 2002, in *The Torture Papers*, p. 135.

20. Memorandum, Secretary of State Colin L. Powell to the Counsel for the President and the Assistant to the President for National Security Affairs, Subject: Draft Decision Memorandum for the President on the Applicability of the Geneva Convention to the Conflict in Afghanistan in *The Torture Papers*, pp. 122–125.

21. Memorandum, William H. Taft IV, the Legal Adviser of the Department of State to the Counsel to the President, Subject: Comments on Your Paper on the Geneva Convention, 2 February 2002, in *The Torture Papers*, p. 129.

22. CAT.

23. Memorandum, J. S. Bybee, Office of Legal Counsel, to Alberto R. Gonzales, Counsel to the President, Subject Standards of Conduct for Interrogation under 18 U.S.C. 2340–2340A, in *The Torture Papers*, pp. 172–217, at pp. 213–214.

24. Report of two committees of the Association of the Bar of the City of New York: the Committee on International Human Rights and the Committee on Military Affairs and Justice, April 2004, in *The Torture Papers*, pp. 557–611.

25. MG Geoffrey Miller's Report: Assessment of DOD Counterterrorism Interrogation and Detention Operations in Iraq, September 2003. The report is printed as an annex to the Tabuga Report, in *The Torture Papers*, pp. 451–450, at p. 451.

26. The Taguba Report: Article 15-6: Investigation of the 800th Military Police Brigade, March 2004, in *The Torture Papers*, pp. 405–465.

27. Independent Panel to Review Department of Defense Detention Operations: the Final Report of the Independent Panel to Review DOD Detention Operations [the Schlesinger Report], August 2004, in *The Torture Papers*, pp. 908–975, at p. 915.

28. Lieutenant General Sanchez, Headquarters, Combined Joint Task Force Seven to Commander, US Central Command, Subject: JTF-7 Interrogation and Counter-Resistance Policy, 14 September 2003, as declassified under a Freedom of Information request by the American Civil Liberties Union.

29. Lieutenant General Sanchez, Headquarters, Combined Joint Task Force Seven to Commander, US Central Command, Subject: JTF-7 Interrogation and Counter-Resistance Policy, 12 October 2003, as declassified under a Freedom of Information request by the American Civil Liberties Union.

30. LTC Diane El Beaver, Staff Judge Advocate, to Commander, Joint Task Force 170, Subject: Legal Brief on Proposed Counter-Resistance Strategies, 11 October 2002, in *The Torture Papers*, pp. 229–235, at pp. 234–235.

31. Memorandum, Secretary of Defense Donald Rumsfeld to the Commander, U.S. Southern Command, Subject: Counter-Resistance Techniques in the War on Terrorism, 16 April 2003, in *The Torture Papers*, pp. 360–365.

32. Lieutenant General Sanchez, Headquarters, Combined Joint Task Force Seven to Commander, US Central Command, Subject: JTF-7 Interrogation and Counter-Resistance Policy, 14 September 2003, as declassified under a Freedom of Information request by the American Civil Liberties Union.

33. Lieutenant General Sanchez, Headquarters, Combined Joint Task Force Seven to Commander, US Central Command, Subject: JTF-7 Interrogation and Counter-Resistance Policy, 12 October

2003, as declassified under a Freedom of Information request by the American Civil Liberties Union.

34. Bob Herbert, "From 'Gook' to 'Raghead,'" The New York Times, 2 May 2005.

35. President George W. Bush's Second Inaugural, 20 January 2005, http:www.washingtonpost.com.

36. Thayer, pp. 157–159.

37. Quincy Wright, A Study of War (Chicago and London: The University of Chicago Press, 2nd edition, 1965), pp. 347, 895–922, 991–999, 1004–1009.

38. Thayer, pp. 224–227.

39. Jonathan Glover, Humanity: A Moral History of the Twentieth Century (New Haven: Yale University Press, 1999), p. 195.

40. Glover, pp. 221–222.

41. Paul Seabury Angelo Cordevilla, War: Ends and Means (New York: Basic Books, 1989), p. 220.

42. Andrew J. Bacevich, The New American Militarism: How Americans Are Seduced by War (New York: Oxford University Press, 2005), pp. 92–93.

*John Ellis van Courtland Moon is professor emeritus of history at Fitchburg State University in Massachusetts. He is the author of Confines of Concept: American Strategy in World War II (New York: Garland, 1988) and coeditor, with Erhard Geissler, of Biological and Toxin Weapons: Research, Development and Use from the Middle Ages to 1945 (New York: Oxford University Press, 1999).

Moon, John Ellis van Courtland. "The Death of Distinctions: From 9/11 to Abu Ghraib." Politics and the Life Sciences 23, no. 2 (September 2004): 2–12.

Used by permission.

Human Rights and Changing Definitions of Warfare

*by Veena Das**

The concept of exceptional circumstances in the application of law is not new, though its relevance for understanding the conduct of normal politics is now beginning to press on scholars and activists alike.[1] The rhetoric of the world having changed after September 11th privileged the experience of North Americans as unique, assuming that forms of terrorism with which other countries, such as Sri Lanka, have lived for more than thirty years, were relevant for those societies but not for humankind in general. The attack on the U.S, on the other hand, has been portrayed as nothing less than an attack on civilization itself. This imaginary of September 11th as having brought about a state of exception in which nothing less than a global civil war was at stake has now made domestic security the overarching discourse within which claims of human rights are framed.

There are some who take it as self-evident that the rhetoric of human rights used with increasing frequency by the Bush administration to justify the war on Iraq is nothing more than an obfuscation to divert attention from what is now increasingly clear—that there were no stockpiles of chemical, biological, or nuclear weapons in Iraq that could have justified the war, and second that there was no clear plan for securing the peace. It does not matter anymore that most sober observers have concluded that the frequently voiced concern with human rights is simply a pretext for other motives. The rhetoric of fear has succeeded in creating a scenario in which the most powerful country in the world lives with a generalized sense of panic that it is under a constant threat of terrorist attacks. No doubt, there are continuities in the present sense of an invisible enemy that surrounds us and the earlier wars—such as the war on Communism or the war on drugs. Yet, it would be interesting to look at the differences and ask what is new in the present situation.

It is well to remember that there were only four military interventions in the past year in Africa even after the announcement of global war on terrorism. Further, in some places such as Liberia there was an expectation that the U.S. would intervene to stop the slaughter of civilians; many took the war in Iraq as a promise that the U.S. would step in more decisively to stop human rights abuses in Liberia. The United States did briefly intervene, but the small number of troops it deployed had little effect. It was openly acknowledged by both President

Bush and Senator Kerry recently in the their debate on foreign policy that with the massive deployment of troops in Iraq, there was no prospect of committing the armed forces to stop the genocide in other places such as Sudan. Clearly the question of whether international interventions will be possible even in the face of genocide depends very much now on whether a particular conflict is seen as affecting American security or not. And finally, the nature of the enemy as perceived by the policy makers in the U.S. has changed so that the enemy is seen as highly mobile and unpredictable since he follows some logic other than that of rational pursuit of self-interest.

In the light of this reading, one of the most important tasks before us is to understand what is happening to democracy in the West. What is the fate of human rights here? The power of the metaphor that civilization was under threat allowed President Bush to gather support of more than half the population of the U.S. and to present the war on Iraq as simultaneously a means to protect the U.S. citizens against terrorism and to bring democracy to Iraq. I will not reprise the arguments about the fact that the U.S. foreign policy had itself supported the regime of Saddam Hussein because these arguments are well-known. My aim, instead, is to ask how the new perceptions of global threats are likely to influence the legitimacy of human rights discourses in the changed configurations of war and peace. The issue for long was posed as the question of cultural relativism versus universal values; that, I think, is not what is at stake now. Instead the question is about the practices through which intervention in grievous circumstances of human right violations is likely to happen and what this will do to the legitimacy of these discourses in countries where human rights violations have become enmeshed within ordinary life either through protracted warfare or through endemic violence.

In a recent paper, Poole et al. examine the implications of a new conception of warfare and a generalized sense of panic for understanding how populations might become themselves complicit in the erosion of their rights, including fundamental rights to due process.[2] Quoting from the writings of Brian Jenkins, who was consultant to RAND as a military expert, they point to the significance of the idea that the threshold between conventional warfare, guerilla warfare, and international terrorism has become vague with "governments, sub-national entities employing them individually, interchangeably, sequentially, or simultaneously— and having to defend against them." The prediction that warfare will cease to be finite, and that the distinction between war and peace will be more ambiguous and complex, means that there is a proliferation of both state and non-state actors who can claim that they are acting within states of exception. This is the common terminology deployed by groups alternately defined as freedom fighters or insurgents or terrorists depending upon your point of view. The state, in its turn, uses the idea of a state of emergency to institute new measures that control such rights as the right to privacy, right to freedom of speech or in some cases, the right to due process. It is well known in countries caught in these protracted conflicts that even when there is formal freedom of speech, one comes to exercise censorship on oneself because of fears of reprisals by both agents of the state and militant groups. In these new configurations when the boundaries between war and peace, combatant and civilian, normal and exceptional have become blurred, we cannot go on pretending that the conceptual work on nature of human rights, their violation, and appropriate institutional mechanisms for securing human rights has already been done. The challenge, it seems to me, is to describe the nature of the present and particularly the question of how we recognize objects in the world. Toward this end, I offer the following suggestions.

The first question, it appears to me, is to ask what kind of new entities have been brought into existence in the name of security that use the instruments of law to institute domains in which the state can act with impunity. The USA Patriot Act, enacted on October 26, 2001, spoke of emergency measures as providing appropriate tools for intercepting and obstructing terrorism. This already included measures for enhancing domestic surveillance and security. However, in itself this could not have produced the categories of detainees who could be subjected to indefinite detention without recourse to legal representation. Under the Patriot Act, any alien suspected of unlawful activities that endangered national security could be taken into custody but had to be charged within seven days with a criminal offence. It was the military order issued by the President on November 13, 2001, that allowed for indefinite detention and trial by military commissions rather than military tribunals. What is important about this order is that it brought a new entity—that of detainees—into being that was outside the realm of both ordinary law and military law. That over a period of time this has been contested is important but does not take away from the fact that states of emergency are productive of new entities that are in great danger of becoming normalized over a period of time.

It is important to note that already the Anti Terrorism Act of 1996 empowers the secretary of state, after consultation with the secretary of the treasury and the attorney general, to designate any foreign organization as one that engages in "terrorist activity" threatening to the security of U.S. nationals or the national security of the United Sates. The dangers of this were spelled out by Philip Heyman in the following terms:

It is a dangerous step to prohibit a political organization from receiving support simply on the determination that it is a terrorist organization by a cabinet official whose factual determinations can be overturned by a court only if they are "arbitrary, capricious, [or] an abuse of discretion." That the law applies only to foreign organizations reduces significantly the danger to our domestic liberties, yet in an increasingly international world, foreign organizations play an increasing part in our politics as well. In earlier years, the African National Congress (ANC) of Nelson Mandela would have been subject to such prohibitions if the secretary of state had said so: even now, the law could apply to the political arms of the Irish Republican Army, depending very largely on the discretion of a cabinet officer reversible only if his judgment is arbitrary."[3]

The expansion of the definition of terrorism to include domestic terrorism points to the way in which extraordinary measures can be normalized and accepted over a period of time. My point is not that the fears of terrorism are unfounded, but that given the fact that they are grounded in experience, how are questions of human rights going to find tools that are subtle enough to distinguish between assessments based on reasonable evidence and those that are put into circulation within a climate of generalized panic?

The second example is from the new landscape in which restrictions of freedom of information operate. Again the relation between research in universities that addresses special needs of the government such as defense needs and that which serves the public interest has been the subject of discussion and debate since the 1960s. However, the well-established distinction between classified research and unclassified research is now put into jeopardy by the emergence of new categories such as "sensitive" research. The agreements arrived at in the '60s in most research universities stated clearly that classified research should not be carried out on campus and that no student, graduate or undergraduate, should be asked to get security clearance for thesis research and that thesis research should not be carried out in areas that require access to classified material. This was consistent with the idea that universities serve public interest and that such an entity as a "classified Ph.D. dissertation" would be a contradiction in terms.

It is salutary that while the war in Iraq is presented as one in which democracy and freedom can be brought to Iraqi people, the state of emergency it has spawned is leading to new restrictions on the circulation of ideas and knowledge in the universities in North America. The USA Patriot Act has defined restricted persons who are prohibited from possessing, transporting, or shipping a number of biological agents and equipments for research. Under the expansions of agents under this act, administrative orders continue to restrict access to many biological agents and equipments even in the laboratories located in the campuses in this country. The Secretary of Health and Human Services has been given special powers to expand the list of restricted items. Further it is now being proposed that research results that are generated in the course of a program could be designated as "sensitive" and free publication and even discussion of these results could be deemed a criminal offence. It remains to be seen whether major research universities will be able to resist this especially if federal grants are at issue.

These changes at home are intimately linked with a sense of fear that has been generated in the general population so that greater restrictions on freedom become acceptable. When it comes to the damage done to prospects of peace in countries in the Middle East, it will be years before we know the results of war. Counts on civilian deaths and injuries are difficult to get despite efforts of organizations, like Iraq body count. The restrictions on freedom of inquiry in universities, research organizations, and think tanks make it unlikely that a sober analysis of the destruction of Iraq will be forthcoming in the near future or that resources for such an analysis will be available. Meanwhile questions continue to be posed in a style of argumentation that there is a feeling of no exit. For instance is the world better after Saddam has been removed or not? Analogies with Hitler and the necessity of war to remove such dangerous dictators are constantly posed in justification of the Iraq war.

My answer to these questions is simple. There are many movements for freedom and democracy within the Middle East, but the problem is that the continuous support from the weapons industry and support from Western governments erodes these fledgling movements. This is in marked contrast with the support that was provided to movements such as Solidarity in Poland. It is not hard to show that whether it is Taliban or Saddam Hussein, what determines the attitudes of Western governments are geopolitical considerations rather than an unwavering commitment to democracy or human rights. So I am convinced that the issue is, indeed, that of preemption, but what is required is not preemptive wars. Instead, it is the building of the pre-political virtues and of institutions in which the habit of democracy can take root.

My own sense is that the "West versus the rest" dichotomy has become more dangerous than ever. We are not likely to find moral resources of nonviolence, readiness to defend freedoms, and dissent in societies that have been eroded of these capabilities. Thus it is important for global alliances to act to stop genocide as in Darfur today, but it is equally important to see that questions on proliferation of small weapons that feed most of the regional wars today are addressed. It is time that the scholarly community stopped framing these issues in terms of cultural relativism *versus* universalism, and started concentrating instead on the institutional mechanisms for addressing the kinds of problems that have emerged. Perhaps the first step would be to reframe the questions of terrorism itself not as a *war* on terrorism but a commitment to strengthen regional systems of democracy even if the costs of that are to give up the idea of American exceptionalism that diminishes the suffering of others and magnifies the idea of America as the motor of history—just as God or the proletariat once occupied that empty signifier.

NOTES

1. See especially, Giorgio Agamben, *Homo Sacer: Sovereign Power and Bare Life*, Stanford University Press, 1998.

2. Deborah Poole et al. "Networks actual and potential," Paper written by the group on Infopolitics under the auspices of The Coming Community, Johns Hopkins University.

3. See Phillip B. Heymann, *Terrorism and America: A Commonsense Strategy for a Democratic Society*, M.I.T. Press, 1998, p. 97.

*Veena Das** is Krieger-Eisenhower Professor of Anthropology and professor of humanities at the Johns Hopkins University. Her most recent books are *Life and Words: Violence and the Descent into the Ordinary* (2006) and *Sociology and Anthropology of Economic Life: The Moral Embedding of Economic Action* (ed., with R. K. Das) (2010).

Das, Veena. "Human Rights and Changing Definitions of Warfare." *Journal of Human Rights* 4 (2005): 113–117.

Reprinted by permission of the publisher (Taylor & Francis Ltd., http://www.tandf.co.uk/journals).

Part 2:

9/11's Impact on International Law

Many of the Bush administration's early responses to 9/11 met with criticism at home and abroad on grounds of illegality. Although many top-level Bush administration officials explicitly stated and strongly maintained that the United States fell outside the jurisdiction of international law, the Bush Justice Department began looking specifically for ways to characterize its actions so as to be able to claim to be at least within the letter of international law.

But, as many have argued, just because an action is governed by international law does not mean it accords with international standards on human rights. When the Bush administration found itself faced with international approbation for dismissing the international legal standards followed by the rest of the world, it changed tack and embarked on a campaign to reinterpret international law in ways that removed the most important restraints on state behavior—and thus effectively removed much of the human rights content that had been constructed over the course of the previous several decades.

Adrian Jones and Rhoda Howard-Hassman are among those documenting both the profound disregard for civil rights and liberties evidenced by the Bush administration's early responses, and the administration's eventual resort to reinterpretation of international law to suit its own purposes. In "Under Strain," they further warn that the gutting of international law will, in the long run, have dangerous consequences for the entire international community and perhaps most of all for the United States.

In "International Human Rights Law and the War on Terrorism," Derek Jinks, too, argues that 9/11 was a fundamental turning point for international law. Most important, an excess of personal freedom was seen as being to blame for providing opportunities to international terror organizations. In response, the Bush administration's "War on Terror" included several key changes in its approach to both international and domestic law and policy. All of these changes called into question what kind of law governed this new war—laws of war, laws of domestic security, some hybrid of the two, or something else altogether. Jinks argues that too little attention has been paid to international human rights law that "...would establish conclusively...that all persons subject to the jurisdiction of the United States . . . are entitled to certain basic rights"[1]—almost all of which have been violated by the Bush administration.

In contrast, David Forsythe ("The United States and International Humanitarian Law") argues that we need to consider the post-9/11 era in the context of the overall U.S. ambivalence about both human rights law *and* international humanitarian law since at least the Vietnam era. In Forsythe's view, the post-9/11 era's willingness to violate internationally recognized standards simply represents the unfortunately predictable end point of American foreign policymakers' increased tendency to place the United States outside the system of international laws and values that it helped to create. Forsythe also encourages observers to disaggregate the foreign policymaking apparatus and consider the differing perspectives held by the intelligence community and the military, as well as the sources of those differences.

As you read the articles in this section, think about the following:

1. Consider the legal structures that the authors in this section most often refer to. Why were they initially constructed and why did so many states ratify them (through a domestic vote, legislatures agreed to treat them as binding laws equivalent with their own country's laws)? In your opinion, have these structures been successful in achieving their initial goals? Is there still a need for them?

2. Can you identify instances in which U.S. interests have benefited from existing international legal structures? Instances in which they have been harmed? On balance, do you think the benefits have outweighed the harms or vice versa?

3. What attitudes about international law have the U.S. Supreme Court's recent decisions reflected? How have these differed from domestic decisions in other countries and the decisions of international courts? Why did these differences arise?

4. What do you think explains the varying positions on international humanitarian law among different parts of the U.S. foreign policy community?

5. What explains the disconnect between the attitudes of the military and civilian leadership? Is this disconnect detrimental to foreign policymaking, in your opinion? Or might it have benefits? If so, what are they?

NOTE

1. Derek Jinks, "International Human Rights Law and the War on Terrorism," *Denver Journal of International Law & Policy* 31 no. 1 (2002): 58.

Under Strain: Human Rights and International Law in the Post 9/11 Era

*by Adrian L. Jones and Rhoda E. Howard-Hassmann**

We have followed with increasing alarm the United States's reaction to the terrorist attacks of September 11, 2001, and its negative implications for human rights and international law. Domestically, anti-terrorist measures such as the Patriot Act unduly compromise fundamental civil liberties and protections.[1] Abroad, the U.S. invasion and occupation of Iraq was undertaken in clear contravention of the United Nations Charter and customary international law. Though we applaud the ouster of Saddam Hussein, and support all efforts to install and consolidate a democratic regime in Iraq, we are concerned that American attempts to balance individual human rights and national security will erode the fundamental principles of liberal democratic society. We are also concerned that unilateral U.S. action in Iraq has undermined the normative and stabilizing framework provided by international law. As a result of these policy stances, the U.S. has severely compromised its legitimacy as a model of democracy and human rights, and its capacity to perform a constructive leadership role in multilateral global governance.

HUMAN RIGHTS: THE BURDEN OF PERSUASION

Mainstream commentators, whether national security hawks or ardent civil libertarians, generally acknowledge that combating global terrorism should be undertaken with the simultaneous preservation of core human rights and democratic principles. Contention focuses on the specific juxtaposition of these objectives, which may sometimes exist in tension, or even conflict. Michael Ignatieff provides a useful framework of legal, political, and ethical principles to guide a reasoned and measured policy approach. His "lesser evil" position eschews undue emphasis on either human rights or national security, with "balance" touted as the appropriate pragmatic and ethical guideline.[2] Ignatieff's position is infused with faith in the resiliency and effectiveness of democratic institutions: "pre-commitments" to democracy and the dynamics of "adversarial justification" will guard against unwarranted human rights infringements.[3]

Although Ignatieff's framework is principled and judicious, we are concerned by his specific calculus, which too closely mirrors or legitimizes prevailing U.S. policy, both domestically and abroad. Our concern is with the implications, not with the intent or sincerity, of Ignatieff's propositions. Middle ground sentiments and discussions, even well-intentioned ones, will almost invariably betray the innocent connotations that those words convey. Ignatieff himself acknowledges the "moral hazard" involved with such a delicate task.[4] Undoubtedly, most U.S. policy-makers claim, or consider themselves, to be acting within such parameters. Nonetheless, the prevailing U.S. approach has been defined by short-term pragmatism and expediency, which threatens irreparable harm to human rights, democracy, and international peace and security.

This approach is exemplified by the Patriot Act: "To deter and punish terrorist acts in the United States and around the world, to enhance law enforcement investigatory tools, and for other purposes."[5] These worthy objectives aside, the fine print is disconcerting. For example, the Act mandates the "authority to intercept wire, oral, and electronic communications *relating to terrorism*" [italics ours].[6] This, like many other provisions, begs the question: How do the authorities know a priori who are the terrorists? The Act has a five-year sunset clause, but may be made permanent, thus tipping the balance far away from civil liberties. Ignatieff acknowledges: "One reason why we balance threat and response poorly is that the political costs of under reaction are always going to be higher than the costs of overreaction."[7] It is the role of the judiciary to protect us against such over-reaction; yet it is not clear that the Supreme Court will consistently be able or willing to quash unconstitutional measures.

The Court's decisions in June 2004 concerning the Guantanamo Bay detainees provide some grounds for optimism. Pursuant to President Bush's 2001 Military Order, where there is "reason to believe" that a non-U.S. citizen is an al Qaeda member, has otherwise aided or abetted terrorism against the U.S., or has harbored terrorists, such person may be detained.[8] At the discretion of the Secretary of Defense, detainees were denied the fundamental right to habeas corpus.[9] Moreover, the President's Order was executed without congressional authorization, and was purportedly sheltered from judicial review.[10] Finally, in June 2004, two U.S. Supreme Court decisions cited due process imperatives—detainees were to have the opportunity to contest the factual bases for their detention—and confirmed the authority of U.S. Courts to consider challenges to the legality of such detentions.[11] Such delay dulls many people's faith in democratic checks and balances: they are not assured by the knowledge that such measures do not affect "us," because "we" are either "Americans" or the "majority." To his credit, Ignatieff cites Dworkin's critical observation that, in such cases, "the trade-off is not between *our* liberty and *our* security, but between *our* security and *their* liberty."[12]

Ignatieff's notion of balance seems reasonable, and even reassuring, but its espousal risks a tacit acceptance of undue human rights infringements. In our view, however well-intentioned this notion may be, it may well represent the "greater evil." The word balance implies that the objectives of combating terrorism and protecting human rights warrant equal prominence in policy formulation. It creates a dangerous and fallacious picture of human rights relativity, and almost invariably implies intrusive surveillance and loss of privacy, restrictions on domestic and international movement, and deprivation of core rights and protections in the criminal justice system. More fundamentally, propositions of this type, especially when espoused by otherwise liberal commentators like Ignatieff, may further propel a fundamental re-evaluation and discounting of the very significance of human rights in American society by policy-makers, nongovernmental elites, and the popular citizenry. Human rights, long embedded in the U.S. collective liberal-democratic political culture, may increasingly be perceived as expendable. Such collective self-doubt and malaise could pose a greater threat to human security than the terrorists themselves. We risk falling prey to the very consequence that Ignatieff warns of: "the politics of the worst (la politique du pire)."[13]

Ignatieff concedes that a "lesser evil morality is antiperfectionist in its assumptions."[14] We, too, acknowledge that some trade-offs are necessary. However, the overwhelming presumption, in every policy domain, toward every individual, and in whatever jurisdiction, should be in favor of fundamental human rights. The starting point should not be a middle ground. A heavy burden of persuasion should be required to legitimize any human rights infringements. Where such a burden is met, we would demand stricter standards of rational connection, minimal infringement, proportionality, and necessity in the formulation and implementation of such measures.

Ignatieff endorses former U.S. Supreme Court Justice Robert Jackson's famous proposition that "the constitution cannot be a suicide pact."[15] We are equally concerned by another type of suicide pact: excessive faith in political exchange and decision-making in an era of unprecedented uncertainly and unease. Global terror threats are a novel challenge for democracy and human rights, and they must not be permitted to undermine human rights and democracy, international law, and the range of multilateral institutions that guard our global and individual security.

INTERNATIONAL LAW: A LONG-TERM PERSPECTIVE

The debate about the relationship between national security and human rights is no longer a philosophical nicety—a stimulating classroom discussion of whether a state can torture a suspected terrorist in order to forestall an imminent threat.

We do not deny the novel transnational nature, unprecedented gravity, and global scope of recent terrorist attacks, including those in Bali and Madrid. The appalling atrocities at a school in Beslan, Russia raise an equally alarming issue: Have broader or separate terrorist networks drawn gruesome inspiration from the 9/11 attacks? Although a response is needed, some states have done so in dangerous, reactionary fashion. Witness the continued consolidation of power by Russian President Vladimir Putin.[16] According to Gray, developments in an "increasingly illiberal Russia" are consistent with the in-vogue realpolitk inclinations of the U.S.[17]

The shocking beatings and humiliations at the Abu Ghraib prison were a gross violation of international humanitarian law.[18] Commentators are asking the right questions: Were the guards acting under orders and, if so, from whom? From how far up the command chain did such instructions come? Was there subtle direction or tacit acceptance by senior officials? Was there a prevailing climate of "anything goes"? Recent revelations suggest that the abuses were not merely the activity of poorly trained and over-exuberant soldiers, as the U.S. Administration has maintained. Rather, they closely reflected the list of "what not to do" provided to members of the Marine Corps in Iraq.[19]

The Abu Ghraib abuses rest uncomfortably close to Ignatieff's fine line separating torture from legitimate coercive techniques.[20] Though publication of The Lesser Evil pre-dated revelations of the abuses, Ignatieff's apparent endorsement of "regulated torture" is particularly alarming.[21] One might conclude that the abuses at Abu Ghraib were the natural extension, if not the officially sanctioned result, of such "balanced" thinking. Although Ignatieff concedes that "torture is probably the hardest case in the ethics of the lesser evil,"[22] he nonetheless proclaims: "The problem lies in identifying the justifiable exceptions and defining what forms of duress stop short of absolute degradation."[23]

The Abu Ghraib affair has also had far broader political ramifications. At a time when the U.S. is seeking to "win the peace"—the hearts and minds of ordinary Iraqis, as well as of the broader Arab world—and mend fences with its own traditional allies, the Abu Ghraib abuses were a disaster. As Wedgwood states: "America's leadership, in battle and in peace, depends on retaining the moral high ground. A successful transition in Iraq also depends upon moral legitimacy. We lost too much of that legitimacy in the cellblocks at Abu Ghraib."[24] Escalated beheadings of kidnapped civilians are express recriminations. Moreover, U.S attempts to narrow the legal definition of torture could backfire when al Qaeda defendants are brought to trial.[25]

In our view, Ignatieff is insufficiently referential to international law and to the global norms required to sustain that system. Admittedly, he identifies the crucial rhetorical question: "Whether a country facing a terrorist emergency should base its public policy exclusively on its own constitution and its own laws, or whether it has any *duty* [italics ours] to pay attention to what other states have to say and what international agreements and conventions require."[26] Realist scholars portray an international climate of mutual suspicion and competition among states, and emphasize the so-called rational pursuit of narrow state interests, primarily the maximization of relative power.[27] Thus, they have long argued that in the absence of a global sovereign, international law should quite readily be disregarded when national interests are at issue.[28] This suggests that we should "balance" international law considerations with national security. Like the initial tension between human rights and national security, this balance may imply a false or exaggerated dichotomy. In our view, states not only have a duty to comply with international law, but it is in their long-term interest to do so. Some scholars have in fact cited the U.S. response to 9/11 as a vindication of realist theory. According to Gray, they support the view that "international order needs a sheriff [the U.S.]," and the rejection of diplomacy is a viable avenue to protect national interests.[29]

In fact, the U.S. has long played a significant role in shaping the priorities and contours of international law.[30] It has benefited accordingly from the stability and predictability that the system provides. Thus, its current posture of heightened unilateralism, and relative disregard for international law, is regrettable. "Operation Enduring Freedom" was initially justified—rhetorically that is—by reference to the dubious legal principle of pre-emptive self-defense. Anticipatory self-defense—the right of first-strike where aggression is imminent—is, perhaps, authorized by the UN Charter and pre-existing customary law.[31] However, the proposition of preemptive self-defense requires no degree of imminence, but merely a threatening "act, intention, *or capability* [italics ours] of an adversary."[32] If taken to its logical conclusion, this principle threatens to wreak havoc on the UN's international peace and security apparatus. Consider India and Pakistan, two mutually suspicious nuclear powers.

The shifting U.S. justifications—from weapons of mass destruction, to the search for bin Laden, to humanitarian intervention—have been extremely detrimental to its global legitimacy and to winning the peace in Iraq. Unfortunately, this precedent threatens to derail the otherwise-positive progression of the customary law of humanitarian intervention. Commentators have increasingly suggested an emerging right of intervention, irrespective of the absence of a threat to international peace and security, where gross human rights or humanitarian atrocities are being committed, or where a natural disaster (e.g., epidemic, famine) is occurring in the target state.[33] A summary of guiding principles for humanitarian intervention is contained in *The Responsibility to Protect: Report of the International Commission on Intervention and State Sovereignty* (the "Report").[34] Ignatieff was a member of the commission that produced this Report. Though not a definitive statement of the law, the Report reflects prevailing progressive thought on how the law has evolved, or should evolve. Thus, it is a useful framework by which to assess the U.S. intervention in Iraq.

The Report lists "Six Criteria for Military Intervention": right authority, just cause, right intention, last resort, proportional means, and reasonable prospects.[35] We are principally concerned with the first three of these. Considering right authority, the Report stresses the pre-eminent role of the Security Council, and appeals to that body to muster the political will to act "pursuant to the collective conscience of humanity [lest] it will diminish in significance, stature and authority."[36] Failing Security Council action, the Report cites the legitimacy of two alternative bases of authority: the General Assembly, acting pursuant to an Emergency Session[37]; and Regional and sub-regional organizations.[38] The U.S.'s blatant disregard for the Council's determinations,[39] and its rather haphazard mobilization of the Coalition of the Willing—the composition of which, apart from the United Kingdom, resembles a ragtag collection of political beggars and debtors, with no true unity of purpose in Iraq—fails to conform to even the most generous interpretation of this provision. Equally importantly, the Coalition is a mere "hub-and-spoke operation" in which the U.S. has retained complete military and political control.[40] The Report critically states: "Interventions by ad hoc coalitions (or, even more, individual states) acting without the approval of the Security Council, or the General Assembly, or a regional or sub-regional grouping of which the target state is a member, do not—it would be an understatement to say—find wide favor."[41]

Fortunately, the pre-emptive self-defense justification was widely condemned by the global community, likely foreclosing any evolution of customary law in that direction. Nonetheless, the U.S. continues to make "exceptional international law," either seeking to shape the general law to its specific liking or, more disconcerting, seeking to reserve to itself exceptional prerogatives contrary to embedded principle of reciprocity.[42] Debates also center on the President's questionable authority to intervene in Iraq without Congressional approval, as generally required by the U.S. Constitution and under federal law.[43]

Regarding just cause, the Report refers to "extreme and exceptional cases,"[44] and specifically cites "civil conflict and repression [which] are so violent that civilians are threatened with massacre, genocide, or ethnic cleansing on a large-scale."[45] Although the Hussein regime committed large scale atrocities, the 2003 Iraqi state of affairs hardly meets the Report's threshold, especially when considered in the midst of human rights and humanitarian atrocities occurring worldwide. Thus, apologists for the U.S. actions in Iraq must confront the following question: Why Iraq, but not Sierra Leone or the Darfur region in the Sudan? Why is the U.S. State Department so disciplined in seeking U.N.-sponsored action in those other cases?

It follows that the right intention criterion is belittled by the shifting justifications of the Bush Administration. Apologists cannot logically maintain that intervention was undertaken with altruistic and humanitarian intentions. Intentions—original intentions—matter because the integrity of any customary norm of humanitarian intervention depends on the good faith of intervening actors. The objective success of an intervention is a separate issue from its legal validity.[46] Moreover, the Report states that "the responsibility to protect implies an evaluation of the issues from the point of view of those seeking or needing support, rather than those who may be considering intervention."[47]

An additional complicating factor concerns widespread perception, if not the reality, that business firms and lobbies with connections to the Bush Administration are improperly profiting from the rebuilding of Iraqi infrastructure. Vice-President Cheney is former chief executive at Halliburton, a company heavily involved in the physical reconstruction of Iraqi oil facilities. He has been the lightning rod for such accusations, particularly during the initial "no-bid" contracting process that excluded firms from nonmember states of the Coalition. This credibility problem continued to fester in an election year, and in the midst of reinvigorated attacks by Democratic Presidential candidate John Kerry.[48]

Underlying the Report's six principles are "Precautionary Criteria," cited separately to underscore the Commission's concern with unwarranted interventions and/or the outright abuse of humanitarian justifications.[49] The Report crucially states: "Our purpose is not to license aggression with fine words, or to provide strong states with new rationales for doubtful strategic designs, but to strengthen the order of states by providing for clear guidelines to guide concerted international action in those exceptional circumstances when violence within a state menaces all people."[50]

To victims of the Hussein regime, the niceties of international law may seem irrelevant. From Nazi Germany to Rwanda, the privileged status of state sovereignty in international law has contributed to, or justified, the dismal failure of the international community to protect the most basic human rights of millions of ordinary citizens. We applaud the progressive evolution of the customary international law of humanitarian intervention and the increasing denial of what the late Leo Kuper described as the "sovereign right to genocide."[51] Unfortunately, the U.S. intervention in Iraq fundamentally contravened the precautionary tone and provisions of the Report, and may have derailed or distorted this progression. The result may well be not international order, which the U.S. so greatly privileges, but a dangerous precedent that may be co-opted as a veiled guise for aggression. Thus, the benefits of ousting the Hussein regime in Iraq, and raising the prospect of democratic governance there, may be outweighed by the longer-term degradation of the international rule of law and the UN system.

GOODWILL, MULTILATERALISM, AND GLOBAL GOVERNANCE

The physical destruction of the 9/11 attacks was perhaps matched by the collective and enduring psychological trauma inflicted on the American people. Understandably, the U.S. felt compelled to respond to these novel terrorist tactics, and lacked the benefit of experience. Somewhat less understandably, it did not rely on the experiences of other states such as the United Kingdom or Spain, with long histories of fighting internal terrorists. Its challenges were magnified in the absence of an international treaty that governs interstate law enforcement and intelligence cooperation.[52] Der Derrian correctly notes that in dealing with terrorists, "the old rules of statecraft, diplomacy, and warfare have been thrown out."[53] However, to the rest of the global community those channels remain critical, and perhaps take on heightened significance in an era of transnational threats that require a concerted global effort. The U.S. received an outpouring of global sympathy in the aftermath of 9/11. The war in Afghanistan was widely accepted as a legitimate response to Taliban support of al Qaeda.[54] Such international acquiescence gave way to a new customary rule concerning the self-defense provisions of Article 51 of the UN Charter: namely, an extension to include military responses against states that support or harbor terrorist groups.[55] However, the Iraq intervention was harshly received by the global community, many traditional allies included. The Canadian government was markedly equivocal in its stance, but the French and German governments soundly denounced the actions of their NATO ally. Elsewhere, governmental and civil society cast vehement condemnations. The United Kingdom's supportive position was anomalous, and its motivations somewhat mysterious.

These critical sentiments have undoubtedly been aggravated by the longstanding and widespread perception of hypocrisy in American foreign policy, particularly concerning human rights.[56] For example, in supporting Hussein against Iran during the 1980s, the U.S. was singularly unconcerned by the mass killings of an estimated 5,000 Kurds in the town of Halabja in March 1988.[57] Regarding nuclear weapons, Pakistani support for the U.S. in Afghanistan earned it elevated status as a "non-NATO ally," in the midst of revelations that its former chief nuclear scientist sold nuclear blueprints and material to Libya and North Korea.[58] The Iraq invasion catalyzed a further downward shift in trust and confidence levels. U.S. unilateralism and isolationism, though it has waxed and waned throughout the 20th century, has taken a heightened turn in recent years.[59] Its retreat to traditional "power politics" has negated its other capabilities, what Nye refers to as "soft power"—the ability to co-opt rather than coerce, through intangible resources such as culture, values, and institutions.[60] The stature of the U.S. as an exemplar of democracy has been greatly diminished, thereby compromising its capacity to lead multilateral initiatives, and its credibility to act as an honest broker in conflict-ridden countries. Everyone loses here.

We hope that the U.S., perhaps under a new administration, will assume a more constructive posture with a longer term view of its own interests, and those of the global community. Unfortunately, as Booth and Dunne crucially note, U.S. policy orientations have hardened since 9/11: "Introspection in the United States is discouraged by the very circumstances of the attack. Such was the sense of homeland violation that it was no surprise when President Bush demanded a loyalty test: 'Either you are with us or you are with the terrorists.'"[61] The State Department's propositions of a "global coalition against terrorism" and endorsement of diplomacy to "promote counterterrorism cooperation that serves our mutual interest" are grossly betrayed by the patently contrary actions taken by the U.S.[62]

On September 21, 2004, President Bush appeared before the U.N. General Assembly, not to explain, much less apologize, but to laud the accomplishments of the Coalition of the Willing for its enforcement of the "just demands of the world."[63] Bush requested a multilateral and UN-sanctioned effort to rebuild and stabilize Iraq: "Freedom is finding a way in Iraq and Afghanistan and we must continue to show our commitment to democracy in those nations. As members of the United Nations, we all have a stake in the success of the world's newest democracies."[64] The irony of this self righteousness and burden-casting does not require elaboration here. Suffice it to say that post-9/11 U.S. policies have placed human rights, international law, and global governance under considerable strain.

NOTES

1. Uniting And Strengthening America By Providing Appropriate Tools Required To Intercept And Obstruct Terrorism (USA Patriot Act) Act of 2001, Public Law 107-56—October 26, 2001. See also the Enhanced Border Security and Visa Entry Reform Act of 2002, Public Law 107-173—May 15, 2002.

2. Michael Ignatieff, The Lesser Evil: Political Ethics in an Age of Terror, Toronto: Penguin, 2004, p. 21.

3. Ignatieff, The Lesser Evil, p. 53.

4. Ignatieff, The Lesser Evil, p. 12.

5. The Patriot Act, Preamble.

6. The Patriot Act, Title II ("Enhanced Surveillance Procedures"), Section 201.

7. Ignatieff, The Lesser Evil, p. 58.

8. November 13, 2001 Military Order Issued by President George W. Bush, Detention, Treatment, and Trial of Certain Non-Citizens in the War Against Terrorism, Section 2(a)(1), The Federal Register.

9. 2001 Military Order, Detention, Treatment, and Trial of Certain Non-Citizens in the War Against Terrorism, Section 4(b) and (c).

10. 2001 Military Order, Detention, Treatment, and Trial of Certain Non-Citizens in the War Against Terrorism, Section 7(a)(2).

11. See Hamedi et al. v. Rumsfeld, Secretary of Defense, et al., Supreme Court of the United States, Certioarari to the United States Court of Appeals for the Fourth Circuit, No. 03-6696, June 28, 2004; and Rasul et al. v. Bush, President of the United States et al., Certioarari to the United States Court of Appeals for the District of Columbia Circuit, No. 03-334, June 28, 2004.

12. Cited in Ignatieff, The Lesser Evil, p. 32.

13. Ignatieff, The Lesser Evil, p. 61.

14. Ignatieff, The Lesser Evil, p. 21.

15. Ignatieff, The Lesser Evil, p. 40.

16. Michael McFaul, "Putin's Strong Hand Is Failing Russia (and His Allies in the West)," New York Times, September 14, 2004. According to McFaul, Putin has "undermined every independent source of political power, starting with the independent national media, then moving on to reign in federal executives, then striking out at Russia's superrich."

17. Colin Gray, "World Politics as Usual after September 11: Realism Vindicated," in Ken Booth and Tim Dunne, eds., Worlds in Collision: Terror and the Future of World Order, Basingstoke, UK: Palgrave Macmillan, 2002, p. 230.

18. See the third Geneva Convention Relative to the Treatment of Prisoners of War (75 UNTS 277, No. 3). Article 13 provides: "Prisoners of war must at all times be humanely treated [and] must at all times be protected against acts of violence or intimidation and against insults and public curiosity." Article 14 provides: "Prisoners of war are entitled in all circumstances to respect for their persons and their honour."

19. Mark Danner, "The Logic of Torture," New York Review of Books, vol. 51(11), June 24, 2004, p. 72. See also Danner, "Torture and Truth," New York Review of Books, vol. 51(10), June 10, 2004, pp. 46–50.

20. Ignatieff, The Lesser Evil, pp. 136–144.

21. Ignatieff, The Lesser Evil, pp. 139–141.

22. Ignatieff, The Lesser Evil, p. 140.

23. Ignatieff, The Lesser Evil, p. 141.

24. Ruth Wedgwood, "The Steps We Can Take to Prevent Another Abu Ghraib," Washington Post, May 23, 2004.

25. Ruth Wedgwood and James R. Woolsey, "Law and Torture," New York Times, Commentary, June 28, 2004.

26. See Ignatieff, The Lesser Evil, p. 7.

27. See Jack Donnelly, Realism and International Relations, Cambridge, UK: Cambridge University Press, 2000, p. 7.

28. See Hans J. Morgantheau, Politics Among Nations, 4th Edition, New York: Alfred Knopff, 1968, pp. 10–11; E. H. Carr, The Twenty Years' Crisis 1919–1939: An Introduction to the Study of

International Relations, 2nd Edition, London: Macmillan, 1962, p. 75; and Kenneth N. Waltz, Theory of International Politics, Reading, Massachusetts: Addison-Wesley, 1979, pp. 108–112.

29. Colin Gray, "World Politics as Usual after September 11: Realism Vindicated," in Ken Booth and Tim Dunne, eds., Worlds in Collision: Terror and the Future of World Order, Basingstoke, UK: Palgrave Macmillan, 2002, pp. 232–234.

30. See David Weissbrodt, "International Law of Economic, Social and Cultural Rights," in Rhoda E. Howard- Hassmann and Claude E. Welch, Jr., Sleeping under Bridges: Economic Rights in Canada and the United States, Philadelphia, PA: University of Pennsylvania Press, forthcoming 2005.

31. Antonio Cassese, International Law, New York: Oxford University Press, 2001, pp. 307–311.

32. Ruth Wedgwood, "Ius ad bellum Dilemmas of Article 2(4) of the UN Charter: Article 51 and Theories of Preemption in a Post-Deterrence Age," Lecture, Salzburg Law School on International Criminal, Humanitarian and Human Rights Law, August 18, 2004. In fact, the so-called "Bush Doctrine" of anticipatory self-defense, while clearly not established in customary international law, has been discussed previously in diplomatic circles, including within the UN Security Council in 1981. See Antonio Cassese, International Law, Oxford UK: Oxford University Press, 2001, pp. 308–309.

33. See generally Martha Finnemore, The Purpose of Intervention: Changing Beliefs About the Use of Force, Ithaca, NY: Cornell University Press, 1996; and J. L. Holzgrefe and Robert O. Keohane, eds., Humanitarian Intervention: Ethical, Legal and Political Dilemmas, Cambridge, U.K.: Cambridge University Press, 2003.

34. International Commission on Intervention and State Sovereignty, The Responsibility to Protect, Ottawa: International Development Research Centre, December 2001.

35. The Responsibility to Protect, Chapter 4, "The Responsibility to React," Paragraph 4.16.

36. The Responsibility to Protect, Chapter 6, "The Question of Authority," Paragraph 6.22.

37. The Responsibility to Protect, Chapter 6, "The Question of Authority," Paragraph 6.29.

38. The Responsibility to Protect, Chapter 6, "The Question of Authority," Paragraphs 6.31–6.35.

39. The Security Council determined that Iraq had "not provided an accurate, full, final, and complete disclosure" of its weapons programs, and warned of "serious consequences as a result of its continued violations of its obligations." See United Nations Security Council Resolution 1441 (2002), November 8, 2002, S/RES/1441(2002). The Council subsequently appealed to states to undertake a range of consultative, collaborative, and implementing measures to address the "proliferation of nuclear, chemical and biological weapons," but did not authorize the U.S. to use armed force. See United Nations Security Council Resolution 1540 (2004), S/RES/1540 (2004).

40. David M. Malone and Yuen Foong Khong, "Resisting the Unilateral Impulse: Multilateral Engagement and the Future of U.S. Leadership," in Malone and Foong Khong, eds., U.S. Foreign Policy: International Perspectives, Boulder, CO: Lynne Rienner Publishers, 2003, p. 426.

41. The Responsibility to Protect, Chapter 6, "The Question of Authority," Paragraph 6.36.

42. Michael Byers, "Terror and the Future of International Law," in Ken Booth and Tim Dunne, eds., Worlds in Collision: Terror and the Future of World Order, Basingstoke, UK: Palgrave, Macmillan, 2002, p. 124.

43. See, for example, The Legality and Constitutionality of the President's Authority to Initiate an Invasion of Iraq, Report of The Committee on International Security Affairs of the Association of the Bar of the City of New York, July 2002.

44. The Responsibility to Protect, Chapter 4, "The Responsibility to React," Paragraphs 4.10–4.14.

45. The Responsibility to Protect, Chapter 4, "The Responsibility to React," Paragraph 4.13.

46. Simon Chesterman, Just War or Just Peace? Humanitarian Intervention and International Law, Oxford, UK: Oxford University Press, 2001, p. 223.

47. The Responsibility to Protect, Chapter 2, "A New Approach: 'The Responsibility to Protect,'" Paragraph 2.29.

48. See David Stout, "Kerry Criticizes Bush and Cheney on Halliburton's Iraq Contracts," *New York Times*, September 17, 2004.

49. The Responsibility to Protect, Chapter 4, "The Responsibility to React," Paragraphs 4.32–4.43.

50. The Responsibility to Protect, Chapter 4, "The Responsibility to React," Paragraph 4.32.

51. Leo Kuper, Genocide: Its Political Use in the Twentieth Century, New York: Penguin, 1981.

52. M. Cherif Bassiouni, "Legal Control of International Terrorism: A Policy Oriented Assessment," (2002), Reprinted in Charlotte Ku and Paul F. Diehl, eds., International Law: Classic and Contemporary Readings, second edition, Boulder, CO: Lynne Rienner Publishers, 2003, p. 316. At p. 317, Bassiouni lists six "modalities" of law enforcement and intelligence cooperation—extradition, transfer of criminal proceedings, recognition of foreign penal judgments, transfer of sentenced persons, and freezing and seizing of assets—which, while present in some bilateral agreements, are not contained in a single integrated international convention.

53. James Der Derrian, "In Terrorem: Before and After 9/11," in Ken Booth and Tim Dunne, eds., Worlds in Collision: Terror and the Future of World Order, Basingstoke, UK: Palgrave Macmillan, 2002, p. 101.

54. On September 18, 2002, the Senate and Congress passed a Joint Resolution authorizing "the President to use all necessary and appropriate force against those nations, organizations, or persons responsible he determines planned, authorized, committed, or aided the terrorist attacks that occurred on September 11, 2001, or harbored such organizations or persons, in order to prevent future acts..." See Joint Resolution to authorize the use of United States Armed Forces against those responsible for the recent attacks launched against the United States, Public Law 107-40—September 18, 2001.

55. Michael Byers, "Terror and the Future of International Law," in Ken Booth and Tim Dunne, eds., Worlds in Collision: Terror and the Future of World Order, Basingstoke, UK: Palgrave Macmillan, 2002, p. 121.

56. See, for example, Julie Mertus, Bait and Switch: Human Rights and American Foreign Policy (New York: Routledge, 2004); Jack Donnelly, "Human Rights and Foreign Policy," in International Human Rights, second edition (Boulder, CO: Westview Press, 1998), pp. 86–114; Robert F. Drinan, "Grading the State Department's Reports on Human Rights," in The Mobilization of Shame (New Haven, CT: Yale University Press, 2001), pp. 84–94; Rosemary Foot, "Credibility at Stake: Domestic Supremacy in U.S. Human Rights Policy," in David M. Malone and Yuen Foong Khong, eds., U.S. Foreign Policy: International Perspectives, Boulder CO: Lynne Rienner Publishers, 2003, pp. 95–166; and Richard A. Falk, "A Half-Century of Human Rights," in Human Rights Horizons: The Pursuit of Justice in a Globalizing World (New York: Routledge, 2000), pp. 37–56.

57. See Vera Beaudin Saeedpour, "Establishing State Motives for Genocide: Iraq and the Kurds," in Helen Fein, ed. Genocide Watch, New Haven: Yale University Press, 1992, pp. 59–69.

58. Amitai Etzioni, "Loose nuclear arms are the biggest threat," *International Herald Tribune*, May 3, 2004.

59. The U.S. has refused to engage constructively in a range of multilateral initiatives, such as the Kyoto Protocol, the proposed additional Protocol on Torture, the Ottawa Convention on Land Mines, the Anti-Ballistic Missile Treaty, and the Rome Statute of the International Criminal Court. See generally, David Malone, "A Decade of U.S. Unilateralism?" in Malone and Yuen Foong Khong, eds., U.S. Foreign Policy:eds., International Perspectives, Boulder, CO: Lynne Rienner Publishers, 2003, pp. 19–38.

60. Joseph S. Nye, The Paradox of American Power: Why the World's Only Superpower Can't Go It Alone, New York: Oxford University Press, 2002, p. 9.

61. Ken Booth and Tim Dunne, "Worlds in Collision," in Booth and Dunne, eds. Worlds in Collision: Terror and the Future of World Order, Basingstoke, UK: Palgrave Macmillan, 2002, p. 2.

62. See U.S. State Department, Diplomacy and the Global Coalition Against Terrorism, On the Diplomatic Front, available at www.state.gov/coalition/dplm/.

63. President George W. Bush, Address to the United Nations General Assembly, September 21, 2004, UN News Centre, p. 3.

64. President George W. Bush, Address to the United Nations General Assembly, September 21, 2004, UN News Centre, p. 5.

*Adrian L. Jones is a Ph.D. candidate in international relations at McMaster University in Hamilton, Ontario. His dissertation research focuses on the global governance implications of the permanent International Criminal Court (established in 1998). In 2004–2005, he was a Graduate Research Fellow at the Institute on Globalization and the Human Condition.

Rhoda E. Howard-Hassmann is Canada Research Chair in International Human Rights at Wilfrid Laurier University, Waterloo, Ontario, where she holds a joint appointment in the Department of Global Studies and the Balsillie School of International Affairs.

Jones, Adrian L., and Rhoda E. Howard-Hassmann. "Under Strain: Human Rights and International Law in the Post 9/11 Era." *Journal of Human Rights* 4 (2005): 61–71.

Reprinted by permission of the publisher (Taylor & Francis Ltd., http://www.tandf.co.uk/journals).

International Human Rights Law and the War on Terrorism

*by Derek Jinks**

The September 11th terrorist attacks prompted a rethinking of the relationship between liberty and security. The attacks exemplify a new mode of organizing sustained violence that poses a fundamental challenge to United States (U.S.) and international law. Indeed, Anne-Marie Slaughter and William Burke-White recently described this critical juncture in global politics as an "international constitutional moment."[1] In the wake of the attacks, the U.S. confronted this challenge by initiating several important changes in its law and policy—the architecture of the "war on terrorism."[2] To be sure, the U.S. response generated substantial controversy concerning three related issues: (1) the most appropriate forum for prosecuting individuals responsible for the September 11th attacks[3]; (2) the international legal status of combatants captured in Afghanistan[4]; and, more generally, (3) the most appropriate role for law in any comprehensive strategy against international terrorism.[5] It is striking that these debates turn on which law, if any, applies in the "war on terrorism." The questions structuring these debates are by now familiar: Does the Constitution protect "enemy aliens?" Do the Geneva Conventions protect "unlawful combatants?" Although these are critical questions, the focus on U.S. constitutional law and international humanitarian law has unfortunately obscured the importance of another potentially relevant body of law: international human rights law. If applicable, international human rights law would establish conclusively—irrespective of the applicability of the Geneva Conventions or U.S. Constitution—that all persons subject to the jurisdiction of the United States, as a matter of law, are entitled to certain basic rights including: the right not to be detained arbitrarily; the right to humane conditions and treatment if detained; and, the right to a fair trial on any criminal charges.

INTERNATIONAL DUE PROCESS STANDARDS

For example, international human rights law informs the legal analysis of the most controversial aspects of U.S. antiterrorism policy including: trial of suspected terrorists by military commission[6]; indefinite detention of citizens designated as "enemy combatants"[7]; and, prolonged detention of aliens suspected of terrorist activity.[8] It is important to note that several international human rights treaties,[9] declarations,[10] and resolutions[11] establish minimum procedural protections for all individuals deprived of their personal liberty. Under Article 9 of the International Covenant on Civil and Political Rights (ICCPR), no one shall be "subjected to arbitrary arrest or detention"[12] or "deprived of his liberty except on such grounds and in accordance with such procedure as are established by law."[13] This provision also specifies that "anyone who is arrested shall be informed, at the time of arrest, of the reasons for his arrest and shall be promptly informed of any charges against him."[14] Article 9(3) provides that all persons arrested or detained on a criminal charge "shall be brought promptly before a judge or other officer authorized by law to exercise judicial power and shall be entitled to trial within a reasonable time or to release."[15] As interpreted by the United Nations (U.N.) Human Rights Committee,[16] the provision requires at a minimum that an individual must be brought before a judge or other officer within "a few days."[17] Finally, The ICCPR provides for the right to habeas corpus, or amparo.[18] Under this provision, anyone deprived of liberty by arrest or detention has the right to "take proceedings before a court, in order that that court may decide without delay on the lawfulness of his detention and order his release if the detention is not lawful."[19] International human rights law has also established an extensive inventory of procedural rights for individuals facing criminal charges. The Universal Declaration of Human Rights (UDHR),[20] ICCPR,[21] African Charter on Human and Peoples' Rights, (Banjul Charter)[22] Inter-American Convention on Human Rights (ACHR)[23] and the European Convention on Human Rights (ECHR)[24] all include detailed fair trial provisions. Specifically, Article 14 of the ICCPR recognizes the right to "a fair trial and public hearing by a competent, independent and impartial tribunal established by law."[25] This provision enumerates the minimum procedural requirements of a "fair trial," including the right to be presumed innocent,[26] the right to be tried without undue delay,[27] the right to prepare a defense,[28] the right to defend oneself in person or through counsel,[29] the right to call and examine witnesses,[30] and the right to protection from retroactive criminal laws.[31]

INTERNATIONAL HUMAN RIGHTS AND U.S. LAW

The central claim of this essay is that international human rights law conditions the exercise of U.S. power in the "war on terrorism."[32] In one sense, international human rights law clearly applies in that the United States has ratified several human rights treaties, including the ICCPR, and all treaties lawfully made under the U.S. Constitution are part of the "supreme law of the land."[33] In addition, agencies of the U.S. government, including the Department of Defense, are required by Executive Order to comply with the ICCPR.[34] Although the U.S. made clear its understanding that the substantive provisions of the ICCPR are "non-self executing," the treaty nevertheless establish international legal obligations binding on the executive and legislative branches of government.[35] Moreover, the nature of international human rights law suggests that it applies in all circumstances. That is, international human rights law defines the minimum rights protections necessary to prevent the arbitrary exercise of power. This body of law reflects the collective normative aspirations of the international community; and, as such, provides an indispensable framework for evaluating specific policy options in the "war on terrorism."

WARTIME AND OTHER "STATES OF EXCEPTION"

The robust regime of procedural rights embodied in the ICCPR would, if applicable, call into question several aspects of U.S. antiterrorism policy. Indeed, the U.N. Human Rights Committee repeatedly declared special military courts and "national security" detention laws inconsistent with the ICCPR.[36] The application of the ICCPR to U.S. action in the "war on terrorism" is, however, complicated by the fact that these actions are undertaken in the context of an ongoing, formally proclaimed national emergency[37] and an international armed conflict.[38] Defining the scope of application of the ICCPR therefore requires an assessment of the degree to which international human rights law applies in times of war and other states of emergency.

International human rights treaties allow the suspension of some rights in public emergencies (such as times of war).[39] Article 4 of the ICCPR provides that in situations threatening the life of the nation, a government may issue a formal declaration suspending certain human rights guarantees provided that: (1) a state of emergency that threatens the life of the nation exists[40]; (2) the exigencies of the situation "strictly require" such a suspension[41]; (3) the suspension does not conflict with the nation's other international obligations[42]; (4) the emergency measures are applied in a non-discriminatory fashion[43]; and, (5) the government notifies the United Nations Secretary-General immediately.[44] Some rights, however, are not subject to derogation even in times of public emergency.[45] The ICCPR specifically identifies several non-derogable obligations including the rights to be freeing from arbitrary killing[46]; torture or other cruel, inhuman or degrading treatment or punishment[47]; and slavery.[48] Although the rights to fair trial and personal liberty are, as a formal matter, derogable provisions,[49] the U.N. Human Rights Committee has made clear that many restrictions of these rights are inappropriate even in times of emergency.[50] Indeed, the Committee, in its General Comment 29, stated that:

> Safeguards related to derogation . . . are based on the principles of legality and the rule of law inherent in the Covenant as a whole. As certain elements of the right to a fair trial are explicitly guaranteed under international humanitarian law during armed conflict, the Committee finds no justification for derogation from these guarantees during other emergency situations. The Committee is of the opinion that the principles of legality and the rule of law require that fundamental requirements of fair trial must be respected during a state of emergency. Only a court of law may try and convict a person for a criminal offence.[51]

The U.N. Human Rights Committee has also emphasized that procedural rights, such as fair trial rights, must be respected even in times of emergency in order to protect other non-derogable rights.[52] Finally, the Committee, following the lead of the Inter-American Court of Human Rights,[53] strongly suggested that, at a minimum, the right to habeas corpus (or amparo) is non-derogable.[54]

The United States has not, and arguably could not, invoke Article 4 to preclude application of the ICCPR in the "war on terrorism." First, the United States has not filed a derogation notice with the other state parties, through the Secretary-General of the United Nations, as required under Article 4 (3). Indeed, the United States has not proclaimed, as matter of domestic law, that emergency conditions necessitating the suspension of fundamental rights exist. Second, substantial evidence suggests that several of the "derogation measures" are not strictly required by the exigencies of the circumstances. Of course, the United States has offered no evidence that specific derogation measures are strictly necessary to meet the immediate threat of catastrophic terrorism. Additionally, the fact that investigation, trial, and conviction of Al Qaeda operatives has been successfully conducted by utilizing ordinary criminal procedure and without compromising national security, strongly suggests that many of the most controversial measures are not necessary to confront the emergency conditions. Third, the nature of the emergency itself may fail to satisfy the threshold requirements of Article 4. Although the September 11th attacks almost certainly constituted an emergency "threatening the life of the nation," the continuing, non-specific and ill-defined threat of terrorist activity does not satisfy this requirement. Moreover, because "states of exception" are, by their nature, of limited duration, the U.S. may not manufacture an ongoing state of emergency by waging a protracted—perhaps indefinite—"war on terrorism." Finally, the derogation measures arguably suspend non-derogable rights (and rights necessary to protect non-derogable rights) by violating the personal liberty and fair trial provisions of the ICCPR.[55]

CONCLUSION

International human rights law recognizes the bare minimum of standards necessary to protect the safety and integrity of individuals from abuses of power. As such, it governs how states treat all people in all circumstances—even in time of war. Nevertheless, this body of law provides for "improved human rights to be matched by accommodations in favor of the reasonable needs of the State to perform its public duties for the common good."[56] In furtherance of this objective, human rights treaties explicitly authorize states to restrict or suspend some rights, subject to several requirements, for an identified set of important public policy objectives. These codified "states of exception" strike a balance between universal human rights norms and national interests by specifying the circumstances in which states may lawfully abrogate treaty obligations. Most important for the purposes of this essay, "derogation clauses" permit the suspension of certain rights in times of war or public emergency. This derogation regime does not, however, preclude application of the ICCPR to the "war on terrorism."

NOTES

1. Anne-Marie Slaughter & William Burke-White, An International Constitutional Moment, 43 Harv. J. Int'l L. 1 (2002).

2. George W. Bush, Address to a Joint Session of Congress and the American People, Sept. 20, 2001, available at http://www.whitehouse.gov/news/releases/2001/09/20010920-8.html (last visited Oct. 21, 2002).

3. See, e.g., Harold Hongju Koh, We Have the Right Courts for Bin-Laden, N.Y. Times, Nov. 23, 2001, at A39 (arguing that any such trials should be conducted in federal district court); Anne-Marie Slaughter, Al Qaeda Should Be Tried Before the World, N.Y. Times, Nov. 17, 2001, at A23 (arguing that the U.N. Security Council should establish another ad hoc tribunal); Paul R. Williams & Michael P. Scharf, Prosecute Terrorists on a World Stage, L.A. Times, Nov. 18, 2001, at M5 (suggesting that the statute of the International Criminal Tribunal for the Former Yugoslavia be amended to confer jurisdiction over the September 11th attacks); Ruth Wedgwood, The Case for Military Tribunals, Wall St. J., Dec. 3, 2001, at A18 (supporting military commissions of the sort envisioned in President Bush's Military Order); Laura Dickinson, Courts Can Avenge Sept. 11: International Justice—Not War—will Honor our Character while Ensuring our Safety, Legal Times, Sept. 24, 2001, at 66 (supporting "internationalized" trials in other national jurisdictions). On the legality of military commissions specifically, see Neal K. Katyal & Laurence Tribe, Waging War, Deciding Guilt: Trying the Military Tribunals, 111 Yale L.J. 1259 (2002); George P. Fletcher, On Justice and War: Contradictions in the Proposed Military Tribunals, 25 Harv. J. L & Pub. Pol'y. 635 (2002); George P. Fletcher, War and the Constitution; Bush's Military Tribunals Haven't Got a Legal Leg to Stand On, The American Prospect, Jan. 1–14, 2002, at 26.; Curtis A. Bradley & Jack L. Goldsmith, The Constitutional Validity of Military Commissions, 5 Green Bag 2d 249 (2002); Abraham D. Sofaer & Paul R. Williams, Doing Justice During Wartime: Why Military Tribunals Make Sense, 111 Pol'y Rev. 3 (2002).

4. The controversy concerns whether detained al Qaeda and Taliban fighters qualify for "prisoner of war" (POW) status under the Geneva Conventions. See Geneva Convention Relative to the Treatment of Prisoners of War, Aug. 12, 1949, 75 U.N.T.S. 287, entered into force Oct. 21, 1950. See e.g., Coalition of Clergy et al. v. Bush, 189 F. Supp. 2d 1036 (C. D. Cal. 2002) (denying habeas petition brought on behalf of Camp X-Ray detainees); John Cerone, Status of

Detainees in International Armed Conflict, and their Protection in the Course of Criminal Proceedings, ASIL INSIGHTS (Jan. 2002) available at http://www.asil.org/insights/insigh81 .htm (last visited Oct. 21, 2002); Alfred P. Rubin, Applying the Geneva Conventions: Military Commissions, Armed Conflict, and al Qaeda, 26 Fletcher F. World. Aff. J. 79 (2002).

5. See generally Sofaer & Williams, supra note 3; Note, Responding to Terrorism: Crime, Punishment, and War, 115 Harv. L. Rev. 1217 (2002); see also Ruth Wedgwood, The Rules of War Can't Protect Al Qaeda, N.Y. Times, Dec. 31, 2001, at A11 (suggesting that the law has no role in war on terror).

6. Military Order of November 13, 2001, Detention, Treatment, and Trial of Certain Non-Citizens in the War Against Terrorism, 66 Fed. Reg. 57,833, (Nov. 16, 2001) [hereinafter Military Order]. The Department of Defense (DOD) has implemented the Order by issuing the rules of procedure and evidence for the commissions. See Department of Defense, Military Commission Order No. 1, Procedures for Trials by Military Commissions of Certain Non-United States Citizens in the War Against Terrorism, (Mar. 21, 2002) [hereinafter DOD Rules]. The use of military commissions in U.S. history is well documented. See generally David J. Bederman, Article II Courts, 44 Mercer L. Rev. 825 (1993); William E. Burkhimer, Military Government and Martial Law 351–69 (Franklin Hudson Pub. 1914) (1892); George B. Davis, A Treatise on the Military Law of the United States 307–13 (John Wiley & Sons, 1915) (1898); William Winthrop, Military Law and Precedents 832–34 (William S. Hein & Co., 1979) (1920).

7. See Amnesty International, Memorandum to the U.S. Government on the Rights of People in U.S. Custody in Afghanistan and Guantanamo Bay (April 2002), available at Amnesty International Online, http://web.amnesty.org/ai.nsf/recent/AMR510532002 (last visited Oct. 21, 2002).

8. See, e.g., David Cole, Enemy Aliens, 54 Stan. L. Rev. 953 (May 2002); David Firestone & Christopher Drew, Al Qaeda Link Seen in Only a Handful of 1,200 Detainees, N.Y. Times, Nov. 29, 2001, at A1.

9. See, e.g., International Covenant on Civil and Political Rights, Dec. 16, 1966, arts. 9, 14, & 15, 999 U.N.T.S. 171 [hereinafter ICCPR]; The African Charter on Human and Peoples' Rights, June 27, 1981, arts. 3, 6, & 7, 21 I.L.M. 58 [hereinafter Banjul Charter]; American Convention on Human Rights, Nov. 22, 1969, arts. 7, 8 & 9, 1144 U.N.T.S. 123 [hereinafter ACHR]; European Convention for the Protection of Human Rights and Fundamental Freedoms, Nov. 4, 1950, arts. 5, 6 & 7, 213 U.N.T.S. 221, E.T.S. 5, as amended by Protocol No. 3, E.T.S. 45, Protocol No. 5, E.T.S. 55, and Protocol No. 8, E.T.S. 118 [hereinafter ECHR]; Convention against Torture and Other Cruel, Inhuman or Degrading Treatment or Punishment, U.N. GAOR, 39th Sess., Supp. No. 51, at 197, U.N. Doc. A/39/51 (1984), entered into force June 26, 1987 (art. 7) [hereinafter Convention Against Torture].

10. See, e.g., Universal Declaration of Human Rights, arts. 9–11, G.A. Res. 217, U.N. GAOR, 3d Sess., at 72, U.N. Doc. A/810 (1948) [hereinafter UDHR].

11. See, e.g., Basic Principles on the Role of Lawyers, Eighth U.N. Congress on the Prevention of Crime and the Treatment of Offenders, Havana, 27 Aug. to 7 Sept. 1990, U.N. Doc. A/CONF.144/28/Rev.1 at 118 (1990); Guidelines on the Role of Prosecutors, Eighth U.N. Congress on the Prevention of Crime and the Treatment of Offenders, Havana, 27 Aug. to 7 Sept. 1990, U.N. Doc. A/CONF.144/28/Rev.1 at 189 (1990); Body of Principles for the Protection of All Persons under Any Form of Detention or Imprisonment, G.A. Res. 43/173, annex, 43 U.N. GAOR 43d Sess., Supp. No. 49, at 298, U.N. Doc. A/43/49 (1988)[hereinafter Body of Principles]; Basic Principles on the Independence of the Judiciary, Seventh U.N. Congress on the Prevention of Crime and the Treatment of Offenders, Milan, 26 Aug. to 6 Sept. 1985, U.N. Doc. A/CONF.121/22/Rev.1 at 59 (1985); Standard Minimum Rules for the Treatment of Prisoners, U.N. Doc. A/CONF/611, annex 1, E.S.C. Res. 663C, 24 U.N. ESCOR Supp. No. 1, at 11, U.N. Doc. E/3048 (1957), amended by E.S.C. Res. 2076, 62 U.N. ESCOR Supp. No. 1 at 35, U.N. Doc. E/5988 (1977) (Part II. A. Prisoners Under Sentence and Part II. C. Prisoners Under Arrest or Awaiting Trial).

12. ICCPR, supra note 9, art. 9(1).

13. Id.

14. ICCPR, supra note 9, art. 9(2).

15. ICCPR, supra note 9, art. 9(3). Note that Article 9(3) of the ICCPR applies only to individuals arrested or detained on a criminal charge, while the other rights recognized in the Article apply to all persons deprived of their liberty. People awaiting trial on criminal charges should not, as a general rule, be held in custody. In accordance with the right to liberty and the presumption of innocence, persons charged with a criminal offence, in general, should not be detained before trial. See id.; id., art. 14(3). International standards explicitly recognize that there are, however, circumstances in which authorities may detain an accused pending trial. See id., art. 9(3); see also Body of Principles, supra note 11, Principle 39; United Nations Standard Minimum Rules for Non-custodial Measures, 14 Dec. 1990, Res. 45/110 Principle 6; ACHR, supra note 9, art.7(5). For example, pre-trial detention is permissible if authorities determine that detention is necessary to prevent flight, interference with witnesses, or when the accused poses a clear and serious risk to others which cannot be contained by less restrictive means. See Van Alphen v. the Netherlands, (305/1988), 23 July 1990, Report of the HRC Vol. II, (A/45/40), 1990, at 115. Therefore, pre-trial detention must not only be lawful, but must also be necessary and reasonable in the circumstances.

16. The ICCPR established the United Nations Human Rights Committee to monitor state parties' compliance with the treaty. See ICCPR, supra note 9, art. 40. This monitoring function involves three complementary procedures. First, the ICCPR establishes a periodic reporting process. See id. art. 40(1). Under the reporting process, the Committee receives periodic written reports from state parties which explain the measures they have taken to protect the rights recognized in the treaties. See id. Government representatives present the reports to the U.N. Human Rights Committee in public sessions; Committee members question the representatives about issues raised in the reports; and the Committee publishes comments and recommendations on how to improve the protection of human rights in the state in question. Second, the Committee drafts "general comments" typically concerning the interpretation of the substantive rights and freedoms contained in the treaty each committee oversees. See United Nations High Commission for Human Rights/United Nations Human Rights Centre, Treaty Database Homepage at http://www.unhchr.ch/tbs/doc.nsf (last visited Oct. 21, 2002) [hereinafter UNHCHR Database] See, e.g., Dominic McGoldrick, The Human Rights Committee 95 (Oxford University Press, 1991) ("The general comments serve rapidly to develop the jurisprudence of the HRC under the Covenant."). Third, and most important, the Committee receives written "communications" or "petitions" from individuals alleging that a State party has violated one or more rights protected by the ICCPR. See Optional Protocol to the International Covenant on Civil and Political Rights, done Dec. 16, 1966, 999 U.N.T.S. 302 [hereinafter Optional Protocol]; Torkel Opsahl, The Human Rights Committee, in The United Nations and Human Rights: A Critical Appraisal (Philip Alston, ed., Oxford University Press, 1992). This procedure is optional, however, and many states party to the ICCPR do not recognize the competence of the Committee to receive individual petitions. See Human Rights Committee, Optional Protocol available at http://www1.umn.edu/humanrts/hrcommittee/hrc-page.html (last visited Aug. 31, 2000) (stating that 95 of the 144 parties to the ICCPR have ratified the Optional Protocol). Under the First Optional Protocol to the ICCPR, the Committee performs a quasi-judicial function when reviewing individual petitions. See Tom Zwart, The Admissibility of Human Rights Petitions (Martinus Nijhoff Pub. 1994). Although the Committee's decisions are not legally binding, they are widely viewed as persuasive authority and several States have implemented the Committee's interpretation of the treaty. See Laurence R. Helfer & Anne-Marie Slaughter, Toward a Theory of Effective Supranational Adjudication, 107 Yale L.J. 273, 344–45 (1997).

17. See Office of the United Nations High Commissioner for Human Rights, Righ to Liberty and Security of Persons (art. 9), 16 [su'th'] Sess., CCPR General Comment 8, para. 2 (1982). Note that this provision does not explicitly recognize a right to counsel for all accused at this stage of the proceedings. The Human Rights Committee has stated, however, that "all persons arrested must have immediate access to counsel." See Concluding Observations on State Part Report: Georgia, Human Rights Committee, UN Doc. CCPR/C/79/Add.74, 9 April 1997, at para. 28. See also Body of Principles, supra note 11, principle 18(1); Basic Principles on the Role of Lawyers, supra note 11, principle 1 (stating that "all persons are entitled to call upon the assistance of a lawyer of their choice to protect and establish their rights and to defend them

in all stages of criminal proceedings."); id., principle 7 (requiring governments to ensure that all persons arrested or detained have access to a lawyer within 48 hours from arrest or detention); see also id., Principle 5 (providing that all persons arrested, charged or detained must be promptly informed of their right to legal assistance); id., principle 8 (requiring authorities to ensure that all arrested, detained or imprisoned persons have adequate opportunities to be visited by and to communicate with their lawyer without delay, interception or censorship, in full confidentiality). It also has been widely recognized that prompt and regular access to a lawyer for all detainees is an important safeguard against torture, ill-treatment, coerced confessions and other abuses. See, e.g., Report of the UN Special Rapporteur on Torture, U.N. Doc. E/CN.4/1992/17, 17 December 1991, at para.284.

18. ICCPR, supra note 9, art. 9(4).

19. ICCPR, supra note 9, art. 9(4).

20. See UDHR, supra note 10, art. 10.

21. See ICCPR, supra note 9, art. 14.

22. See Banjul Charter, supra note 9, arts. 7, 26. The African Commission on Human and Peoples' Rights has adopted a resolution on the Right to Recourse Procedure and Fair Trial which elaborates on article 7 (1) of the Banjul Charter and guarantees several additional rights, including: notification of charges, appearance before a judicial officer, right to release pending trial, presumption of innocence, adequate preparation of the defense, speedy trial, examination of witnesses and the right to an interpreter. See Doc. No. ACHPR/COMM/FIN (XI)/Annex VII, 9 March 1992.

23. See ACHR, supra note 9, art. 8.

24. See ECHR, supra note 9, art. 6.

25. ICCPR, supra note 9, art. 14(1).

26. See ICCPR, supra note 9, art. 14(2); ECHR, supra note 9, art.6(2).

27. See ICCPR, supra note 9, art. 14(3)(c); ECHR, supra note 9, art. 6(1).

28. See ICCPR, supra note 9, art. 14(3)(d); ECHR, supra note 9, art. 6(3)(b).

29. See, ICCPR, supra note 9, at art. 14(3)(d); ECHR, supra note 9, at art. 6(3)(d): In the determination of any criminal charge against him, everyone shall be entitled to the following minimum guarantees, in full equality: (d) To be tried in his presence, and to defend himself in person or through legal assistance of his own choosing; to be informed, if he does not have legal assistance, of this right; and to have legal assistance assigned to him, in any case where the interests of justice so require, and without payment by him in any such case if he does not have sufficient means to pay for it.

30. See, ICCPR, supra note 9, at art. 14(3)(e). See also ECHR, supra note 9, at art. 6(3)(d); ACHR, supra note 9, at art. 8(2)(f): In the determination of any criminal charge against him, everyone shall be entitled to the following minimum guarantees, in full equality: (e) To examine, or have examined, the witnesses against him and to obtain the attendance and examination of witnesses on his behalf under the same conditions as witnesses against him.

31. See ICCPR, supra note 9, art. 15(1) ("No one shall be held guilty of any criminal offence on account of any act or omission which did not constitute a criminal offence, under national or international law, at the time when it was committed").

32. Whether any particular U.S. policy contravenes the substantive provisions of the ICCPR is beyond the scope of this essay. I will therefore analyze the substantive requirements of the treaty only insofar as these provisions inform analysis of the conditions under which the ICCPR is applicable. See ICCPR, supra note 9.

33. See U.S. Const. art.VI, .2.

34. Executive Order 13,107 directs all members of the executive branch to comply with the ICCPR. See Exec. Order No. 13,107, 63 Fed. Reg. 68,991 (1998), reprinted in 38 I.L.M. 493 (1999). [hereinafter Executive Order]. The preamble of the Executive Order names three human rights treaties in particular: the ICCPR, supra note 9; the Convention Against Torture, supra note 9;

and the International Convention on the Elimination of All Forms of Racial Discrimination, Mar. 7, 1966, 660 U.N.T.S. 195, reprinted in 5 I.L.M. 352 (1966). However, it also recognizes that the Executive Order shall apply to "other relevant treaties concerned with protection and promotion of human rights to which the United States is now or may become a party in the future." Executive Order 13,107, supra, at 68,991.

35. See Louis Henkin, Foreign Affairs and the U.S. Constitution 198-204 (Foundation Press, 2nd ed. 1996). In addition, the "non-self executing" declarations arguably do not preclude defendants from invoking treaty rights defensively. See United States v. Duarte-Acero, 132 F. Supp.2d 1036, 1040 (S.D. Fla. 2001) (holding the prohibition against private causes of action does not apply when raising "ICCPR claims defensively"); See also John Quigley, Human Rights Defenses in U.S. Courts, 20 Hum. Rts. Q. 555, 580–82 (1998); David Sloss, The Domestication of International Human Rights: Non-Self-Executing Declarations and Human Rights Treaties, 24 Yale J. Int'l L. 129, 210–214 (1999).

36. See, e.g., Acosta v. Uruguay, Comm. No. 110/1981 (1983), U.N. Doc. Supp. No. 40 (A/39/40) at 169 (1984); Scarrone v. Uruguay, Comm. No. 103/1981 (1982), U.N. Doc. Supp. No. 40 (A/39/40) at 154 (1984); Barbato & Barbato v. Uruguay, Comm. No. 84/1981, (1981), U.N. Doc. Supp. No. 40 (A/38/40) at 124 (1983); Schweizer v. Uruguay, Comm. No. 66/1980 (1980), U.N. Doc. Supp. No. 40 (A/38/40) at 117 (1983); Conteris v. Uruguay, Comm. No. 139/1983 (1985), U.N. Doc. Supp. No. 40 (A/40/40) at 196 (1985); Machado v. Uruguay, Comm. No. 83/1981 (1982), U.N. Doc. Supp. No. 40 (A/39/40) at 148 (1984); Lluberas v. Uruguay, Comm. No. 123/1982 (1983), U.N. Doc. Supp. No. 40 (A/39/40) at 175 (1984); Nieto v. Uruguay, Comm. No. 92/1981 (1981), U.N. Doc. Supp. No. 40 (A/38/40) at 201 (1983); Caldas v. Uruguay, Comm. No. 43/1979 (1979), U.N. Doc. Supp. No. 40 (A/38/40) at 192 (1983); Magana ex-Philibert v. Zaire, Comm. No. 90/1981 (1981), U.N. Doc. Supp. No. 40 (A/38/40) at 197 (1983); Altesor v. Uruguay, Comm. No.R.2/10 (1977), U.N. Doc. Supp. No. 40 (A/37/40) at 122 (1982); Pietraroia v. Uruguay, Comm. No.R.10/44 (1979), U.N. Doc. Supp. No. 40 (A/36/40) at 153 (1981); Bouton v. Uruguay, Comm. No. R.9/37 (1978), U.N. Doc. Supp. No. 40 (A/36/40) at 143 (1981); Touron v. Uruguay, Comm. No. R.7/32 (1978), U.N. Doc. Supp. No. 40 (A/36/40) at 120 (1981); Motta v. Uruguay, Comm. No. R.2/11 (1977), U.N. Doc. Supp. No. 40 (A/35/40) at 132 (1980); Muteba v. Zaire, Comm. No. 124/1982 (1983), U.N. Doc. Supp. No. 40 (A/39/40) at 182 (1984); Borda v. Columbia, Comm. No.R.11/46 (1979), U.N. Doc. Supp. No. 40 (A/37/40) at 193 (1982).

37. President George W. Bush, Remarks by the President in Photo Opportunity with the National Security Team, (September 12, 2001), available at http://www.whitehouse.gov/news/releases/2001/09/20010912-4.html (last visited DATE).

38. Mike Mount, U.S. Mounts New al Qaeda Hunt in Afghanistan, available at CNN.com, http://www.cnn.com/2002/WORLD/asiapcf/central/09/09/afghanistan.sweep/index.html (last visited on Oct. 21, 2002).

39. See, e.g., ECHR, supra note 9, at art. 15(1); ICCPR, supra note 9, at art.4(1); ACHR, supra note 9, art. 27(1). For useful surveys of this area of law, See Anna-Lena Svensson-McCarthy, The International Law of Human Rights and States of Exception (M. Nijhoff Publishers, 1998); Joan Fitzpatrick, Human Rights in Crisis: the International System for Protecting Rights During States of Emergency (University of Pennsylvania Press, 1994); Jaime Oraa, Human Rights in States of Emergency in International Law (Oxford University Press, 1992).

40. See Svensson-McCarthy, supra note 39, at 195–281; Fitzpatrick, supra note 39; Fionnuala Ni Aolain, The Emergence of Diversity: Differences in Human Rights Jurisprudence, 19 Fordham Int'l L. J. 101, 103 (1995) (arguing that the concept of a "state of emergency refers to those exceptional circumstances resulting from temporary factors of a political nature, which, to varying degrees, involve extreme and imminent danger that threaten the organized existence of the state"); Lawless Case (Ireland), 1961 Y.B. Eur. Conv. On H.R. (Eur. Ct. H.R. 438, 472, 474) (holding that the ECHR's derogation clauses may be invoked only in "an exceptional situation of crisis or emergency which affects the whole population and constitutes a threat to the organized life of the community of which the State is composed"). The concept of emergency does include circumstances other than armed conflict. For example, national disasters and extreme economic crises may constitute "public emergencies." See R. St. J. MacDonald, Derogations under Article 15 of the European Convention on Human Rights, 36 Colum. J.

Transnat'l L. 225, 225 (1997). Furthermore, the emergency must be temporary, imminent, and of such a character that it threatens the nation as a whole. See Svensson-McCarthy, supra; Oraa, supra note 39, at 11–33.

41. This requirement incorporates the principle of proportionality into derogation regimes. This principle requires that the restrictive measures must be proportional in duration, severity, and scope. Implicit in this requirement is that ordinary measures must be inadequate; and the emergency measures must assist in the management of the crisis. See, e.g., Oraa, supra note 39, at 143; MacDonald, supra note 40, at 233–35.

42. See Svensson-McCarthy, supra note 39, at 624–639.

43. Id. at 640–682.

44. Id. at 683–718; ICCPR, supra note 9, at art. 4(3); ECHR, supra note 9, at art. 15(3); ACHR, supra note 9, at art. 27(3). The Human Rights Committee has emphasized the importance of notification for effective international supervision of derogations in states of emergency. See Report of the Human Rights Committee, U.N. GAOR, 36th Sess., Supp. No. 40, Annex VII, at 110, U.N. Doc A/36/40 (1981).

45. Each convention containing a derogation clause provides an explicit list of non-derogable provisions. See ICCPR, supra note 9, at art. 4(2) (prohibiting derogation from Articles 6 (right to life), 7 (prohibition on torture), 8 (prohibition of slavery and servitude), 11 (imprisonment for failure to fulfill contractual obligation), 15 (prohibition on retrospective criminal offence), 16 (protection and guarantee of legal personality), and 18 (freedom of thought, conscience and religion); ECHR, supra note 9, at art. 15(2) (prohibiting derogation from Articles 2 (right to life), 3 (freedom from torture), 4 (freedom from slavery), and 7 (retrospective effect of penal legislation)); ACHR, supra note 9, at art. 27 (prohibiting suspension of Articles 3 (right to juridical personality), 4 (right to life), 5 (right to humane treatment), 6 (freedom from slavery), 9 (freedom from ex-post facto laws), 12 (freedom of conscience and religion), 17 (right of the family), 18 (right to name), 19 (right of child), 20 (right to nationality), and 23 (right to participate in government)).

46. See ICCPR, supra note 9, art. 6.

47. See ICCPR, supra note 9, art. 7.

48. See ICCPR, supra note 9, art. 8.

49. Proposed drafts of ICCPR Article 4 submitted by French and U.S. representatives would have made the prohibition on arbitrary arrest, the right to prompt notice of charges, and the right to fair and prompt trial non-derogable. Both proposals, however, would have made derogable the right to take prompt judicial proceedings to challenge the lawfulness of detention. U.N. Doc. E/CN.4/324 (1949) (French draft); U.N. Doc. E/CN.4/325 (1949) (U.S. Draft). The representative of the U.K. argued that the prohibition against arbitrary arrest and the right to a fair trial might be impossible to respect during wartime or other grave emergency. U.N. Doc. E/CN.4/SR.126, at 4–5 (1949). The U.K. view prevailed when the list of non-derogable rights was agreed to provisionally in 1950. See Joan Hartman, Working Paper for the Committee of Experts on the Article 4 Derogation Provision, 7 Hum. Rts. Q. 89, 115–18 (1985).

50. Although the Human Rights Committee recommended against adopting an Optional Protocol to the ICCPR re-categorizing Articles 9 and 14 as non-derogable, the Committee noted that states should not derogate from several of the protections included in these articles. The Committee reasoned that: The Committee notes that the purpose of the possible draft optional protocol is to add article 9, paragraphs 3 and 4, and article 14 to the list of non-derogable provisions in article 4, paragraph 2, of the Covenant. The Committee is satisfied that States parties generally understand that the right to habeas corpus and amparo should not be limited in situations of emergency. Furthermore, the Committee is of the view that the remedies provided in article 9, paragraphs 3 and 4, read in conjunction with article 2 are inherent to the Covenant as a whole. Having this in mind, the Committee believes that there is a considerable risk that the proposed draft third optional protocol might implicitly invite States parties to feel free to derogate from the provisions of article 9 of the Covenant during states of emergency if they do not ratify the proposed optional protocol. Thus, the protocol might have the undesirable effect

of diminishing the protection of detained persons during states of emergency. Annual Report of the Human Rights Committee, U.N. G.A.O.R., 49th Sess., Supp. No. 40, at 120, U.N. Doc. A/49/40, at para.2 (1994).

51. UN Human Rights Committee, General Comment No. 29: States of Emergency (Article 4), UN Doc. CCPR/C/21/Rev.1/Add.11 (2001) at para. 16, available at http://www.unhchr.ch/tbs/doc.nsf (last visited Oct. 21, 2002).

52. The Committee concluded that: It is inherent in the protection of [non-derogable] rights that they must be secured by procedural guarantees, including, often, judicial guarantees. The provisions of the Covenant relating to procedural safeguards may never be made subject to measures that would circumvent the protection of non-derogable rights. Thus, for example, as article 6 [the right to life] is non-derogable in its entirety, any trial leading to the imposition of the death penalty during a state of emergency must conform to the provisions of the Covenant, including all the requirements of articles 14 [fair trial] and 15 [prohibition on retroactive penalties]. Id. at para. 15.

53. See Habeas Corpus in Emergency Situations (Arts. 27(2), 25(1) and 7(6) American Convention on Human Rights), 8 Inter-Am. Ct. H.R. (ser. A) at 33, OEA/ser.L./V/111.17, doc. 13 (1987); See also Judicial Guarantees in States of Emergency (Arts. 27(2), 25 and 8 American Convention on Human Rights), 9 Inter-Am. Ct. H.R. (ser. A) at 40, OEA/ser.L./VI/111.9, doc. 13 (1987). The Court unanimously held that "'essential' judicial guarantees which are not subject to derogation, according to Article 27(2) of the Convention, include habeas corpus (Art. 7(6)), amparo, and any other effective remedy before judges or competent tribunals (Art. 25(1))." Id.

54. Annual Report of the Human Rights Committee, U.N. G.A.O.R., 49th Sess., Supp. No. 40, at 120, U.N. Doc. A/49/40, at para.2 (1994).

55. The derogation measures do not, however, necessarily violate the prohibition on discrimination in Article 4(1). Of course, many of the derogation measures are applied in a discriminatory fashion. For example, the Military Order providing for trial by military commission facially discriminates on the basis of citizenship. Military Order, supra note 6 (applying only to noncitizens). Article 4(1) prohibits discrimination "solely on the ground of race colour, sex, language, religion, or social origin." ICCPR, supra note 9, art. 4(1). Unlike Articles 2(1) and 26—the substantive provisions on discrimination—Article 4(1) does not prohibit discrimination on the grounds of "national origin." Compare ICCPR, supra note 9, arts. 2(1) and 26 with id.art. 4(1). The travaux preparatoires of the treaty makes clear that states acknowledged that discrimination based on "national origin" might be essential in times of war. See, e.g., Svensson-McCarthy, supra note 39, at 643–646.

56. See Rosalyn Higgins, Derogations Under Human Rights Treaties, 48 Brit. Y.B.I.L. 281, 281 (1976–77).

*Derek Jinks is the Marrs McLean Professor in Law at the University of Texas School of Law and a senior fellow at the Robert S. Strauss Center for International Security and Law at the University of Texas.

Jinks, Derek, "International Human Rights Law and the War on Terrorism." *Denver Journal of International Law and Policy* 58 (2002): 58–68.

Used by permission.

The United States and International Humanitarian Law

by David P. Forsythe*

From the time of the Vietnam War and its My Lai massacre, the United States showed increased attention to international humanitarian law (also known as the laws of war) until the terrorist attacks on New York and Washington on September 11, 2001. From the time of those attacks until about 2005, the Bush Administration reversed course and downplayed both IHL and international human rights law in the treatment of enemy prisoners. At the time of writing the U.S. view toward IHL is much debated, with important congressional and judicial challenges to Bush policies. The U.S. military has returned to a more sensitive appreciation of IHL, while the CIA position is not clear.

States profess, as a matter of principle, their commitment to various forms of international law. It is a fact that formal commitment to international humanitarian law (IHL) is universal; all extant states having ratified or legally adhered to the Geneva Conventions of August 12, 1949 for the protection of victims of war. It is true that the three additional protocols (AP) to these 1949 Geneva Conventions have not reached universal acceptance. The two 1977 protocols (API for the further development of the law for international armed conflict, and APII for internal armed conflict) have been formally accepted (ratified or formally adhered to) by a bit more than 80% of the UN's 192 member states, while the 2005 protocol (APIII on neutral emblems in armed conflict) is of recent vintage and was always as controversial—if not more so—as the first two. Still, in principle, states do not contest the old adage that whoever says war, says law. That is, states do not contest that international law, and specifically IHL, exists for the legal management of armed conflict. (Some do contest the nomenclature, with some preferring the old semantics about laws of war or law of armed conflict, compared with IHL. It seems that IHL has only been widely used since the early 1950s.)

It has been said by a British author that the United Kingdom and the United States "make the weather" regarding international human rights, taken to include IHL.[1] One might quibble about the British role, but it seems evident enough that the United States, with its size, power, and relatively transparency, has great impact on world affairs. Some data indicate that because of US tough policies after the terrorist attacks of September 11, 2001, many states, taking their cue from Washington, increased repression—and thus in general violations of many human rights.[2] This article examines the US record on IHL both before and after 9/11 in broad brush terms in a search for major trends.

THE UNITED STATES AND IHL UP TO 2000

The United States often presents itself to the world as an exceptional nation, and "American exceptionalism" has become a feature of political and legal discourse. But in matters of IHL, the United States might seem anything but exceptional at first glance. In its Civil War of 1861–1865 the Federal side devised (and somewhat implemented) the Lieber Code as a set of rules to mitigate that war's human destructiveness (even as General Sherman pillaged and burned his way across the Confederacy). The United States eventually ratified the various Hague and Geneva conventions that made up the core of the laws of war between 1864 and the Second World War. It played a leading role in the negotiation of the 1949 treaties, with those four interlocking instruments constituting the main legal firewall against barbarism in war after that time, designed to ensure that belligerents did not become barbarians. Washington ratified them in 1955. And while it has yet to ratify API and APII, it played a leading role in their negotiation and further supported the development of APIII. (The latter instrument, by establishing a Red Crystal as a neutral emblem, paved the way for Israel's official emergency response society, Magen David Adom, which agreed to use the new emblem, to be recognized by the International Committee of the Red Cross, to join the International Federation of Red Cross and Red Crescent Societies, and thus to become a full member of the International Red Cross and Red Crescent Movement.) True, the United States did not accept the treaty banning antipersonnel land mines, but Washington did accept a protocol to the Convention on the Rights of the Child banning child soldiers even though the latter caused US changes in military assignment.

In its various wars between 1949 and 2000 the United States compiled a record on implementing IHL that was probably no worse than, and sometimes clearly better than, other fighting parties. In most if not all of these wars, the US record of implementation was mixed, with some serious and genuine attention to IHL combined with various violations. Whether any other state or nonstate party, or particularly any other liberal democracy, did better overall is a large subject worthy of careful comparison—a comparison that will not be attempted here.

It seems that the Korea War of 1950–1953 was rather typical in this regard. On the one hand, the United States paid far more attention to the newly minted 1949 GC # 3 for detained combatants, even though it was too new to be legally binding on any of the fighting parties, than North Korea. The latter's refusal of cooperation with the International Committee of the Red Cross (ICRC), and its abuse of American and South Korean prisoners of war is well known, leading to a much inferior record of compliance compared with the United States. On the other hand, we now know that the US military sometimes committed massacres, at times firing into ostensibly civilian populations because of fear that North Korean infiltrators were hiding amongst the civilians.

If we move to the American phase of the war in Indochina, and if we again look at only treatment of detained combatants, again we find the same mixed record on the US side. On the one hand the US authorities, in quest of reciprocity for its soldiers held by the other side, adopted a reasonably generous approach to military detention and interrogation. In particular, from about 1966 the United States agreed that "main force Viet Cong" detainees, captured with arms visible in combat or immediately prior to combat, should be treated as prisoners of war. Thus, not only (eventually) North Vietnamese regular military personnel but also irregular fighters out of uniform and presumably fighting for a nonstate party should be afforded de facto or de jure POW status. Moreover, military tribunals were utilized to determine who was a combatant entitled to such POW status and who was, by contrast, a civilian, including "terrorists" posing as civilians.[3]

Furthermore, the United States did officially agree that for all detainees not entitled to better treatment, at least Common Article Three (CA3) from the 1949 Geneva Convention (GCs) applied. That article, common to the four 1949 legal instruments, provided a baseline of humanitarian protections. CA3 prohibits torture, as well as humiliating and degrading treatment.

So the official US guidelines for its military detention facilities were in keeping with, and maybe even in excess of, what the 1949 GCs required. And these standards were over time made officially applicable to the South Vietnamese authorities as well, through such arrangements as a combined interrogation center in Saigon. Some abuse of detainees occurred of course, especially by the South Vietnamese authorities when dealing with "political prisoners," but the official US military policy was to prohibit it. The same could not be said regarding North Vietnamese policies toward detained US military personnel, particularly US airmen shot down over the north, who were regularly tortured and otherwise abused in captivity.

On the other hand, the United States ran the Phoenix program of torture and murder through the Central Intelligence Agency (with some military personnel seconded to the Agency).[4] This program was a "pump and dump" operation in which Washington used torture and mistreatment in quest of actionable intelligence, then often killed its victims including by throwing them out of airborne helicopters. Thus while the US military authorities showed interest in military honor and legal obligations, the CIA, with approval from high authorities, engaged in covert murder and torture. (The US record in Vietnam was not significantly different from the French in Algeria. The French finally recognized the relevance of Common Article 3 to the situation, as well as a humanitarian regime for irregular combatants. At the same time, to combat "terrorists," the French engaged in torture and murder. The Algerian fighters, for their part, attacked civilian as well as military targets and refused almost all cooperation with the ICRC.)

After Vietnam, and in the light of such events as the 1968 My Lai massacre in which US military units killed some three hundred unresisting and nonthreatening Vietnamese civilians, the Pentagon made a concerted effort to improve attention to IHL. This may have been in part because US military lawyers were keen on legal obligations. But it was also in part because high Pentagon authorities recognized various expedient concerns entangled with the moral and legal factors associated with IHL. Attention to IHL's protections that were afforded to the civilian population was compatible with military discipline and a desire to win the hearts and minds of local populations in the theatre of conflict. Attention to IHL's protections that were afforded to combatants was compatible with military morale and quest for humane treatment offered by the other side. No less important, a serious attention to IHL was important for avoiding scandals and controversies that could sap support on the home front. Given that American domestic opposition to the Vietnam War often focused on US-alleged war crimes, and similar controversies on the part of South Vietnamese allies, Pentagon authorities after 1975 resolved to try to avoid similar difficulties in the future. This was a matter of maintaining crucial support in Congress and public opinion for the war effort.

In the rather conventional wars fought by the United States in 1991 (to expel Iraq from Kuwait) and 1999 (to oppose Serbian policies in Kosovo), US attention to IHL was considerable. Probably never before had military lawyers played such an important role in such things as target selection for bombing and artillery attacks. This is not to say that the US record was without blemish. With regard to Kosovo in 1999, for example, there was debate about the wisdom and legality of US attacks on such "dual use" (military and civilian) targets as bridges and communication centers in Belgrade. There was also controversy about the altitude of US and NATO bombing runs, with "the West" choosing higher altitudes to minimize dangers to pilots even if this resulted in more "collateral damage" to civilians on the ground. Was it legal, and was it morally justified, to increase dangers to innocent civilians for the sake of minimizing dangers to professional military personnel? Still, on balance, one could document a serious effort on the part of the United States to examine the intersection of IHL with military operations and to limit relatively often the latter in the light of the former.[5]

In summary to this point, the United States between 1945 and 2000 helped negotiate and formally accepted many of the legal instruments that make up contemporary IHL, and its record of implementation in actual armed conflict was increasingly serious as time progressed—even if Washington's record on both counts (standard setting and enforcement) fell short of perfection. (Again, I leave to others the interesting question of whether the Israeli, British, French, or other military establishments in Western-style liberal democracies compiled a comparable record.)

THE UNITED STATES AND IHL AFTER 2000

After the al-Qaeda terrorist attacks on New York and Washington on September 11, 2001, the George W. Bush administration was at first determined to avoid serious and limiting reference to IHL. Later in places like Iraq after 2003 it was negligent regarding many aspects of that law. The Congress and courts were slow to provide corrective measures. Only from about 2005 did a serious "blowback" in favor of IHL occur in Washington. At the time of writing, IHL has once again become an important part of the political debate about how to conduct what the Bush administration called its long "war against terrorism."

The al-Qaeda attacks were a shock to the government and nation, comprising as they did the greatest intentional damage to the homeland inflicted by a foreign party in the history of the country. The 2001 attacks killed just under three thousand, almost all of whom were civilians. By comparison, the Japanese attack on Pearl Harbor on December 7, 1941, killed some 1,500 persons, virtually all of whom were military personnel. The United States has been fortunate in fighting most of its wars on foreign soil, and with the exception of the British burning of Washington in 1812, it has escaped much direct homeland damage from armed conflict. This is a primary reason why US nationalism is quite different from European nationalism, Europe having seen catastrophic damage at home from the playing out of intense nationalism and the concomitant glorification of state sovereignty.

Whereas the Europeans have devised such arrangements as the Council of Europe, with its major focus on the regional protection of human rights, and the European Union, both with supranational courts, the United States under particularly the governments of Ronald Reagan and George W. Bush have glorified the virtues of US sovereignty. Whereas the Europeans mostly look to international law and organization to constrain the dangers of chauvinistic nationalism, the United States often displays a nationalism that has more in common with Venezuela and other developing countries than with Europe. Whereas Europe through bitter experience has learned the need to transcend the nation-state system through accepting measures such as the International Criminal Court, the United States still emphasizes its strictly national virtues while retaining deep suspicions about international law and organization. For particularly the George W. Bush administration, American exceptionalism translates into American exemptionalism, and exempts itself from most international regimes that seriously constrain its independence, the World Trade Organization being the primary exception that proves the general rule. A primary tenet of so-called neoconservatism is skepticism about international law and organization and a concomitant desire The U.S. and International Humanitarian Law 29 to unilaterally project US hard power in behalf of the US view of morality, freedom, and democracy.[6]

The Bush administration, driven by a determination to avoid further terror attacks on the homeland and fueled by a sense of self-righteous indignation that the virtuous and divinely blessed United States had been attacked, tried to avoid any serious limitations on its policymaking stemming from IHL (and international human rights law). With reference to IHL in particular, some respected international lawyers referred to Bush decision making as a "criminal conspiracy" to violate the 1949 Geneva Conventions. According to this former JAG officer, when looking at Bush decision making principally in 2001–2002, not since the Nazi era had so many government lawyers been complicit in war crimes.[7]

When in the fall and winter of 2001 the United States used military force in Afghanistan against the Taliban and al-Qaeda, the Bush administration, with civilian lawyers playing a key role, tried to argue that IHL applied to neither Taliban fighters nor al-Qaeda personnel. Disregarding US policies in Vietnam, Bush declared that enemy combatants out of uniform would not be given 1949 GC3 protections, nor would al-Qaeda operatives since they were associated with a nonstate party operating on an international basis. US military and exmilitary lawyers in the government, many independent international lawyers, and various advocacy groups all argued otherwise, as did the ICRC. Citing various provisions in the 1949 GCs, these actors noted that GC3 protected irregular (unprivileged) as well as regular combatants, and those in a war zone not considered combatants were protected by GC4 pertaining to civilians. Moreover, CA3 applied to those involved in an internal armed conflict, including all associated with a nonstate actor.

The Bush administration, however, anticipating the capture of various types of enemies, was determined from the start to engage in abusive or coercive interrogation. It therefore tried to maintain its position that, while IHL did indeed apply to the then ongoing international armed conflict in Afghanistan, law did not pertain to captured fighters who were detained in Afghanistan and at the US detention facility at Guantanamo Bay, Cuba. The latter US site, leased in perpetuity from Cuba, and dating from the Spanish-American War of 1898, was chosen as a principal prison in the hopes of avoiding legal review by US courts. The Bush administration argued that because Cuba was the sovereign there, US courts had no jurisdiction. Guantanamo was intended as a legal black hole, where neither IHL nor US law would apply. Complicating legal analysis was the fact that certain persons were seized by the United States in places like Pakistan, Macedonia, Egypt, Gambia, and other places not involved in any armed conflict, international or internal, and then were transferred to either Afghanistan or Guantanamo or both.

It must be noted that the United States is a party to the UN Convention Against Torture, which prohibits both torture and lesser forms of mistreatment. According to the terms of the treaty, these provisions pertain in all situations, whether characterized by armed conflict or not. The same prohibitions and material field of application are found in the International Covenant on Civil and Political Rights, to which the United States is also a party. In the latter treaty, prohibitions on torture and mistreatment are nonderogable and thus cannot be suspended in national emergencies.

Bush lawyers, being aware of these provisions in international human rights law, tried to argue that: (1) these treaties pertained only to the US homeland, not to international or foreign areas; (2) that if a US official did not intend to inflict serious pain on a prisoner, but resulting pain was only a by-product of other intentions such as collecting information, then the norms were not violated; or (3) that if coercive interrogation did not result in conditions approaching organ failure and death, then the United States was not in violation of international human rights standards.[8]

Various legal authorities, inside and outside the United States, contested these interpretations. *The New York Times* eventually called them "legal sophistries."

As 2002 progressed, the following situation manifested itself "on the ground." First, at Guantanamo, by late 2002 harsh conditions and abusive interrogation were part of a conscious policy implemented by regular military personnel at a regular military installation. Secretary of Defense Rumsfeld had dispatched General Geoffrey Miller to implement coercive interrogation, with the approval of the Joint Chiefs of Staff. The intention was to improve actionable intelligence. Military police were instructed to "soften up" the prisoners for military intelligence; the latter being instructed to use various abusive techniques. Other parties were part of the process, including the CIA on occasion, and also certain foreign intelligence officials. This situation, a radical departure from the position of the US military in other wars, especially in Vietnam, had the approval of the highest US authorities, certainly including Vice President Cheney. Various documents that eventually found their way into the public domain, from the FBI, from ICRC reports, and from various military sources, leave no doubt as to the general situation. Only the exact techniques, and the number of prisoners involved, remain to be fully resolved.

Second, from spring 2002 the CIA began to hold another set of prisoners, presumably "high value detainees," in secret sites. Whereas, in a sequence that has yet to be explained, the ICRC was allowed to visit most detainees at Guantanamo, that agency was not permitted access to the CIA "black sites." Circumstantial evidence suggests that at least some of the perhaps one hundred detainees held from time to time in these black sites were subjected to "water boarding," "short shackling," exposure to extremes of heat and cold, sleep deprivation, and other forms of coercive interrogation. Given that the CIA has considerable experience with these measures, referred to as "no touch torture," there is less and less reason to question the general situation.[9] Given that various US officials, including the former head of the CIA, George Tenet, have acknowledged the use of "enhanced" or "aggressive" interrogation techniques, there is no reason to question the general situation, only the specifics of how many, how often, for how long, and with what effect, etc. There is circumstantial evidence that certain foreign high officials, and certainly foreign security managers, were involved in the black sites. President Bush announced the transfer of fourteen of these prisoners to Guantanamo in September 2006, after which they were visited by the ICRC, whose subsequent confidential report was indirectly leaked to the press. Thus as a matter of US policy, we find the practice of forced disappearance and abusive interrogation in violation of international human rights standards (and IHL if it applies, depending on whether the prisoner has some connection to armed conflict as properly referenced by international law).

Third, in both Afghanistan from late 2001 and in Iraq from spring 2003, where one finds armed conflict and for a time occupation in the legal sense, again there is much circumstantial evidence of a pattern of harsh detention conditions and abusive interrogation in military and CIA installations. As far as we know, the number of deaths while in US custody was much higher in Afghanistan and Iraq than at Guantanamo and in the black sites. In fact, General Miller, having instituted a harsh regime at Guantanamo, was transferred to Iraq in late summer 2003 in order to effectuate tough policies toward prisoners. It was in this context that the scandal at Abu Ghraib prison in the fall of 2003 became known in early 2004. It became perfectly clear that given a policy of abusive interrogation at Guantanamo and in the black sites, this policy spun out of control at Abu Ghraib given the chaotic conditions there, the lack of fully trained and fully disciplined military personnel assigned to the prison, and the emphasis on pacifying the country that required better actionable intelligence. One also finds contract employees at work in the interrogation process who The U.S. and International Humanitarian Law 31 were not clearly regulated under military law and who were not tightly controlled by the CIA. Abu Ghraib represented "a perfect storm" of negative factors that combined to produce the equivalent of the My Lai massacre—a violation of human rights and humanitarian standards so shocking that, when brought to public attention, it eventually helped to produce important changes.

From the summer of 2005, various Senators of the Republican Party in Congress became publicly concerned about events. Led by Senators McCain, Warner, and L. Graham, all of whom had military connections, they began to insist on greater attention to IHL and issues of military honor and tradition. Their position was important given Republican control of both houses of Congress at that time. After the congressional elections in November 2006, the Democratic Party won control of both houses, thus intensifying congressional oversight of administration policies, including a review of many policies at play in the so-called war on terrorism. Congressional oversight of Bush foreign policy had been essentially absent during 2001–2006.

At more or less the same time, various legal cases wound their way through the US federal court system that touched upon detention and interrogation. By slim margins the US Supreme Court ruled that it did have jurisdiction over Guantanamo, and that it would hear claims pertaining to habeas corpus from prisoners there. Most importantly, in its Hamdan judgment of June 2006, the Supreme Court ruled that at least 1949 GC CA3 pertained to prisoners taken in the war on terrorism. This ruling was directed at the use of military commissions to try certain Guantanamo prisoners, and the necessity of congressionally approved standards of due process, but the ruling implied no torture or humiliating or degrading treatment.

It is impossible to say what was the exact role of transnational criticism concerning Bush policies, particularly regarding treatment of terror suspects and other enemy detainees. Various international advocacy groups, UN officials, European officials, and others had made various critiques concerning how Bush policies failed to measure up to proper understandings of IHL (and human rights norms). But it was particularly the Hamdan judgment that required the Bush administration to rethink some of its policies regarding IHL. After Hamdan, the US military began to rewrite its military manuals regarding interrogation, making

sure to implement CA3 standards. It increasingly prosecuted various lower rank-
ing military personnel for violations of military law, not only regarding prisoner
treatment but the more general abuse of civilians as well during military operations. The Congress adopted several pieces of legislation incorporating IHL standards. And the administration itself announced changes in interrogation policies
in the black sites that seemed to rule out water boarding, short shackling, and
uses of extreme temperature manipulation as part of the interrogation process.
Several Bush officials indicated a desire to close Guantanamo as a detention site.

To be sure, the administration seemed to keep certain coercive options open.
It did not renounce the use of forced disappearances in the future. It seemed to
endorse sleep deprivation as an interrogation technique. And it refused to grant
permission to the ICRC to see all prisoners in the future. The president issued
"signing statements," added to various legislative acts prohibiting torture of prisoners that implied he had the constitutional authority to violate international
and domestic law if necessary for national security.

It is reasonable to suppose that increasingly several high Bush officials understood that particularly in Europe and the Islamic world it had damaged its image,
reputation, and soft power through highly publicized abuse of detainees, whether
calculated as at Guantanamo and the black sites or out of control as at Abu
Ghraib. With waning domestic support for the bungled invasion of Iraq, perhaps
the Bush administration might learn that serious attention to IHL (and certain
human rights norms) was compatible with many of its national interests, and
that in any event the US Supreme Court had compelled some shift in policies.
Increasingly there were many dissident views in Washington prepared to leak
the latest unfavorable report about Bush interrogation policy, whether from the
ICRC or other sources.

CONCLUSION

There is no doubt but that the Bush administration played fast and loose with IHL
in the aftermath of 9/11. Administration officials declared the 1949 GCs quaint
and proceeded to violate various prohibitions found therein particularly regarding the detention and interrogation of enemy prisoners. This was a clear departure from a progressive trend that had been manifesting itself in favor of greater
attention to IHL in the United States from the time of the Vietnam War forward.

What is perhaps most important in the long run were not the US calculated
violations of IHL, or the military and political negligence that contributed to
the Abu Ghraib scandal, but the strength of the blowback against those IHL
violations. International and domestic advocacy groups, courageous individuals,

certain congressional circles, some foreign and international circles, including the ICRC, and above all a dominant set of judges on the US Supreme Court had interacted to force the Bush team to rethink a number of its policies.

Of course a number of prisoners had been badly abused, and sometimes even killed, while this opposition was struggling to assert itself.

Underlying the specifics about the laws of war, Common Article 3, whether legal obligations stopped at national boundaries or applied offshore, etc., was a "big picture" debate about the nature of world affairs.

On the one side were the likes of Ronald Reagan and George W. Bush and other American exemptionalists. They saw the United States as the motor for freedom and democracy (and prosperity) in the world, whose virtuous policy making was not to be constrained by the lowest common denominator approach to decision making in international organizations, or by an international law fashioned to considerable degree by authoritarian and weak and poor states. Thus nothing could be worse than attacks on the US homeland, or an interpretation of the laws of war (IHL) that interfered with the quest for actionable intelligence for the sake of US national security.

On the other side were the likes of John McCain who used a different version of American exceptionalism: Americans are above torture and mistreatment; it is not part of American character to do such things. They were joined by the more pragmatic moral consequentialists like John D. Rockefeller, III, after 2006 the Democratic chair of the Senate Intelligence Committee, who argued that while some actionable intelligence might be gained from coercive interrogation, the many negatives for the United States involved in the process (e.g., loss of reputation abroad) might outweigh the gains. This latter group gave great weight to the Geneva Conventions and UN human rights law, if for overlapping reasons. This latter group was more interested than the former in robust and muscular international law and organization.

Given globalization in its many forms, it is doubtful that in historical terms American exemptionalism is sustainable. As the word is integrated in intrusive and delicate ways, there will be a greater need for muscular international law and organization to regulate the predictable conflicts. The outlines of the trend are clear, from the World Trade Organization to the mini-regime to protect the ozone. But the so called neo-cons still constitute a powerful force in US politics and foreign policy. Their defense of a mighty US Gulliver who should not be tied down by the international Lilliputians remained a principal feature of debates about the United States and world affairs, including whether IHL should be taken seriously.

NOTES

1. Conor Gearty, *Can Human Rights Survive* (Cambridge: Cambridge University Press, 2006), 107.

2. Sonia Cardenas, *Conflict and Compliance: State Responses to International Human Rights Pressure* (Philadelphia: University of Pennsylvania Press, 2007), 10.

3. For a good review of US directives in Vietnam regarding treatment of enemy prisoners, see Major James F. Gebhardt, U.S. Army (Ret.), "The Road to Abu Ghraib: US Army Detainee Doctrine and Experience," *Global War on Terrorism Occasional Paper* 6 (Fort Leavenworth, KS: Combat Studies Institute Press, n.d.).

4. Douglas Valentine, *The Phoenix Program* (New York: Harper Collins, 1992).

5. See further regarding 1975–1995 Marc L. Warren, "Operational Law—A Concept Matures," *Military Law Review*, 151 (1996), 33–73.

6. For a readable overview see Robert Kagan, *Of Paradise and Power: America and Europe in the New World Order* (New York: Knopf, 2003).

7. Jordan J. Paust, *Beyond the Law: The Bush Administration's Unlawful Responses in the "War" on Terror* (Cambridge: Cambridge University Press, 2007).

8. The best source on the early US memos denigrating the international legal framework designed to protect prisoners, both in war and in general, is Karen J. Greenberg and Joshua L. Dratel, eds., *The Torture Papers: The Road to Abu Ghraib* (Cambridge: Cambridge University Press, 2005).

9. See especially Alfred W. McCoy, *A Question of Torture: CIA Interrogation from the Cold War to the War on Terror* (New York: Henry Holt, 2006).

*David Forsythe is a University Professor and Charles J. Mach Distinguished Professor in the Department of Political Science at the University of Nebraska, Lincoln.

Forsythe, David P. "The United States and International Humanitarian Law." *Journal of Human Rights* 7 (2008): 25–33.

Reprinted by permission of the publisher (Taylor & Francis Ltd., http://www.tandf.co.uk/journals).

Part 3:

Freedom from Terror: Should It Trump Other Rights and Freedoms?

One of the trickiest parts about balancing security and human rights priorities stems from the fact that security considerations have frequently been cloaked in the verbiage of human rights, especially once it became clear that the majority of the international community did indeed care about rights. To be certain, physical safety is a crucial right that is a prerequisite for the others. It is appropriate, however, to ask how we weigh and prioritize these rights and to what extent the right to security has come at the cost of the protection and promotion of other rights.

In "Human Rights and Terrorism," Paul Hoffman, chair of the International Executive Committee of Amnesty International, argues that it is not so much the pursuit of safety that is problematic, but rather the unique *way* the Bush administration chose to pursue it that has been so destructive to the international human rights framework. Written before the Abu Ghraib revelations became public, Hoffman argues that abandoning human rights in times of crisis is shortsighted and self-defeating. Miroslav Nincic and Jennifer Ramos ("Torture in the Public Mind") demonstrate that the extreme measures embraced by the Bush administration fly in the face of popular values in the United States and that most people are firmly opposed to them. Finally, Julie Harrelson-Stephens and Rhonda Callaway ("The Empire Strikes Back") read the signs rather differently and trace a history of surprising resilience in the international human rights regime.

As you read the articles in this section, consider the following:

1. In your opinion, which other human rights are most important for assuring security rights? How do they enhance physical security?

2. How did the U.S. leadership's attitude toward international humanitarian law change after 9/11? Which of those changes have persisted? Which have been reversed? Describe another hypothetical event that might have a similarly far-reaching effect on the U.S. foreign policymaking apparatus's approach to international law. What would be the likely nature of the effect?

3. Why are most members of the public opposed to torture? What led the Bush administration to adopt policies so at odds with apparent public values? Was the administration right or wrong to do so? Why?

4. Why has the human rights regime been able to persist despite the U.S. "assault" on it? What are its likely prospects for the future according to the authors? Do you agree with them? Why or why not?

Human Rights and Terrorism

*by Paul Hoffman**

[…]

III. Human Rights as a Casualty of the "War on Terrorism"

Since the September 11 attacks, the United States, with the support of many governments, has waged a "war on terrorism".[15] This "war" puts the human rights gains of the last several decades and the international human rights framework at risk. Some methods used in detaining and interrogating suspects violate international human rights and humanitarian norms in the name of security. Throughout the world, governments have used the post-September 11 antiterrorism campaign to crack down on dissidents and to suppress human rights. These actions are documented by Amnesty International and many other human rights groups.[16]

Of course, not all of the antiterrorism efforts of the last thirty months deserve such criticism. There are many examples of cooperative law enforcement efforts to prevent terrorist acts and to bring suspected perpetrators to justice taken within a human rights paradigm. The allocation of additional resources and attention to these efforts in light of massive attacks on civilians is understandable. Governments have a wide degree of discretion in identifying threats to national or international security, and such discretion is recognized in existing human rights and humanitarian law.[17]

The analysis that follows is a review of the human rights consequences of the "war on terrorism" as it has been waged in the last thirty months that is presented in order to illustrate the ongoing threat to the human rights framework.[18]

A. The "War" Paradigm

At the heart of the challenge to the human rights framework is the question of whether the "war on terrorism" is a "war," and if so, what sort of a war it is. To date, one of the characteristics of the "war on terrorism" is a refusal to accept that anybody of law applies to the way this "war" is waged. Central to the human rights framework is the idea that there are no "human rights free zones" in the world, and that human beings possess fundamental human rights by virtue of their humanity alone. In addition, contrary to the picture painted by many in Washington DC, there is no gap between human rights law and humanitarian law in which a "war on terrorism" may be waged, free from the constraints of international law. The essence of the rule of law requires that executive action be constrained by law.

The refusal to accept that the rule of law governs the conduct of the "war on terrorism" has created tremendous uncertainty and has also led to the erosion of individual rights.[19] For example, in April 2003 the United States took the position, in response to questions posed by the UN Special Rapporteur on Extrajudicial, Summary or Arbitrary Executions about the November 2002 killing of six men in Yemen by a missile shot from an unmanned drone, that this attack was against enemy combatants in a military operation and, thus, was beyond the competence of the Special Rapporteur and the UN Human Rights Commission.[20]

The US carried out this operation in cooperation with the Yemeni government. Thus, it is not an example of an act of last resort because a government is alleged to be hiding or assisting suspected terrorists. Capturing persons suspected of planning or having engaged in criminal actions, whether considered "terrorism" or not, is the quintessential law enforcement activity; an activity that is ordinarily subject to the restrictions of international human rights law. Those ordinary restrictions require the governments of United States and Yemen to capture these men and try them under applicable criminal laws. By defining the "war on terrorism" as a "war," the United States and cooperating governments conveniently eliminate all of the protections of human rights law, even in circumstances in which international humanitarian law does apply. It is not clear why this precedent would not be applicable to any government seeking to target dissidents, national liberation movements, or anyone opposed to a regime as being a "terrorist" and an appropriate military threat in this global "war."

The substantive, temporal, and geographic scope of the "war on terrorism" are unbounded and unknown. The "war on terrorism" exists in a parallel legal universe in which compliance with legal norms is a matter of executive grace or is taken out of diplomatic or public relations necessity.[21] The concept of "terrorism" put forward is any act perceived as a threat by those waging the war against it. The battlefield is the entire planet, regardless of borders and sovereignty. The "war on terrorism" might continue in perpetuity, and it is unclear who is authorized to declare it over. Human rights protections simply do not exist when they conflict with the imperatives of the "war on terrorism."

B. The Guantanamo Detainees

The continuing detention of more than 600 alleged "terrorists" at a military base in Guantanamo is becoming the most visible symbol of the threat to the human rights framework posed by the "war on terrorism".[22] The Guantanamo detainees essentially have been transported to a "human rights free zone" or "legal black hole,"[23] where only visits by the International Committee of the Red Cross (ICRC) stands between them and the arbitrary, unreviewable exercise of executive power.[24]

The detainees are beyond the reach of any body of law and receive the treatment that their captors deem reasonable in the circumstances. The US says the detainees are to be treated consistent with the laws of war. Yet, they are denied hearings required by Article 5 of the Third Geneva Convention before a "competent tribunal" to determine whether they are prisoners of war[25] as the ICRC presumptively believes them to be. In the eyes of their captors, they are conclusively determined to be "enemy combatants" or "enemy aliens," who may be tried before military commissions and detained indefinitely whether they are convicted by those commissions or not.

The Military Order of November 13, 2001—Detention, Treatment and Trial of Certain Non-Citizens in the War Against Terror, authorizes the detention and trial of "terrorists" and uses a broad definition of "individuals subject to this order".[26] Thus, US authorities may take any person in the world they believe fits this broad definition and transport them to the "human rights free zone" in Guantanamo. There the US is not subject to judicial oversight by domestic[27] or international authorities, and the detainees can be treated in any manner until they are tried, released, or held in these conditions indefinitely.

The Military Order applies only to noncitizens, leading to a stark double standard between the treatment of US citizens accused of being involved in terrorist activity and noncitizens, who are not entitled to the panoply of rights accused US "terrorists" will receive.[28] There is no reason to believe that US citizens may not also engage in terrorist activity. Indeed, before September 11, the worst terrorist act on US soil was committed in Oklahoma City by US citizen Timothy McVeigh. The idea that noncitizens are not entitled to international fair trial standards because they are unworthy "terrorists" is at odds with international antidiscrimination and fair trial norms as well as the presumption of innocence.

Trials before the military commissions, established pursuant to the November 2001 order, will not comply with essential international fair trial safeguards or guarantees of an independent judiciary. Indeed, the proceedings appear to be no different from military tribunals the international community has criticized in many other settings as a violation of international human rights standards.[29]

The availability of the death penalty in these military commissions undermines the human rights goal of eventual abolition of the death penalty; especially in light of the important strides the international community has made toward abolition of the death penalty in the Rome Statute and elsewhere, for even the most egregious crimes. These commissions also inhibit international cooperation to combat terrorism given the strong views of many states that abolition of the death penalty is an important human rights issue.[30]

The conditions under which the detainees are held also raise serious human rights issues. Historically, incommunicado and secret detentions have often led to torture and other forms of ill treatment. Now, there is evidence that suggests that the conditions of detention on Guantanamo, secure from outside oversight, violate these international standards. Based on reports emerging from released detainees, detainees are subjected to repeated interrogations and to techniques designed to wear them down and seemingly humiliate them. These techniques reportedly include twenty-four hour illumination, sleep deprivation, and standing for long periods of time. Detainees have also been kept in cramped detention cages or small cells and denied adequate exercise in violation of basic humanitarian and human rights norms.[31] The fact that these detentions are outside any established legal framework has resulted in a negative impact on the mental state of the detainees;[32] establishing a detainee's status in a fair process and providing humane conditions to detainees are fundamental norms of both international human rights and humanitarian law.[33]

In the post-September 11 environment, the absolute prohibition against torture has been questioned, but there is no logical stopping point to any relaxation of the prohibition of torture. Would it be used only on those who might know of the existence of a terrorist sleeper cell determined to use a weapon of mass destruction? This logic would surely undermine the categorical prohibition of torture achieved, though not yet consistently implemented, after decades of human rights campaigning. There is also no evidence that a policy of allowing torture would actually make the world any safer from terrorist attack.

There is more to say about the conditions of confinement in Guantanamo Bay, especially after recent revelations about the widespread abuse of prisoners in Iraq and elsewhere. The central challenge it presents to the human rights framework is that the detainees are left without the protection of law or judicial or international oversight. Although the ICRC is allowed to visit the detainees, the United States does not agree that the detainees are prisoners of war or even entitled to the full protections of international humanitarian or human rights law.

The United States has labeled the detainees as "enemy combatants,"[34] but this label cannot avoid the requirement of a determination of every detainee's status by a "competent tribunal." Humanitarian law requires that such determinations be made by tribunals and under procedures that guarantee fair treatment, protect vulnerable detainees, and restrain the detaining power.[35] Instead, the detainees, like the six men killed in Yemen, are subject only to the discretion of an unrestrained executive authority.

Fundamental human rights norms require that detentions be subject to judicial oversight.[36] As the UN Working Group on Arbitrary Detention stated in December 2002, if prisoner of war status is not recognized by a competent tribunal,

> [T]he situation of detainees would be governed by the relevant provisions
> of The [International Covenant on Civil and Political Rights] and in
> particular by articles 9 and 14 thereof, the first of which guarantees that
> the lawfulness of a detention shall be reviewed by a competent court,
> and the second of which guarantees the right to a fair trial".[37]

The United States has rejected the UN's position and every other form of international oversight of these detentions.

As a result, the identity of the detainees are secret, and there is no international or domestic oversight of the detentions. There is no way of knowing whether there is any basis for the continued detention of particular detainees, which includes children as young as thirteen. Over time, a number of detainees have been released, and so far the released detainees have not been charged with any criminal offense. Thus, raising substantial questions about the grounds for their detention in the first place and even more concern about the length of the detentions. Despite assurances by United States officials, there are examples of mistakes coming to light.

The case of Sayed Abassin, a taxi driver from Afghanistan, lends a human face to these human rights violations.[38] In April 2002, Abassin was arrested in Gardez. He had the misfortune of driving the wrong passengers from Kabul to Khost. Abassin was detained and subjected to sleep deprivation, shackling, and repeated interrogations at Bagram Air Base and a base in Kandahar. He had no access to a court, a lawyer, or to a "competent tribunal" guaranteed under the Third Geneva Convention. He was transferred to Guantanamo, where he was detained for nearly a year. For the last ten months he was not even interrogated. He was released without charge or trial in April 2003. The disruption to his life and to the lives of his family members was substantial and could have been avoided had international human rights or humanitarian standards been respected.

There is no way of knowing how many similar cases will emerge from the "human rights free zone" in Guantanamo. The whole point of judicial oversight is to ensure that there is a legitimate basis for the continued detention of individuals. Even if judges give substantial deference to detaining authorities given the context of these detentions, as seems likely, there must be some independent check on the arbitrary exercise of executive authority.

C. The Problem of Discrimination

One of the features of the "war on terrorism" so far is that minority groups have paid most of the cost for antiterrorism efforts, presumably undertaken for the benefit of society as a whole. Such discrimination is not only unfair, it is corrosive to legitimate security efforts. In this section, the focus is again on US examples, but there are examples in many other contexts which could be cited.

In the aftermath of September 11, thousands of Arab nationals and Muslims have been rounded up and detained in the United States in a massive form of preventive detention. These detentions were undertaken in secret, and the government opposed bail for post-September 11 detainees as a matter of course. Detainees were kept in harsh conditions, often with those charged with criminal offenses. Contacts with family and lawyers were heavily circumscribed.[39] Government investigative reports confirm that widespread abuses of noncitizens were perpetrated during the course of these activities.[40]

In addition to detainees picked up in the immediate aftermath of September 11, the government continues to arrest and detain persons from these cultural backgrounds. Additionally, the government conducted a special registration program limited to nationals of only certain backgrounds and has engaged in other activities considered viably to be racial profiling, thus, exacerbating feelings of exclusion and anger.

Almost all of the detainees have been held on minor immigration law violations, which ordinarily would not warrant detention or deportation. One commentator reports that only three of the estimated 5,000 noncitizens detained by these efforts have been charged with any offense remotely related to terrorism, indicating the ineffectiveness of such strategies.[41] Yet, these activities make life within the United States insecure for thousands of vulnerable noncitizens based on their national or religious background.

These transgressions on immigrant communities are just a part of the "collateral damage" of the "war on terrorism." International norms clearly prohibit discrimination on the basis of ethnicity, nationality, or religion. There is a growing recognition of the harms caused by discrimination in the social fabric of our communities. By targeting immigrant communities, the government fosters the discrimination and exclusion that human rights law has struggled so hard to eradicate, making it all the more difficult to engender understanding and cooperation between communities in the fight against terrorism.

The United States is not alone in using new antiterrorism powers against minority groups or noncitizens. Antiterrorism legislation in the United Kingdom is also targeted at noncitizens, so British citizens will receive the full panoply of protections if suspected of terrorism, while noncitizens can be detained indefinitely without trial or charge.

Discrimination is also counterproductive in the fight against terrorism. The statistics showing that such dragnet arrests and detentions have produced virtually no terrorists indicate the extremely limited utility of using such tactics in the fight against terrorism. Instead, it has been demonstrated that such tactics create enmity between law enforcement authorities and the affected communities. The voluntary cooperation so essential to uncovering and to preventing terrorist actions is now less likely to occur. Why would Arab nationals or Muslims in the United States or targeted minority groups in any country voluntarily assist the same governmental authorities who take arbitrary action against their innocent relatives, friends, and coreligionists?

D. Renditions Without Rights

The case of Maher Arar raises another troublesome aspect of the way the "war on terrorism" is being waged. Arar was detained at JFK airport on 26 September 2002 while in transit to Canada on a Canadian passport.[42] He was held in US custody for thirteen days, during which time he was interrogated about his links to Al-Qaeda. After this, he was transported to Syria through "expedited removal," without a hearing and without his lawyer, family, or the Canadian consulate being notified. He was held without charge in Syria for a year, during which time he suffered torture as well as cruel, inhumane, and degrading treatment and punishment. His rendition to Syria violated US obligations under Article 3 of the Convention Against Torture, which prohibits sending an individual to a country in which there is reason to believe that he will be subjected to torture. There is evidence that this is not an isolated event and that secret renditions are taking place outside any judicial oversight, often in violation of the Convention Against Torture.

Another lesser known challenge to the rule of law has been the manner in which many of the detainees held in Guantanamo have been brought there.[43] Although it has been claimed that the Guantanamo detainees are "battlefield" captives, this is true only if the battlefield is anywhere a "terrorist" suspect is found. Though it appears that most Guantanamo detainees were captured in Afghanistan, an unknown number of detainees have been seized in other circumstances and places usually outside normal legal channels or judicial oversight.

An intricate web of extradition and mutual assistance treaties exists, which could be used to render persons accused of crime to the custody of the United States or other governments seeking them upon sufficient evidence. These agreements ordinarily provide for judicial supervision and some minimal guarantees of procedural and substantive fairness to persons accused of criminal acts.

In the "war against terrorism," this web of international cooperation is seen as optional and the lawless rendition of suspects more convenient. Perhaps the most egregious example of this phenomenon was the transportation of six Algerian suspects from Bosnia at a time when their cases were under judicial review by the appropriate judicial body in Bosnia. Rather than await a legal ruling, the suspects were spirited out of Bosnia to Guantanamo, where they remain without charge or trial.

There may well be circumstances in which international cooperation and the rule of law in the rendition of suspects cannot be observed without threatening national security. An example of such a time being when a government hides terrorists who are planning an attack. However, casual circumvention of these legal obligations and the failure to abide by human rights norms undermines respect for the rule of law in general.

IV. A HUMAN RIGHTS FRAMEWORK IS ESSENTIAL IN THE RESPONSE TO TERRORISM

For the most part, the international community has responded to the events of September 11 and their aftermath with an insistence that the response to terrorism must unfold within basic standards of human rights and international law. For example, the United Nations Security Council in Resolution 1456 (2003) insisted that any measure taken to combat terrorism must comply with international law obligations, "in particular international human rights law, refugee, and humanitarian law".[44]

The question is whether these norms will actually govern the conduct of states and what the international community will do if they do not. The detainees in Guantanamo are in a "human rights free zone" with the active cooperation of many governments and the absence of an adequate response by the international community as a whole. It is not too late to repair this damage to the human rights framework.

A. A Right to Security

At the heart of antiterrorism efforts is a recognition that all human beings have a right to security and to life. All governments have a responsibility to respect, ensure, and fulfill these rights and, to that end, to employ effective strategies to prevent and to punish acts of mass murder and destruction. No human rights advocate would deny this responsibility. The human rights framework is built on this recognition, but the right to security must be fulfilled within the framework of human rights protection, not at the expense of human rights. Just as the state must prevent human rights violations from occurring within its territory, whether they are committed by nonstate actors or officials, it must protect those within its borders from "terrorism."

Recognizing the existence and force of universal human rights norms does not mean that international society has entered into a collective suicide pact, placing individual rights invariably over pressing security needs. To the extent a "war on terrorism" is meant to imply a marshaling of the resources to address this pressing threat, this "war" must respect the basic human rights everyone has a right to have fulfilled. The purpose of this article is not to voice a problem with the rhetorical use of the "war" metaphor but to argue against the rhetoric becoming policy and altering the international legal regime.

The right to security is not absolute in theory or in reality. No society can be protected completely from those who would use violence to achieve their desired ends. There will always need to be some balance between liberty and security. Indeed, the development and implementation of international human rights standards and humanitarian law have always been sensitive to the balance between liberty and security. These are not new questions. There have always been threats of violence, including violence leading to the deaths of thousands of civilians; and in the last sixty years the human rights framework has not been an obstacle to legitimate government action designed to respond to those actions and threats.

In fact, the human rights framework has been forged out of the experiences of the devastation societies suffered when human rights were exchanged too easily in a fight against terrorists, subversives, or whatever name is placed on the threat. Using these terms, governments have been able to justify political murder and torture. In today's world there are more people who must endure the loss of loved ones or personal suffering because of the failure of states to adhere to human rights standards than there are victims of terrorist attacks.

The author does not mean to elevate one form of suffering over another or to denigrate any efforts to end terrorist attacks. The point is that there are real and well documented risks involved when the fabric of human rights protection is torn asunder or ignored. The cost of abandoning human rights standards in the fight against terrorism may not be immediately apparent, but it is as real as the suffering of the victims of a terrorist attack. One less obvious impact is that massive human rights catastrophes have been allowed to unfold without sufficient international attention or action, while the war on terrorism receives a disproportionate amount of attention and resources.[45]

B. A Human Rights Framework Does Not Impair the Fight Against Terrorism

Implicit in the design of the "war on terrorism" is the notion that the international human rights framework necessarily complicates the fight against terrorism. However, there is nothing in the existing human rights framework that need impair international efforts to fight terrorism. Indeed, it is difficult to see how international cooperation in the fight against terrorism can be maintained without respect for the rule of law.

Nothing in international human rights law prevents governments from passing laws that impose criminal penalties on those who would conspire or act to commit mass murder and destruction. Indeed, many nations have already enacted such laws. Governments may not enact laws that infringe on freedom of expression, religion, or other freedoms or that are so vague they invite abuse. Antiterrorism laws can be fashioned within these basic requirements. Some post-September 11 legislation raised these concerns, but the scope for legislation that addresses terrorist acts remains broad.

Even if one assumes the detainees are not covered by international humanitarian law,[46] the international human rights framework still requires they be tried for a recognizable criminal offense and be granted the internationally recognized guarantees of a fair trial. The United States had no difficulty complying with these requirements in response to the first World Trade Center bombing,[47] showing it is possible for governments to create special procedures for handling classified or sensitive evidence in such trials in accordance with their legal systems. Many countries have experience trying alleged terrorists in ordinary courts under procedures that comply, or at least arguably comply, with international standards. There can be increased cooperation at every level of government within a human rights framework.

Many human rights standards, beginning with Article 29 of the Universal Declaration of Human Rights, explicitly recognize limitations based on the requirements of public order or security. There is a substantial body of international, regional, and domestic jurisprudence in balancing liberty and security in a wide variety of specific contexts. These standards should be respected and enforced, not ignored.

International human rights law also explicitly recognizes that there may be emergencies that justify suspension of some international human rights protections during times of crisis.[48] For example, Article 4 of the ICCPR allows for measures derogating from obligations assumed under the Covenant in a time of "public emergency" that is "officially proclaimed" and "threatens the life of the nation." Notification of this declaration must be given to other state parties through the Secretary-General. Derogating measures must only be to the extent "strictly required by the exigencies of the situation," and cannot involve discrimination on the ground of race, color, sex, language, religion, or social origin and cannot conflict with other international law obligations. While the Bush administration has used the rhetoric of national security to justify the incognito detention of hundreds of Arab residents in the US for minor immigration violations since September 11, it has yet to notify the Secretary-General of declaration of an emergency under Article 4.

Moreover, there are some obligations (e.g., the right to life, the prohibition against torture, and other forms of cruel, inhumane, and degrading treatment or punishment) that are nonderogable. In addition to these explicit nonderogable rights, the Human Rights Committee has determined that the obligation to treat detainees with humanity, the prohibition of the arbitrary deprivation of liberty, and the presumption of innocence have become peremptory rules of international law. These new rules further restrict what may be done in a crisis situation.[49]

International human rights bodies, especially regional human rights bodies, have had substantial experience in adjudicating cases arising out of alleged terrorism attacks and terrorist groups.[50] The international human rights framework was developed with the possibility of crisis threatening the life of a nation in mind. There are no grounds to abandon the framework altogether because of the events of September 11 or because of the threat of similar attacks.

C. A Human Rights Framework Is Essential for Real Human Security

Without denying the legitimacy of responding to threats of terrorist attacks, a central problem with the "war on terrorism" is that it ignores other equally or more pressing challenges to human security. For hundreds of millions of people in the world today, the most important source of insecurity is not a terrorist threat but grinding, extreme poverty. More than a billion of the world's six billion people live on less than one dollar a day.

The Universal Declaration of Human Rights and the entire human rights framework is based on the indivisibility of human rights. This includes not only civil and political rights but also economic, social, and cultural rights. The discrepancy between these human rights promises and the reality of life for more than one-sixth of the world's people must be eliminated if terrorism is to be controlled.

[. . .]

NOTES

[. . .]

15. This section focuses primarily on actions taken by the United States; however, the ramifications of the "war on terrorism" reverberate throughout the world and there are many governments which have taken antiterrorism measures, sometimes repelling US measures, which undermine international human rights norms.

16. Numerous reports and updates may be found on the websites of Amnesty International, *available at* www.amnesty.org, Human Rights Watch, *available at* www.hrw.org, as well as many other NGOs.

17. This article does not address the legality of the military actions in Afghanistan or Iraq. An analysis of those actions is beyond the scope of this article and raises a host of additional issues and challenges. It should be noted, however, that the new US doctrine of preemptive attack also challenges basic assumptions about the way the international community is structured and exacerbates the dangers the "war on terrorism" poses for international human rights protection.

18. There is a large and growing literature about the human rights consequences of the "war on terrorism." *See, e.g.,* AMNESTY INTERNATIONAL, UNITED STATES OF AMERICA: THE THREAT OF A BAD EXAMPLE: UNDERMINING INTERNATIONAL STANDARDS AS "WAR ON TERROR" DETENTIONS CONTINUE (2003), AMR/51/114/2003, *available at* web. amnesty.org/library/Index/ENGAMR511142003); *See also* AMNESTY INTERNATIONAL, UNITED STATES OF AMERICA: RESTORING THE RULE OF LAW: THE RIGHT OF GUANTANAMO DETAINEES TO JUDICIAL REVIEW OF THE LAWFULNESS OF THEIR DETENTION (2004), AMR 51/0931/2004, *available at* web.amnesty.org/library/Index/ENGAMR510932004?open& of=ENG-USA.

19. *See generally* Joan Fitzpatrick, Sovereignty, Territoriality, and the Rule of Law, 25 HASTINGS INT'L & COMP. L. REV. 303 (2002). *See generally* RESTORING THE RULE OF LAW, *supra* note 18.

20. *Civil and Political Rights, Including the Questions of: Disappearances and Summary Executions,* U.N. Doc. E/CN.4/2003/G/80 (2003), *available at* www.unhchr.ch/Huridocda/Huridoca.nsf/e06 a5300f90fa0238025668700518ca4/9b67b6687466cfcac 1256d 2600514c7f/$FILE/G0313804.pdf.

21. In February 2002, President Bush declared that the detainees held at Guantanamo Bay, Cuba, would be treated "humanely and, to the extent appropriate and consistent with military necessity, consistent with the principles" of the Geneva Convention. *See* John Yoo, *With "All Necessary and Appropriate Force,"* L.A. TIMES, 11 June 2004, at B 13, *available at* www.aei.org/news/ filter.,newsID.20688/news_detail.asp.

22. There are also detentions in other locations including Bagram Air Base in Afghanistan and in other secret detention facilities. *See* HUMAN RIGHTS FIRST, ENDING SECRET DETEN-TIONS (2004), *available at* www.humanrightsfirst.org/usJaw/PDF/EndingSecretDetentions_web.pdf.

23. The Queen on the Application of Abbasi and Another v. Sec'y of State for Foreign and Commonwealth Affairs, EWCA Civ 1598, ¶64 (U.K.) Sup. Ct. Judicature, (C.A.) (6 Nov. 2002), *available at* www.courtservice.gov.uk/judgmentsfiles/j1354/abassi_judgment.htm.

24. For a more comprehensive discussion of the rights possessed by the detainees in Guantanamo and Afghanistan, *See* AMNESTY INTERNATIONAL, UNITED STATES OF AMERICA: MEMORANDUM TO THE US GOVERNMENT ON THE RIGHTS OF PEOPLE IN US CUSTODY IN AFGHANISTAN AND GUANTANAMO BAY (2002), AMR 51/053/2002, *available at* web.amnesty.org/library/Index/ENGAMR510532002. *See also* RESTORING THE RULE OF LAW, *supra* note 18. For a recent examination of the legal issues surrounding the detention in Guantanamo, *See* Dianne Marie Amann, *Guantanamo*, 42 COLUM. J. TRANS-NATIONAL L. 263 (2004).

25. Geneva Convention (III) Relative to the Treatment of Prisoners of War (Geneva III), *adopted* 12 Aug. 1949, 6 U.S.T. 3316, T.I.A.S. No. 3364, 75 U.N.T.S. 135, art. 5 (*entered into force* 21 Oct. 1950) (*entered into force* for U.S. 2 Feb. 1956). The convention also requires humane treatment, limits interrogation, and requires repatriation at the end of hostilities.

26. Sec. 2. Definition and Policy states:

    (a) The term "individual subject to this order" shall mean any individual who is not a United States citizen with respect to whom I determine from time to time in writing that:

    (1) There is reason to believe that such individual, at the relevant times,

    (i) is or was a member of the organization known as al Qaida;

    (ii) has engaged in, aided or abetted, or conspired to commit, acts of international terrorism, or acts in preparation therefore, that have caused, threaten to cause, or have as their aim to cause, injury to or adverse effects on the United States, its citizens, national security, foreign policy, or economy; or

    (iii) has knowingly harbored one or more.

    Military Order of November 13, 2001—Detention, Treatment, and Trial of Certain Noncitizens in the War Against Terrorism, 66 Fed. Reg. 57,833, 57,834 (13 Nov. 2001), *available at* www.cnss.org/milordet.pdf.

27. On 28 April 2004, the United States Supreme Court heard oral arguments in two cases in which family members of Guantanamo detainees are asserting that US courts have habeas corpus jurisdiction to consider the legality of detainees' detention under US law. The argument did not focus on whether there was an international obligation to provide some means for the detainees to obtain judicial oversight of their detentions. Hamdi v. Rumsfeld, 124 S. Ct. 2633 (2004); Rumsfeld v. Padilla, 124 S. Ct. 2711 (2004).

28. This double standard is reflected in the treatment of John Walker Lindh, who was captured while fighting for the Taliban in Afghanistan and was charged in an ordinary federal court and received all of the rights ordinary criminal defendants would receive in US courts.

29. For a comparison of the rules governing military commissions and international standards, *See* HUMAN RIGHTS WATCH, HUMAN RIGHTS WATCH BRIEFING; PEOPLE ON U.S. MILITARY COMMISSIONS (2003), *available at* www.hrw.org/backgrounder/usa/military-commissions.pdf.

30. *See* European Parliament Resolution on EU judicial Co-operation with the United States in combating terrorism, B5-081 3/2001 (11 Dec. 2001), *available at* www.epp-ed.org/Activities/doc/b5-813en.doc (encourages mutual assistance with US in combating terrorism while urging complete abolition of the death penalty).

31. *See* Geneva III, art. 38, *supra* note 25; *See also* Geneva Convention (IV) Relative to the Protection of Civilian Persons in Time of War (Geneva IV), *adopted* 12 Aug. 1948, 6 U.S.T. 3516,

T.I.A.S. No. 3365, 75 U.N.T.S. 287, art. 94 (*entered into force* 21 Oct. 1950) (*entered into force* for U.S. 2 Feb. 1956). *See also Standard Minimum Rules for the Treatment of Prisoners, adopted* 30 Aug. 1955, E.S.C. Res. 663C (XXIV), U.N. ESCOR, 24th Sess., Supp. No. I, at 11, U.N. Doc. E/3048 (1957), 21(1), *amended* by U.N. Doc. E/5988 (1977), *available at* www1.umn.edu/humanrts/instree/g1smr.htm (requires at least one hour of suitable open air exercise a day.)

32. The ICRC has expressed concern about the mental state of detainees especially as the length of their detentions grows. There have been reports of a substantial number of suicide attempts. *Red Cross Finds Deteriorating Mental Health at Guantanamo*, USA TODAY, 10 Oct. 2003, *available at* www.usatoday.com/news/world/2003-10-10-icrc-detainees_x.htm.

33. International Covenant on Civil and Political Rights, *adopted* 16 Dec. 1966, G.A. Res. 2200(XXI), U.N. GAOR, 21st Sess., Supp. No. 16, art. 10, U.N. Doc. A/6316 (1966), 999 U.N.T.S. *171* (*entered into force* 23 Mar. 1976); Common Article Three of the Geneva Conventions. *See* Geneva III, *supra* note 25; Geneva IV, *supra* note 31.

34. The US Supreme Court is considering whether the president may label US citizens as "enemy combatants" and deprive them of Constitutional rights. *See* Hamdi, *supra* note 27; Padilla, *supra* note 27. These cases do not concern the fate of the non-citizen "enemy combatants" in Guantanamo.

35. *See generally* RESTORING THE RULE OF LAW, *supra* note 18.

36. As ICRC President, Jakob Kellenberger emphasized in a 17 March 2004 speech to the UN Commission on Human Rights:

> For example, fundamental judicial guarantees are a cornerstone of protection in peat clime and in armed conflict. This is confirmed by the wording of Article 75 of Additional Protocol I of 1977, which is applicable in international armed conflicts, a provision clearly influenced by human rights law. Similarly, the application of human rights standards is needed in non-international armed conflicts in order to supplement humanitarian law provisions governing the treatment, conditions of detention and rights regarding a fair trial of persons deprived of liberty.

Jakob Kellenberger, 60th Annual Session of the UN Commission on Human Rights— Statement by the President of the ICRC (17 Mar. 2004), *available at* www.icrc.org/Web/Eng/siteengo.nsf/htmlall/5X6MY5?OpenDocument&style=custo_print.

37. *Civil and Political Rights, Including the Question of Torture and Detention: Report of the Working Group on Arbitrary Detention, Louis Joinet Chairperson-Rapporteur, Executive Summary*, U.N. ESCOR, Comm'n on Hum. Rts., 59th Sess., Agenda Item 11 (a), U.M. Doc. E/CN.4/2003/8 (2002), *available at* www.hri.ca/fortherecord2003/documentation/commission/e-cn4-2003-8 .htm. The United States rejected this position. *Civil and Political Rights, including the Questions of: Torture and Detention: Response of the Government of the United States of America to the December 16, 2002 Report of the Working Group on Arbitrary Detention*, U.M. ESCOR, Comm'n on Hum. Rts., 59th Sess., Agenda Item 11 (a), U.N. Doc. E/CN.4/2003/G/73 (2 Apr. 2003), *available at* www.unhchr.ch/Huridocda/Huridoca.nsf/e06a5300f90fa023802566870051 8ca4/35a53be 3c4b5a245c1256d050036ff03/$FILE/C0312799.pdf. The United States is a party to the ICCPR, yet no other party has *Seen* fit to bring a state-to-state complaint challenging the US position on these detentions. The Inter-American Commission on Human Rights has taken a similar position on the Guantanamo detainees and the United States has rejected this position as well.

38. *See* THREAT OF A BAD EXAMPLE, *supra* note 18, at 23.

39. For a more comprehensive description of these events, *See* DAVID COLE, ENEMY ALIENS: DOUBLE STANDARDS AND CONSTITUTIONAL FREEDOMS IN THE WAR ON TERRORISM (2003). *See also* AMERICAN CIVIL LIBERTIES UNION, AMERICA'S DIS-APPEARED: SEEKING INTERNATIONAL JUSTICE FOR IMMIGRANTS DETAINED AFTER SEPTEMBER 11 (2004), *available at* www.aclu.org/Files/OpenFile.cfm?id=14799. The ACLU has filed a complaint on behalf of the post-September 11 detainees with the UN Working Group on Arbitrary Detention. *See also* Marjorie Cohn, *Rounding up the Unusual Suspects: Human Rights in the Wake of 9/11: Human Rights, Casualty of the War on Terror*, 25 SAN DIEGO JUSTICE J. 317 (2003). *See also* Kareem Farhim, *The Moving Target: Profiles in Racism*,

AMNESTY NOW, Winter 2003, *available at* www.amnestyusa.org/amnestynow/racial_profiling .html.

40. U.S. DEPARTMENT OF JUSTICE: OFFICE OF THE INSPECTOR GENERAL, THE SEP-TEMBER 11 DETAINEES: A REVIEW OF THE TREATMENT OF ALIENS HELD ON IMMIGRATION CHARGES IN CONNECTION WITH THE INVESTIGATION OF THE SEPTEMBER 11 ATTACKS (2003), *available at* www.usdoj.gov/oig/special/0306/index.htm. In contrast to Guantanamo at least immigrants detained within the United States were allowed to have counsel and were placed within a process where there was the possibility, however limited, of administrative and judicial oversight.

41. *See* COLE, *supra* note 39, at 188.

42. Press Release, Amnesty International, USA: Deporting for Torture? (14 Nov. 2003), AMR 51/139/2003, *available at* web.amnesty.org/library/index/engamr511 392003.

43. *See* Joan Fitzpatrick, *Rendition and Transfer in the War Against Terror: Guantanamo and Beyond,* 25 LOY. L.A. INT'L & COMP. LJ. 457 (2003).

44. S.C. Res. 1456, U.N. SCOR, 58th Sess., 4688th mtg., ¶ 6, U.N. Doc. S/RES/1456 (2003), *available at* www.unhchr.ch/Huridocda/Huridoca.nsf/(Sytnbol)/S.RES. 1456+(2003).En? Open document. *See* a/so Report on Terrorism and Human Rights, Inter-Am. C.H.R., OEA/ser.L/V/ II.1 16, doc. 5 rev. 1 corr. (2002), available afwww.cidh.org/Terrorism/Eng/toc.htm.

45. One example are the events unfolding in the Darfur region of the Sudan. Just as millions may have died in recent years, without much public notice, in the Democratic Republic of the Congo, thousands may be dying now in Darfur; yet the world is not mobilizing adequately to prevent this impending catastrophe.

46. If deemed prisoners of war then there is a well-defined regime of humanitarian law under which the detainees must be treated.

47. *See* United States v. Yousef, 327 F.3d 56 (2d Cir. 2003) (affirming convictions of those respon-sible for the 1993 World Trade Center bombing).

48. *See generally* JOAN F. FITZPATRICK, HUMAN RIGHTS IN CRISIS: THE INTERNA-TIONAL SYSTEM FOR PROTECTING RIGHTS DURING STATES OF EMERGENCY (1994).

49. General Comment on Article 4, General Comment No. 29, U.N. GAOR, Hum. Rts. Comm., 1950th mtg., ¶11, U.N. Doc. CCPR/C/21/Rev.1/Add 11 (2001).

50. *See, e.g.,* Brogan and Others v. United Kingdom, 24 Eur. Ct. H.R. (ser. B) at 145-B (1988), *available at* www.worldlii.org/eu/cases/ECHR/1988/24.hlml (emphasizing the requirement of judicial oversight); *See also* Habeas Corpus in Emergency Situations (Arts. 27(2) and 7(6) of the American Convention on Human Rights), Advisory Opinion OC-8/87 of 30 January 1987, Inter-Am. C.H.R. (Ser. A) No. 8 (1987), *available at* heiwww.unige.ch/humanrts/iachr/tM 1_4h .htm. *See* a/so American Convention on Human Rights, *signed* 22 Nov. 1969, O.A.S.T.S. No. 36, O.A.S. Off. Rec. OEA/Ser.L/V/ll.23, doc. 21, rev. 6 (1979) (*entered into force* 18 July 1978), *reprinted* in 9 I.L.M. 673 (1970).

*Paul Hoffman is the chair of the International Executive Committee of Amnesty International. He is a civil rights and human rights lawyer with the Venice, CA–based law firm of Schonbrun, DeSimone, Seplow, Harris & Hoffman LLP. He also teaches international human rights law at USC Law School and Oxford University.

Hoffman, Paul. "Human Rights and Terrorism." *Human Rights Quarterly* 26, no. 4 (2004): 932–955.
© 2004 by The Johns Hopkins University Press.

Reprinted with permission of The Johns Hopkins University Press.

Torture in the Public Mind

*by Miroslav Nincic and Jennifer Ramos**

[...]

THE ISSUE IN PERSPECTIVE

At least since the imperative of containing communism at the height of the Cold War, few foreign policy objectives have garnered as much national support as the struggle against international terrorism. [...] At the same time [...] many believe that even praiseworthy national objectives should not trump core norms that define the American character. [...]

Such core values encompass reliance on ethically acceptable instruments of foreign policy and the appropriate treatment of prisoners taken in the context of the war. The bitterest disagreements have centered on [...] coercive interrogation techniques, some of which amount to generally accepted notions of torture.

[...]

The [American] cultural revulsion [to torture] has been buttressed by institutional and normative rules. These include the US Constitution's Fifth Amendment (barring self-incrimination) and its Eighth Amendment (involving cruel and unusual punishment). Abusive practices also are proscribed by international conventions to which the United States is party. Article 5 of the United Nations Universal Declaration of Human Rights unambiguously states that "No one shall be subjected to torture or cruel, inhuman or degrading treatment or punishment." The United Nations Convention Against Torture prohibits "any act by which severe pain or suffering is intentionally inflicted on a person."[5] The Geneva Conventions, dealing with captured enemy combatants and enemy civilians, forbid "violence to life and person, in particular murder of all kinds, mutilation, cruel treatment, and torture" as well as "outrages upon personal dignity, in particular humiliating and degrading treatment."

The normative restraints are overwhelming, and until recently and with certain exceptions [...] there has been little reason to think that the United States could be found culpable in this area.[7] Such perceptions were dramatically altered by the manner in which the war on terror has been conducted. The most graphic evidence of torture by US personnel was provided by the treatment of detainees at the Abu Ghraib prison in Baghdad, in 2004 and 2005. The official report commissioned by the Department of Defense on this matter (the Taguba Report 2004) indicated severe abuse of prisoners at that facility, and the media reported extensively on the matter. According to the *New York Times*, prisoner mistreatment included such degrading practices as urinating on detainees, jumping on wounded legs and pounding them with a metal baton, pouring phosphoric acid on detainees, tying ropes to their legs and penises and dragging them across the floor, sodomizing prisoners with a baton, and so forth (Zernike 2005).

Comparable mistreatment of prisoners was reported at other US-run facilities. According to an FBI report, the detention facility at Guantanamo saw such practices as chaining detainees in a fetal position on the floor for over 18 hours, as they urinated and defecated on themselves (*Guardian.co.uk* 2007). Revelation that confessions by one terrorist suspect at Guantanamo were obtained by torture, led Susan J. Crawford, the convening authority of the military commission, to decide against referring his case to trial (Glaberson 2009). The military jail at Bagram Air Base in Afghanistan, at which many al-Qaeda suspects are held, witnessed the death of two detainees when they were chained to the ceiling and beaten (Golden 2005). One variant of abuse at the center of much controversy has been the practice of "waterboarding" whereby a prisoner is strapped to a downward-inclined board, with plastic bag over his head, and, via water introduced into his nose, given the sensation of drowning.

The problem is that most Americans, both at the elite and mass levels, firmly support the need to combat terrorism (Table 1). When the Chicago Council on Global Affairs asked citizens the degree to which they viewed terrorism as a threat: "Below is a list of possible threats to the vital interest of the United States in the next 10 years. For each one, please select whether you see this as a critical threat, an important but not critical threat, or not an important threat at all … terrorism," an overwhelming majority consistently viewed it as a critical threat. In this climate, the Bush administration was able to base its justification

Table 1. Terrorism as a Critical Threat

Year	Percent of the Public Who View Terrorism as a Critical Threat
2004	75
2006	74
2008	72

(*Notes.* Source: Chicago Council on Global Affairs)

Table 2. Is Torture Justified?

Year	Response Options	Percent Concurring
2006*	Sometimes	35
	Never	36
2008**	Often/Sometimes	48
	Rarely/Never	50
2009***	Favor use	43
	Oppose use	48

(*Notes.**CBS News/*New York Times* Poll. September, 2006. **Pew Research Center for the People and the Press Political Survey. February, 2008. ***Fox News/Opinion Dynamics Poll. January, 2009.)

for practices that many deem torture, or cruel and inhumane treatment, on the imperatives of the war on terror. The dilemma for many Americans is obvious, for, while a slight majority claims to oppose the proscribed methods, a sizable minority does not (Table 2).

This trend has continued over the years. In 2006, when Americans were asked "Do you think it is sometimes justified to use torture to get information from a suspected terrorist, or is torture never justified?," 56% replied "never", but 35% considered it a possibility. Similarly, in 2008, the public was asked, "Do you think the use of torture against suspected terrorists in order to gain important information can often be justified, sometimes be justified, rarely be justified, or never be justified?", 48% responded if can be "often" or "sometimes" justified, while 50% answered "rarely" or "never" (See Table 2). More recently, in 2009, a poll asked "Do you favor or oppose allowing the CIA (Central Intelligence Agency) in extreme circumstances, to use enhanced interrogation techniques, even torture to obtain information from prisoners that might protect the United States from terrorist attacks?", and found that 43% agree that torture can be justified, while 48% opposed the use of torture, regardless of the circumstances.

The question is how, in the face of the apparent imperatives of the US war on terror, an ethically based judgment on the acceptability of torture and related practices can be reached by most Americans. When ethical dilemmas arise because important policy objectives are pursued by means inconsistent with deeply held norms, cognitive dissonance must be dealt with. The usual outcome is that either support for the controversial means is abandoned or the conflicting values are interpreted such that they no longer seem incompatible with these means. Our purpose is to examine the nature of the analytic choices behind these decisions. A first step is to identify the basic sources of the ethical beliefs people hold.

[...] [E]thical impulses do not always point in the same direction. Thus, while torture might be judged as bad in and of itself, it could also be regarded as consequentially desirable (if it helped save innocent lives), or undesirable (for example, if it made it more likely that American prisoners abroad would be tortured). A person's ultimate decision on whether or not to endorse a policy would, then, depend on how the individual criteria are weighed, from which a judgment on the net value of the policy may be assumed to follow.

Torture and Terror: The Relevant Context

It is important that torture and terrorism be placed in a context reflecting the ethical and practical issues as they appear in the real world. In this regard, we must address the thought experiment, often referred to as the ticking time bomb scenario, which seeks to show how torture could be ethically justified and which is fundamental to most attempts to justify the occasional resort to torture. One is asked to contemplate a situation in which a terrorist has hidden a time bomb (in some variants a nuclear bomb) in a public place, such that, unless the bomb is defused, it would soon detonate, killing a catastrophically large number of innocent people. If the terrorist had been apprehended, and if only torture could force him to reveal the bomb's location, would anyone seriously consider its use unethical? Most people would almost surely consider the decision an easy one, and this scenario is often invoked by those who object to a blanket ban on torture. In this vein, Justice Richard Posner (2002) has argued that, "If torture is the only means of obtaining the information necessary to prevent the detonation of a nuclear bomb in Times Square, torture should be used and will be used to obtain the information" (2006). [...]

The ticking time bomb scenario, while compelling, is often considered a dubious foundation on which to argue the necessity for torture in the context of the war on terror, as is evident when the scenario's hidden assumptions are considered. A first assumption is that we are absolutely sure that there is a bomb, that it is not a matter of misinformation, or a scare engineered by the enemy to create a sense of panic. The second is that the prisoner being tortured is, in fact, the person who planted the bomb (or who could reveal the information needed to locate it). The third is that there is no other way of obtaining the information, at least not within the applicable time constraints. The fourth is that the torture will effectively elicit the truth. If *any* of these assumptions is wrong, torture would fail to serve its purpose. [...]

No known case of torture conducted as part of the US campaign against terror has met the ticking time bomb assumptions. Although many subjected to cruel and degrading treatment undeniably had terrorist affiliations, in none of the reported cases was it apparent that the person was associated with an imminent attack. Thus, the first two assumptions of the ticking time bomb scenario have not been met. Had they been, it would remain unclear whether torture was the only way of obtaining the information and whether the truth can reliably be extracted from a person with a strong incentive to lie in order to end to his torment. Thus, it is hard to argue that the mind game used to justify torture in the most unique set of circumstances conceivable is a useful guide to the ethical issues involved in more plausible scenarios. [...]

The issue of how torture and abuse may be justified must refer, not to a contrived and wildly implausible scenario but to the situation of a war on terror conducted under conditions of uncertainty regarding the fund of relevant knowledge possessed by suspects, regarding the imminence of the threats involved, regarding the effectiveness of torture, and regarding methods of eliciting information. If any of the ticking time bomb's assumptions were to prove erroneous after the fact, torture would have no justification. If uncertainties exist *before* the fact, any justification for torture is substantially weakened; whether it could be sustained depends on how much uncertainty a person is willing to accept, and whether the information about the threat is highly compelling, or, as the *Washington Post* expressed it, a matter of a "fishing expedition for morsels of information that might prove useful but usually don't" (Luban 2005). To these uncertainties must be added qualms about possible secondary consequences: the most frequently mentioned of which bear on the nation's moral authority, a crucial component of what is referred to as "soft power," (Nye 2004), as well as the more tangible danger that US military or covert operatives might be subjected to similar treatment when in the enemy's hands.

Accordingly, the matter is not one of crisp certainties in the face of immense and immediate stakes, but of generally murky information on ambiguous stakes. A further preliminary issue concerns the extent of mistreatment needed to qualify as torture. It may be claimed that mistreatment meted out in the US case is not so great that it could not be offset by its utilitarian benefits. The argument rests on the difference between torture as it was practiced, say, in the Middle Ages, and what has been done to prisoners at US military facilities. It is not a matter of torment on the rack or of pulling out fingernails, but of nonlethal forms of physical violence, psychological humiliation, and so forth. At the extreme end of opinion, Rush Limbaugh, commenting on the events at Abu Ghraib and the legal trouble that responsible military personnel encountered as a result, indignantly exclaimed: "This is no different than what happens at the Skull and Bones initiation and we're going to ruin people's lives over it and we're going to hamper our military effort, and then we're going to really hammer them because they had a good time" (Sontag 2004). Related views are occasionally also found, in a far more muted and thoughtful form, at the political center. Thus, Jean Bethke Elshtain observes that the concept of torture is insufficiently disaggregated and that there are forms of physical and mental abuse (say, slapping, or sleep deprivation) that could be termed "torture lite," a practice that should not be excluded when the stakes are great enough (Elshtain 2004:85–89). At the same time, there is the view according to which, "Whenever people resort to euphemisms, they shouldn't be engaged in the activity" (Barrett 2008: 3).

[…] At the moment, we will retain the concept's meaning as implied by international conventions, and remembering that the UN Declaration on human rights proscribes not only torture but also any form of cruel and inhuman treatment. […]

SUPPORT FOR TORTURE AND THE WAR ON TERROR

As pointed out, two sorts of ethical reasoning could be invoked in support of torture, the one deontological and the other utilitarian. We will begin by outlining views expressed at the level of opinion-making elites, subsequently comparing them to the distribution of opinions held by the general public.

Deontological Arguments

[Deontology derives the rightness or wrongness of one's conduct from the character of the behavior itself rather than the outcomes of the conduct]. A principled deontological argument generally describes torture as unambiguously bad, although the core principle it violates may be conceived in several ways. Lindsey Barrett, writing for the Center for American Progress, argues a pure deontological position, saying that "People are bound by a common humanity, but denigrating fellow humans ruptures that bond and destroys the basic spiritual principle of the Golden Rule, which commands that we treat others as we would want to be treated ourselves. Torture tears this principle to shreds. It also corrupts the hearts of the perpetrators, just as it destroys the bodies and souls of its victims." (Barrett 2008). Senator Patrick Leahy's deontological position is rooted in the sanctity of a fundamental political principle: "If we do not protect the civil rights that distinguish us from terrorists, the terrorist have also won. Torture is among the most heinous of crimes, and there is no justification, in law or otherwise, for its use" (Leahy 2003). The deontological view is ultimately also about a sense of identity, a matter of, according to the *New York Times*, "Is this who we really are?" (2007). With that question in mind, a letter by 29 retired US generals and admirals stated that such practices are "anathema to the values Americans have held dear for generations."[11]

No matter how one describes the core principle justifying rejection of torture, there are other deontological concerns that could modify the initial taboo. Arguing the acceptability of torture and abuse, one might observe that the basic principle is the sanctity of life and body and that in as much as torture violates this sanctity, so does the killing of innocent people—a defining feature of terrorism. Thus, a fundamental and principled argument might allow for torture if it were a matter of saving innocent lives. Nudging aside the fact that this implies a ticking time bomb setting, with its implicit utilitarian assumptions (for example, torture *would* save these lives), a person considering an appropriate, deontologically based attitude toward torture as an instrument of the war on terror would have to weigh the bad that is torture against the good implied by saving innocent lives. If the root of the principle is the sanctity of human life and body, the issue becomes one of seeking the lesser evil.

[...]

The deontological argument, then, could pit a belief in the intrinsic evil of torture, fortified by the realization that innocent people might be tortured, against the intrinsic value of saving innocent lives against terrorism. If no further utilitarian considerations intruded, the respective values assigned to these considerations should determine final judgment on torture's permissibility in the global war on terror. But consequentialist positions [those that hold actions should be judged based on their ultimate effects, rather than simply their content] inevitably also shape such judgments. [...]

Consequentialist Arguments

One important consideration involves the actual effectiveness of torture at extracting the truth needed to save lives from the threat believed to be hovering over them, and there is considerable disagreement on the issue of this effectiveness. Former vice president Cheney, referring to the waterboarding of Khalid Sheikh Mohammed, an al-Qaeda operative and architect of the 9/11 attacks, waxed enthusiastic about the method's effectiveness, claiming that, at least in that case, "it's been remarkably effective" (ABC News Online 2008). An editorialist for the *National Review* agreed, maintaining that "to declare that torture never works is inaccurate and a dodge" (Wehner 2004).

At the same time, many claim that torture does not work, at least not well enough to justify the undeniable moral bad. One problem is that victims of torture have a strong incentive to lie in order to end it. Thus, after the 9/11 attacks when the Bush administration was considering the invasion of Iraq, Ibn al Shaykh al Libbi, a high-raining al-Qaeda operative in US custody, was turned over to Egyptian authorities whom he informed, under torture, that Iraq's military leaders had trained al-Qaeda and other terrorist groups to use chemical and biological weapons. The Administration used this information to justify invading Iraq. Later, the CIA admitted that al Libbi "had no knowledge of such training or weapons, and fabricated the statements because he was terrified of further harsh treatment" (Barrett 2008:2). Referring in a more general context to torture, a former CIA official described it as "bad interrogation. I mean you can get anyone to confess to anything if the torture's bad enough" (ABC News Online 2005). The previously cited letter by a number of generals and admirals to Senator McCain pointed out that "torture and cruel treatment are ineffective methods, because they induce prisoners to say what their interrogators want to hear, even if it is not true."

Another argument against torture, involving one of its secondary consequences, is that torture practiced by the United States could make it more likely that captured Americans would be subjected to similar treatment, through revenge or because of a general erosion of the norm against detained abuse. Senator Lindsey Graham explained that "If we let our chief of state decide the law is getting in the way, what's to prevent some other [foreign] chief of state from saying 'That American pilot we've captured, he knows where the next bomb wave is coming, do what you got to do'" (Isikoff 2006). Similarly, Senator McCain, argued that "While our intelligence personnel in Abu Ghraib may have believed that they were protecting US lives by roughing up detainees to extract information, they have had the opposite effect. Their actions have increased the danger to American soldiers, in this conflict and in future wars" (McCain 2004). The *New York Times* adopted the same position, writing that torture "will add immeasurably to the risk facing any man or woman captured while wearing America's uniform or serving in the intelligence forces" (*New York Times* 2007).

Accordingly, a person's views on the likelihood that US mistreatment of suspected terrorists would expose captured Americans to greater probability of abuse could also shape their final views on the acceptability of torture practiced by the United States.

The Structure of Support for Torture

The question, at this juncture, is how are these different concerns weighted, absolutely and relative to each other, by people contemplating the justifiability of torture? [...]

[...]The Program on International Political Attitudes (PIPA),[12] at the height of the torture debate in the United States, surveyed its respondents in 2004 on all three issues. Those interviewed were asked whether or not they found the following statement convincing (Statement 1): "Torturing and abusing people is morally wrong. The United States as a great nation, and as a moral leader of the world, should not set a bad example by engaging in cruel or degrading treatment." The unqualified statement that such practices are morally wrong comes as close as we can reasonably hope to the expression of a pure deontological principle.

At the same time, PIPA sought to provide a broader range of deontological options, implying that such practices might be for a greater good. It asked respondents whether or not they found this statement convincing: "Because we often do not know for sure that someone actually has useful information or is in fact a terrorist, if torture or abuse is allowed a significant number of innocent people will end up being tortured or abused." Respondents were asked whether they found this convincing or unconvincing (Statement 2). In addition, PIPA asked, "Because getting information from suspected terrorists could save many innocent people's lives, it would be immoral to limit ourselves from using whatever methods may be useful for getting that information." Respondents were asked whether they found that statement convincing or not (Statement 3). Table 3 displays the distribution of responses to these statements.

A strong majority shares the view that torturing and abusing people is "morally wrong," a result consistent with what most would have expected. At the same time, a very significant majority also believes that such practices would imply the torture and abuse of many innocent people. A less stark plurality does not condone these methods, *even* if they help save innocent lives.

On the consequentialist side, respondents were asked whether they thought the coercive methods were ineffective, because people would simply lie under the circumstances (Statement 4): "Research says that torture and abuse is not an effective way to get information out of people because people will lie to get the

Table 3. Views on the Deontological Arguments	
Statement	Percent Agreeing
Statement 1 (torture is morally wrong)	77
Statement 2 (innocent will be tortured)	71
Statement 3 (torture saves lives)	48

(*Notes.* Source: Program on International Policy Attitudes (PIPA) (2004))

Table 4. Views on the Consequentialist Arguments

Statement	Percent Agreeing
Statement 4 (victims will lie)	70
Statement 5 (Americans will be mistreated)	77

(*Notes.* Source: Program on International Policy Attitudes (PIPA) (2004))

torture to stop. Rather, it is better to use positive incentives." Yet another question, with further implications for consequentialist judgments, inquired whether these practices make it more likely that captured Americans would be exposed to harsh treatment should they fall into hostile hands (Statement 5): "If the US makes exceptions to international laws against torture and abuse, other countries and groups will feel freer to make exceptions, thus making it more likely that when Americans are detained they will be tortured or abused." Table 4 summarizes the opinions on these matters.

Plainly, people seem to take consequentialist arguments seriously, with 70% saying torture and abuse are ineffective because people will lie just to get the torture to stop and 77% reckoning that torture and abuse of foreigners makes it more likely that captured Americans would be treated in the same way. The widely held feeling that torture may be both ineffective and counterproductive could make it less likely that it would be found acceptable, deontological views notwithstanding.

In any case, knowing the emphasis placed on different arguments for or against torture does not furnish a definitive picture of their respective impact when a concrete judgment on its acceptability is sought. This requires their joint incorporation into a model via which the relative impact of each circumstance can be assessed. Since, moreover, it is possible that the impact of each would depend on the level of abuse involved—ranging from physical torture to various forms of humiliating treatment—the degree of mistreatment must also be considered. Once again, we turn to PIPA (2004) and employ questions that bear on the level of torture that respondents believe the government should use. Specifically, the PIPA survey asks respondents the degree to which they agree with the following statements: "Government should never use physical torture," "Government should never threaten physical torture," "Government should never use mental torture," and "Government should never use humiliating or degrading treatment."

[…]

EXPERIMENTAL ANALYSES: THE IMPACT OF FOREIGN THREATS

One limitation of the above analyses is that they do not consider the impact of external conditions on public responses to torture-ignoring, in particular the gravity of the foreign threat that torture is meant to address. Perhaps these attitudes are rooted in core values, implying that they would not be affected by the presence or absence of a foreign threat. But it also is possible that a dramatic threat would increase popular acceptance of torture, under the rule that the end justifies the means. To test this possibility, we conducted an experiment mirroring some of the preceding analyses, while focusing on the possible impact of external threats. Employing a randomized experiment in this context will allow us to control for other influences, such as political knowledge and news-gathering habits, that may be impacting survey responses. Under controlled conditions, as in our quasi-experiment, we are able to isolate the causal variable of foreign threat since the only variation between the two groups of subjects is their exposure to threat. [...] [However] The survey evidence does not allow us to conclude that one's views on torture are or are not conditioned by circumstance. We, therefore, proceed with the following experiment.

Subjects in the experiment were randomly assigned to one of two groups: for the first, a security threat was suggested, and the second (control group) faced no threatening condition. We created a post-test design, such that subjects were first exposed to a treatment group or control group, and then asked to answer a series of questions regarding views on torture, while various demographic variables were taken into account.

Participants and design—The study ran from May 4–5, 2009; 93 research subjects were recruited from undergraduate classes at a liberal arts university in California. They were compensated $7 for their time (approximately 15 minutes). Self-reported demographic data for the sample revealed that the average age was 20, 55% were White (13% Hispanic / Latino, 10% Asian), 64% were women, 21% were Republican, 49% were Democrat, and 31% identified as Independent or Other. The average ideological score (1 = very liberal, 7 = very conservative) was 3.43.

Procedure—Subjects were recruited via an online experimental recruitment program, ORSEE, which advertised a politics and public opinion study.[13] In the experimental laboratory, they were randomly assigned to one of the two conditions: *Security Threat* or *Control Group* (no-threat). The groups had 47 and 46 participants, respectively. Subjects were seated at desks with partitions so that answers would be completely confidential and anonymous. The study began with exposure to the treatment (or lack thereof), which was followed by a series of questions related to torture as well as basic demographic information.

Table 9. Comparing Attitudes toward Torture across Contexts (% Who Favor Certain Prohibitions)

	Control Group (%)	Security Crisis Group (%)	Statistical Significance? p > .10
Governments should never use physical torture	63.04	65.22	No
Governments should never threaten physical torture	39.13	34.04	No
Governments should never use mental torture	47.83	55.32	No
Governments should never use humiliating or degrading treatment	63.04	61.7	No

Experimental Treatments

We designed a series of one-page newspaper articles for subjects in the two conditions. Each of the articles highlighted real news information from various Web sites. The goal of the *Security Threat* treatment was to stimulate awareness of possible terrorist attacks, drawing on security information from government officials and news agencies—such as, for example, the statement that "multiple intelligence estimates have warned that al-Qaeda is actively planning attacks on the US homeland from its safe haven in Pakistan." In contrast, those in the *Control Group* read a positive article about advances the United States is making in the areas of science, health, and education: "the quality of life keeps getting better." The article made no reference to any kind of threat.

Experimental results—The first and most obvious question we sought to answer was whether an individual exposed to the threat condition would be more receptive to the need for torture than one not so exposed. We employed the same question wording as in our survey analyses in order to enhance our ability to cross-validate our findings. The results are presented in Table 9. Apart from the fact that threats of torture are not as widely rejected as is its actual practice, and that physical torture is considered somewhat less unacceptable than mental torture, Table 9 reveals no statistically significant (even at the relatively undemanding .10 level) difference between our two groups when acceptability of torture is examined. On the basis of this experiment, different attitudes are grounded in beliefs too deeply entrenched to be affected by perceptions of international conditions.

Even if a threat condition does not seem to affect overall views on the permissibility of torture, it might have some impact on a person's views on the attitudes that are generally invoked for or against this practice, affecting the impact of either deontological or consequentialist arguments, are of some subsets thereof. For example, the issue of whether torture is, or is not, morally wrong may become less relevant in the presence of a threat, whereas the practical issue that it may do no good because victims would lie may become more salient. Comparing responses to the various arguments of both groups reveals, however, that, here again, the suggestion of an external threat makes no statistically meaningful difference (See Table 10).

As Table 10 indicates, the experiment shows that there is no statistically significant difference across treatment and control groups when it comes to views on torture. Whether a deontological or consequential argument was invoked, opinions remained stable whether or not an external threat was suggested. Perhaps counter-intuitively, whether or not one is subject to threatening conditions, they seem to play little role in an individuals' commitment to their stances on torture.

The addition of the experimental evidence solidifies the findings in the previous section and reassures us that there remains a commitment among citizens to the values upon which our country was founded, even when our government strays from these ideals. Moreover, the study contributes to the increasing focus on core values in academia and suggests that views on torture be considered within such research. This would be especially useful in exploring the link between domestic and foreign policy preferences.

Table 10. Comparing Views on Torture Across Context
(% Who Agree Argument is Convincing)

	Control Group (%)	Security Crisis Group (%)	Statistical Significance? p > .10
Deontological Arguments			
Statement 1 (torture is morally wrong)	82.22	72.34	No
Statement 2 (innocent will be tortured)	80.43	72.34	No
Statement 3 (torture saves lives)	28.26	36.17	No
Consequential Arguments			
Statement 4 (victims will lie)	73.91	76.6	No
Statement 5 (Americans will be mistreated)	56.52	55.32	No

CONCLUSION

Foreign policy often implies choosing between incompatible objectives, as well as between desirable objectives and the unappealing means they sometimes imply. Rarely, however, has the issue of "dirty hands" presented itself as starkly as in the debate on the admissibility of torture as a tool of the global war on terror. Values deeply embedded in the nation's culture and political principles have collided with policy imperatives claimed by its top decision makers. As the White House has changed hands, the dilemma has been resolved by decisively rejecting the repugnant practices, but the conundrum may reemerge under altered political circumstances; in any event, not every American would agree that the practices were unjustified. In a democratic context, the ultimate decision on the (in)admissibility of such practices will rest with the American public, and it is interesting to know what considerations weigh most heavily in the public's mind.

The two sentiments that appear to compete most powerfully in many minds, are, on the one hand, a deep moral abhorrence of torture, and, on the other hand, a desire to do whatever it takes to save innocent lives. It is likely that the abstract character of the former makes it hard to offset the more concrete need implied by the latter; still, the two are in very close competition, and the force of the abstract moral belief is reinforced by an aversion to the prospect that innocent suspects could be tortured or otherwise abused. The desire to save innocent lives must further contend with the more utilitarian conviction that many of those subjected to torture would gladly lie in order to end their pain and anguish. The ultimate outcome is that most Americans reject the desirability of torture, even when attempts are made to justify it by the claims of the war on terror. Our experimental study confirms this; attitudes toward torture are a part of one's core values, an area of foreign policy studies that only recently has begun to gather scholarly interest. At least in the post-9/11 era, views on torture are not significantly affected by international conditions—in particular, by the presence or absence of a security threat to Americans.

NOTES

[...]

5. It continues, "for such purposes as obtaining from him, or a third person, information or a confession, punishing him for an act he or a third person has committed or is suspected of having committed, or intimidating or coercing him or a third person, or for reason based on discrimination of any kind, when such pain or suffering is inflicted by or at the instigation of or with the consent or acquiescence of a public official or other person acting in an official capacity. It does not include pain or suffering arising only from, inherent in, or incidental to, lawful sanctions."

[...]

7. However, critics may point out that the existence of the death penalty in the United States is a form of torture. We acknowledge that Americans' perceptions of themselves as "moral" on the issue of torture may be subject to considerable debate.

[...]

11. This letter is reprinted at http://www.humanrightsfirst.org/wp-content/uploads/pdf/090108 -ETN-oct3-ret-mil-ldrs-ltr-senmccain-support-amend.pdf. (Accessed June 23, 2011.)

12. We are fortunate to have the publically available data gathered by PIPA, as it is well regarded and has a long-standing reputation as a data source.

13. ORSEE, or online recruitment system for economic experiments, was created by Ben Greiner (2003–2004).

REFERENCES

ABC NEWS ONLINE. (2005) CIA's Harsh Interrogation Techniques Described. November 18. Available at http://abcnews.go.com. (Accessed December 3, 2009.)

ABC NEWS ONLINE. (2008) Cheney Defends Harsh Tactics. December 16. Available at http:// abcnews.go.co,/politics/story. (Accessed November 24, 2009.)

[...]

BARRETT, LINDSEY. (2008) Torture is a Moral Issue. Center for American Progress, July 7. Available at http://www.americanprogress.org/2008/07/torture_moral.html. (Accessed November 24, 2009.)

[...]

ELSHTAIN, JEAN BETHKE. (2004) Reflection on the Problem of Dirty Hands. In *Torture: A Collection*, edited by Sanford Levinson. New York: Oxford University Press.

GLABERSON, WILLIAM. (2009) Detainee Was Tortured, a Bush Official Confirms. *New York Times*, January 14. Available at http://www.nytimes.com. (Accessed September 22, 2010.)

GOLDEN, TIM. (2005) In Us Report, Brutal Details of 2 Afghan Inmates. *New York Times*, May 20. Available at http://www.nytimes.com. (Accessed September 24, 2010.)

[...]

ISIKOFF, MICHAEL. (2006) What America Stands for. *Newsweek*. Available at http://www .newsweek.com/2006/09/17/what-americans-stand-for.html. (Accessed August 24, 2010)

[...]

LEAHY, PATRICK. (2003) Torture Is A Crime. Statement of Senator Patrick Leahy. Available at http://leahy.senate.gov/issues/foreignpolicy/torture. (Accessed November 22, 2009.)

[...]

LUBAN, DAVID. (2005) Torture, American Style. *Washington Post*, November 27. Available at http://www.washingtonpost.com. (Accessed September 27, 2010.)

[...]

MCCAIN JOHN, SENATOR. (2004) In Praise of Do-Gooders. Available at: http://mccain.senate .gov/public/index.cfm?FuseAction=PressOffice.OpEds&ContentRecord_id=a9398047-de31 -404d-9a6f be9d14855ac8&Region_id=&Issue_id=73379446-ed00-4a32-8ef1-9f1e12737746. (Accessed June 23, 2011)

[...]

NEW YORK TIMES. (2007) On Torture and American Values. October 7. Available at http://www .ny-times.com. (Accessed November 24, 2009.)

[...]

NYE, JOSEPH S. (2004) *Soft Power: The Means to Success in World Politics.* New York: Public Affairs Books.

[…]

POSNER, RICHARD. (2002) Review of Alan Dershowitz, Why Terrorism Works. *The New Republic* September 2: 28.

PROGRAM ON INTERNATIONAL POLICY ATTITUDES (PIPA). (2004) Americans on Detention, Torture and the War on Terrorism. Survey conducted July 9–15.

[…]

SONTAG, SUSAN. (2004) Regarding the Torture of Others. *New York Times Magazine*, May 23. Available at http://www.nytimes.com/2004/05/23/magazine/regarding-the-torture-of-others.html. (Accessed August 24, 2010).

TAGUBA REPORT. (2004) Treatment of Abu Ghraib Prisoners in Iraq. Article 15–16 Investigation of the 800th Military Police Brigade. Available at http://www.Findlaw.com

[…]

TRAN, MARK. (2007) FBI Files Detail Guantanamo Torture Tactics. *The Guardian*, January 3. Available at http://www.guardian.co.uk/world/2007/jan/03/guantanamo.usa. (Accessed June 27, 2011.)

WEHNER, PETER. (2004) Tortured Position. *National Review Online*, November 4. Available at http://www.nationalreview.com/articles/222719/tortured-positions/peter-wehner. (Accessed August 20, 2010)

ZERNIKE, KATE. (2005) Detainees Describe Abuses by Guard at Iraq Prison, New York Times, and January 12. Available at http://www.nytimes.com. (Accessed September 25, 2010.)

*Miroslav Nincic** is professor of political science at the University of California, Davis. His areas of specialization include international security, U.S. foreign policy, and research methods.

Jennifer M. Ramos is assistant professor of political science at Loyola Marymount University. Her work has appeared in *Journal of Politics, Public Opinion Quarterly, International Studies Perspectives, Journal of Political Ideologies, Foreign Policy Analysis* and *Human Rights Review.* Her most recent book is *Changing Norms through Actions: The Evolution of Sovereignty* (2013).

Nincic, Miroslav, and Jennifer Ramos. "Torture in the Public Mind." *International Studies Perspectives* 12 (2011): 231–249. ©2011 International Studies Association.

"The Empire Strikes Back": The US Assault on the International Human Rights Regime

by Julie Harrelson-Stephens and Rhonda L. Callaway*

[...]

PHASE I: HEGEMONIC SUPPORT

In developing an international human rights regime, that is, the expectation of state behavior when it comes to human rights, the United States played an initial, significant role. After refusing to accept hegemonic responsibility after World War I, the United States sought to assume the role even before the World War II was over. In a succession of meetings with its allies, the United States forged a vision of the post-war international order that reflected its primary belief in individual liberty and freedom, both in the economic and political realm. Economically, the United States developed a monetary and trade regime based upon free market principles and trade openness and developed international organizations to support these norms in the form of the IMF, the World Bank, and the GATT. The emphasis of capitalist ideology, specifically the role of the individual in the market, is mirrored in the US emphasis of individual rights internationally, particularly notable in its support of democratization efforts around the world. Politically, the United States acted to first punish the perpetrators of the Holocaust by spearheading the establishment of the Nuremberg Tribunal as well as push for an international organization that would provide peace and security. In the formation of the UN, the United States helped create an organization that would be the initial focus of the forthcoming human rights regime.

There is a general consensus that the human rights regime was a product of World War II as Forsythe notes that the "greatest war to date, World War II, led to the greatest effort to promote human rights" (Forsythe 1989, 10). However, the seeds to developing a post-war institution focusing on human rights are found in the beliefs and norms promoted by the United States and its allies. During the War, President Franklin D. Roosevelt (1941) looked "forward to a world founded upon four essential human freedoms" the freedom of expression and religion and the freedom from want and fear.[10] It was the reality of the Holocaust, however, which provided the final impetus for the creation of the human rights regime. As Dorsey points out "it is well known that Western reaction to fascism and militarism in the 1930s and 1940s led to human rights norms being written into the UN Charter, and widespread knowledge of the Holocaust gave the human rights movement a further push" (Dorsey 2000, 176). Thus, in terms of US hegemony, a certain amount of consensus with regard to the importance of human rights, with an emphasis on security rights, existed among the great powers during the regime's early development.

The primary focus of the United States has traditionally been in the area of security rights. These beliefs of individual freedom, liberty, and the right to life are found in the Declaration of Independence and have subsequently been the cornerstone of US foreign policy, particularly since the end of World War II. While US ideology favored security rights, it is important to note that the United States experienced a particular, albeit brief, point in history where significant support for subsistence rights existed as well. The Great Depression created a unique atmosphere where the executive and Democratic congressional leadership favored economic rights (Forsythe 2000). Moreover, there was a general agreement among all the participants crafting the UDHR about the inclusion of such rights, even if there were disagreements over fine points.

While the United States possessed many forms of hegemonic power immediately after World War II, its most persuasive weapon was that of ideological power (Nye 1990; Pease 2003; Sikkink 1993). The idea of democracy, with individual freedoms brought about by limited government, was extremely influential in the wake of fascism. The war was not even over before the Allied Powers met to hammer out the details of a post-war organization designed to maintain peace internationally.[11] Along with American support for the establishment of the UN, many NGOs within the United States were also instrumental in promoting human rights. Given the atrocities of the war, both the United States and Great Britain agreed that human rights should be regulated at the international level.

The UN Charter addresses human rights in several sections, but Article 55 lays out the most succinct statement regarding human rights focusing on the "principle of equal rights and self determination of peoples." More specifically, the article outlines three distinct areas of concern: economic and social development within states, increased international cooperation regarding such development, and "universal respect for, and observance of, human rights and fundamental freedoms for all without distinction as to race, sex, language, or religion." It is this last section that the United States has traditionally emphasized ideologically and to a lesser degree in its foreign policy. Article 55, as well as other sections of the UN Charter, serves as the foundation of what would later be an independent document addressing international human rights. President Harry S. Truman demonstrated American support for both the UN Charter and the development of international norms regarding human rights at the closing session of the founding conference when he stated that "[w]e have good reason to expect the framing of an international bill of rights...that...will be as much a part of international life as our own Bill of Rights is a part of our Constitution" (Farer 1992, 228). The UDHR (1948) served to further explicate internationally agreed upon human rights. The participation of the United States, in the person of Eleanor Roosevelt, was instrumental in forging this agreement between the East and the West and between developed and newly independent countries. The UDHR was adopted by the General Assembly signaling both the universalization and internationalization of human rights.

PHASE II: PASSIVE SUPPORT

After the brief post-war period of strong support for human rights, a second phase begins. This phase of passive support is marked by continued growth of human rights laws and norms internationally, while US support for the regime falters in the wake of an intensifying Cold War. The United States continues to overtly support the tenets of human rights, particularly security rights while simultaneously and covertly utilizing repressive tactics in the name of fighting communism.[12] Security rights remain a stronghold of US ideology while subsistence rights were perceived to be more in line with Soviet ideology. The struggle for human rights during the height of the Cold War was marked by this ideological division between the communist emphasis on subsistence and the democratic emphasis on individual rights. The human rights regime would, to some extent continue to grow, but also constantly find itself at odds with Cold War politics. This division would dominate the struggle for human rights until the end of the Cold War.

As the Cold War intensified, US support for human rights changed to the extent that it refused to ratify most of the international covenants and laws that would follow the UDHR. This refusal is reflective of several developments: first the increasing attention to second generation rights at the international level and second, the tendency of the United States to link human rights to foreign policy. Between the 1950s and early 1970s, the United States failed to lead on any international human rights effort as well as neglected human rights bilaterally. The regime continued to grow with only tacit US support. In fact, the international preferences for security rights led by European states actually surpassed the US definition of what constitutes security rights. Most notable was the issue of the death penalty. European countries began to openly condemn the US practice and refuse to extradite prisoners who could face capital punishment.

In the 1970s, the US Congress and President Jimmy Carter confronted US ambivalence towards human rights practices during the Cold War by placing a high priority on human rights. During this period, the United States attempted to link human rights practices to foreign policy while at the same time continued to forgo multilateral efforts. Consequently, as the international community and regional organizations signed and ratified a plethora of human rights treaties and covenants on topics ranging from economic and social rights to rights of the child, the United States opted to address human rights bilaterally by tying human rights to such things as trade agreements and foreign aid. One of the lone multilateral efforts came in the form of ratifying the Convention on the Prevention and Punishment of the Crime of Genocide during the Reagan Administration.

The end of the Cold War witnessed a renewal of ratifications on the part of the United States, signaling a willingness to support international human rights norms in practice as well as in rhetoric. In the early 1990s, the Senate ratified the Convention on the Abolition of Forced Labor, the Covenant against Torture and Other Cruel, Inhuman, or Degrading Treatment or Punishment, and finally in 1992 the United States ratified the International Covenant on Civil and Political Rights that had been in force since 1976. US participation in these covenants further signifies the type of rights the United States is committed to, that is security rights. However, this movement toward multilateralism did not include social and economic rights and the trend towards greater international commitment quickly came to an end with American refusal to submit to the jurisdiction of the ICC. While the initial phase was marked by an environment of relative consensus and cooperation with regard to crafting the UDHR, the United States began to challenge the idea of subsistence rights as the Cold War intensified. The second phase was characterized by tacit acceptance of security rights, which remained a stronghold of US ideology while openly questioning subsistence rights, which were perceived to be more in line with Soviet ideology.

PHASE III: HEGEMONIC ASSAULT

As discussed above, the early period of human rights regime formation was marked by strong hegemonic support based largely on ideological consistency with the values of security rights. The hegemon's willingness to undertake the costly responsibility of building the international human rights regime was underscored by a more general international environment supportive of human rights, a rather unique consequence of the Holocaust. As the Cold War waged throughout the 1970s and 1980s, American support for the human rights regime remained overtly steadfast while covert actions in the name of fighting communism often played fast and loose with the ideals and values of the regime. While there seemed to be increased support for the international institutions supporting human rights in the form of personal freedom and liberty after the Cold War, the terrorist attacks on the World Trade Center and Pentagon on September 11, 2001 would usher in a third phase of the human rights regime.

In this phase, the United States begins actively and overtly attacking security rights, the area of human rights where it had exhibited the strongest support. Although American commitment to security rights has never been absolute, the post-9/11 era marks a distinct change in support for the human rights regime. As part of the US-led war on terror, the United States has overtly rejected the idea of security rights and asserted its right to torture in the name of national security. Its rejection of basic international standards promised by the Geneva Convention, as well as the Convention against Torture with respect to the prisoners held at Guantanamo Bay, may be seen as the first sign that the United States was about to launch an aggressive campaign against its long held commitment to security rights.[13] The move to hold detainees at Guantanamo by the Bush Administration was an attempt specifically designed to create an arbitrary distinction that would allow them to argue that neither national law nor international law applied. Then came the US decision to reconsider its long-held ban on torture. The need to fight the war on terror, so the argument goes, necessitates abandoning the prohibition against torture.

The assault by the United States on the human rights regime would take three forms. First, the government would attempt to rename torture in order to hide it in plain sight. The military began calling its interrogation methods, stress and duress techniques, in order to distinguish them in name from torture (Massimino 2004). Such techniques focus on sleep and sensory deprivation and include requiring prisoners to remain standing or kneeling for hours, keeping prisoners in awkward and uncomfortable positions for prolonged periods of time, keeping the prisoners in black out situations by using black hoods or spray-painting goggles and interrogating prisoners while they are nude (Priest and Gellman 2002; Human Rights Watch 2004). According to an article in The Washington Post (Roth 2004, A29), the "Defense Department has adopted a 72-point 'matrix' of types of stress to which detainees can be subjected ... the more stressful techniques must be approved by senior commanders, but all are permitted. And nearly all are being used, according to testimony taken by Human Rights Watch from post-Sept. 11 detainees released from U.S. custody." In spite of the fact that even the United States agreed in June of 2003 that in ratifying the Convention against Torture such activities were illegal, the Bush Administration continued to authorize the use of stress and duress techniques.

Second, the government began a policy which embraced widespread use of torture. The first hint of the new policy was news that the US military tortured prisoners at Abu Ghraib. Even if this can be attributed to just a few bad apples, the use of language such as stress and duress techniques suggests that the government had created, at best, an environment ambiguous to and, at worst, an environment conducive to the use of torture. Moreover, evidence suggests that the abuse has been widespread, involving more than 460 detainees.[14] Beyond the overt use of torture after September 11th, the United States also engaged in increased covert support of torture with the use of black sites, or off the record detention facilities and the practice of extraordinary rendition where torture is outsourced to another state. In defending the practice, US officials "say the prisoners are sent to these third countries not because of their coercive questioning techniques, but because of their cultural affinity with the captives . . . They look to foreign allies more because their intelligence services can develop a culture of intimacy that Americans cannot" (Priest and Gellman 2002).[15] Other officials have been more forthright. For example, Priest and Gellman, in the same Washington Post article, quoted one official that was directly involved in such renditions that the understanding is "[w]e don't kick the [expletive] out of them. We send them to other countries so they can kick the [expletive] out of them."

Third, and perhaps most important, the administration began to justify torture to the American population in a direct attempt to counter longstanding US values. The administration, followed by society at large, began to reconsider its prohibition on torture. The Bush Administration contributed to this by making the argument that water boarding was not, in fact, torture. This argument was presented in a series of torture memos written by the Justice Department at the behest of the Bush Administration and CIA requests to be allowed to engage in more aggressive interrogation techniques.[16] Political pundits and academics alike joined the discussion with the argument that in the more dangerous war on terror world, the prohibition against torture no longer made sense. According to this line of reasoning, if terrorists are willing to blow themselves up and terrorist organizations are actively seeking more powerful weapons, then torture may be a necessity. For example, neoconservative commentator Charles Krauthammer (2005) staunchly defends a state's right to torture. In a 2005 column he contends that "[i]t would be a gross dereliction of duty for any government not to keep Khalid Sheikh Mohammed isolated, disoriented, alone, despairing, cold, and sleepless, in some godforsaken hidden location in order to find out what he knew about plans for future mass murder."[17] Even a well-known liberal academic argued that the government's ability to torture be sanctioned by the domestic legal framework by utilizing judicially issued torture warrants (Dershowitz 2002). As recently as

2008, the Bush Administration continued to protect the government's right to torture when it vetoed legislation that would have explicitly prevented the CIA from utilizing water boarding, sexual humiliation, and similar techniques. In addition to pundits, the US population at large witnessed an increase in support for torture, particularly in regards to the war on terror which seemed inconceivable prior to 9/11 (WorldPublicOpinion.org 2008). Thus, the third phase represents not only a significant policy shift in the United States but a seemingly important ideological shift as well.

The US assault on the human rights regime entails reverberations felt worldwide. Many states have used the US war on terror as justification for their own crackdown on security rights. Russian repression in Chechnya was defended as an extension of the war on terror, as was repression in China, Egypt, and Zimbabwe, to name a few examples. UN High Commissioner for Human Rights, Louise Arbour, expressed her frustration with this practice: "If I try to call to account any government, privately or publicly, for their human rights records, the first response is: first go and talk to the Americans about their human rights violations" (2007).[18] Thus, states that were torturing their citizens can now claim to be in line with hegemonic norms. Seven years into the war on terror, the cumulative effect of these actions by the United States constitutes a significant departure from its long standing commitment to individual freedom and the rule of law and amounts to a sustained attack on the human rights regime.

Again, surprisingly the norm of human rights has continued to grow even in spite of this attack. Some of America's closest allies have openly criticized its abandonment of security rights in the fight against terrorism. As noted above, the international community has continued to go further than the United States in calling for universal jurisdiction, or the idea that in the case of serious violations such as genocide or disappearances, states can claim jurisdiction regardless of where the crime occurred. A second expansion of security rights in the post-9/11 environment is the idea that humanitarian assistance implies an international responsibility to protect individuals when their states fail to do so. Moreover, it is in the post-9/11 environment that more countries, as well as international and regional organizations, advocate the abolition of the death penalty. According to Amnesty International (2009), in 1977 only 16 countries had abolished the death penalty whereas, as of 2008, more than two-thirds of countries have abolished the death penalty in law or practice. Beyond security rights, the human rights regime has continued to focus on the issues of subsistence as evidenced by the UN Millennium Development Goals (2000) which call for measurable improvements in rights that have been historically marginalized by the hegemon. This movement towards a more holistic view represents a significant expansion of the concept of human rights and further illustrates the growth and resiliency of the regime.

THE HUMAN RIGHTS REGIME: PROSPECTS FOR THE FUTURE

We now turn to a theoretical discussion of how regimes in general are maintained and what the theoretical implications are for the human rights regime in particular. As previewed above, the regime literature is divided into three main camps: power based theories grounded in realism, interest-based theories with roots in liberalism, and knowledge-based theories in line with constructivism or cognitive theories (Hasenclever et al. 1996, 1997). All have something to say about the maintenance of regimes and the role of the hegemon. We are specifically interested in whether a regime, in this case the human rights regime, is likely to persist when faced with a direct hegemonic attack. Hegemonic stability theory, which is the strongest realist or power-based view of regimes, suggests that hegemons continue to support international regimes that represent and further their own self-interests. Hegemonic leadership is based primarily on power distribution which can confer legitimacy; the more legitimate a hegemon is viewed within the system, the stronger the international regimes (Kindleberger 1981; Gilpin 1981, 1987). As the support of hegemon wanes, the strength of the regime can falter. The hegemon's commitment to the regime may diminish as other states begin to grow at a faster rate than the hegemon while its own growth begins to level off leaving the hegemon less willing and able to manage the system. For hegemonic stability theorists, a hegemon is required for both the creation and ongoing survival of a regime (Kindleberger 1981; McKeown 1983; Gilpin 1987). Rather than viewing regimes as a constraint on states, in the realist view "... the basic function of regimes is to coordinate state behavior to achieve desired outcomes in particular issue-areas" (Krasner 1983, 7). From this perspective, regimes merely reflect the existing power distribution of the international system.

The human rights regime is viewed from the realist perspective as a relatively weak regime that, at the end of the day, does not constrain the behavior of states. Whereas regimes with more tangible payoffs in terms of state power, such as monetary regimes, may be used by the hegemon to increase its power and influence in the international system, the human rights regime does little to overtly affect the power distribution of states. Realists' explanations do little to further our understanding of the persistence of the human rights regime. Therefore, examining the regime from a power-based perspective fails to adequately explain either its initial creation, or its continued growth, particularly as Cold War politics began to supersede ideological considerations within the United States. Moreover, the realists' view would suggest that waning commitment by the United States would constitute the beginning of the end of the human rights regime. By contrast, we find that the human rights regime is not only persisting but actually growing even as US support for the regime subsides.

Whereas realists view regimes as a tool of the state used to further its interests, the liberal view of regimes argues that institutions and international law serve to regularize the behavior of states. One of the most cogent statements on regimes comes from institutionalists who argue that regimes are supported by a benign hegemon to overcome suboptimal outcomes and facilitate cooperation. From this perspective, regimes matter as they fundamentally change the decision-making calculus of states (Keohane 1984). For institutionalists, shared interests among major powers can motivate them to continue the regime absent hegemonic support and regimes may become even more important absent a hegemon in order to promote international cooperation. From this perspective, regimes endure, in part, because international actors are aware of the difficulty of creating regimes. Moreover, once created, regimes can take on a life of their own and "commitments made to support such institutions can only be broken at a cost to reputation" (Keohane 1984, 26). Other institutionalists have begun to argue that regimes can be maintained without a hegemonic presence or support. Snidal (1985), for one, has argued that oligopolistic groups can maintain regimes absent hegemonic leadership. Likewise, Young (1989) argues that exogenous shocks or crises can play a significant role in regime maintenance. Such shocks can serve as reminders to states of the common interests enshrined by regimes. Institutionalists, then, are more likely to view regimes as a genuine constraint on state behavior, as it can make cheating less likely and therefore facilitate more cooperation among states.

However, it is important to note that previous research on regimes from both the realist and institutionalist perspectives has concentrated largely on issues of political economy where shared interests may be more obvious. The common interests of states are more easily discernible in economic issues such as trade or security issues such as arms control but much less obvious in the area of human rights. The human rights regime is largely based on ideology, and even when shared interests exist, they are obscure at best. A state violating the human rights of its citizen may well be viewed as cheating but that cheating does not have the same tangible effects on the state as war or economic loss. As noted by realists, for example, if a state cheats with regard to security issues in an anarchical system, the result might well be that other states cease to exist. Cheating in terms of human rights involve reputational costs for the cheaters but typically no costs for other states. The institutional perspective suggests that such cooperation occurs where there are shared gains for major powers. Absent a discussion of ideological motivations, the liberal perspective also falls short in explaining the growth of the human rights regime.

Institutions, international norms, and acceptance into a community of states all constitute inducements to create an environment where state repression is unacceptable. Consequently, international human rights norms and institutions have less to do with strategic or economic interests than with ideological interests which leads to a third view of regimes: the knowledge-based or constructivist approach. For constructivists, the ideas and identities of international actors matter and the realist and liberal focus on interests, absent the actor's understanding of those interests, presents an incomplete view of the world. For example, to a constructivist the anarchical nature of the system is only important based on how states understand and interpret that concept (Wendt 1992). Perceptions of decision-makers, shaped by their ideas about the world, influence their understanding of interests. As such "interests should be treated analytically, as contingent on how actors understand the natural and social world and the nature of their preferences" (Hasenclever et al. 1996, 206). Thus, the realist focus on power and institutionalist focus on interests misses the point that "ideas and communicative processes define in the first place which material factors are perceived as relevant and how they influence understandings of interests, preferences, and political decisions" (Risse and Sikkink 1999, 7).[19] Moreover, the importance of norms and ideas can become stronger when organizations are created to reinforce those ideas, so that "once ideas have become embodied in institutional frameworks, they constrain public policy as long as they are not undermined by new scientific discoveries or normative change" (Hasenclever et al. 1996, 207). Ultimately, the constructivist approach serves as an important bridge between realists and institutional explanations of behavior and reality by emphasizing the important role that ideas, knowledge, and norms can play in international regimes. As the constructivist position suggests, human rights has been intrinsically linked to international legitimacy and the identity of liberal states has been created and identified with that legitimacy.

The teeth of the human rights regime are most obvious in terms of reputation costs and questions of legitimacy. While other inducements, such as attempting to attract foreign aid, may come into play in the adherence to the human rights regime, it is likely the question of reputation that is critical in the persistence of the regime. Ultimately, the United States did not forge the human rights regime based solely on strategic interests. Rather this regime was created on the basis of a moral ideal, that is, as a reaction of the horrors of the Holocaust as well as a reflection of the value that the United States places on individual liberty.

Traditional concerns of regime theorists, such as relative gains, transaction costs, and cheating, make less sense in terms of the human rights regime where strategic interests are largely absent. Ideological regimes are not, in and of themselves, necessarily strong regimes. However, ideological regimes are strong to the extent that they can garner near universal consensus. The United States along with other major powers have pointed to a state's human rights practices, particularly security rights, to distinguish between rogue states and those that are accepted into the international community. The Hitler and Stalin regimes created the template for how states should not behave while the US ideological emphasis on individual rights helped identify how civilized states should behave. Consequently, democracy and human rights represent the most important identifying factors for the acceptance into the community of states.

We can conceive of an argument tying human rights and strategic interests only in indirect terms. The spread of democracy as an ideological counter to communism became central to the Cold War. For the United States, their experience in the interwar period suggested that international leadership was necessary to prevent future great wars. Moreover, US hegemony was based, at least in part, on support for the Kantian model of a pacific federation of republican states as the best way to insure peace. Theoretically, as states become more democratic, their respect for personal integrity rights improves dramatically, as subsequent evidence has born out. It is in the context of fighting the ideological battle of the twentieth century that we can envision a strategic element in the creation and maintenance of the human rights regime. The next question is whether this strategic interest is enough to maintain the regime when faced with a hegemonic attack? We would argue that it is not likely to be sufficient. Fairly quickly in the Cold War, the United States appears to abandon the Kantian vision as it supports one right-wing dictator after another, thereby placing human rights goals second to other strategic goals. After the end of the Cold War, the United States rejects multilateral cooperation for unilateral action and renews its support for repressive dictatorships in the name of fighting terrorism. This makes it difficult to argue that the pursuit of a human rights regime represents a strategic interest as human rights consistently take a backseat to other strategic interests.

[...]

The current strength and endurance of the human rights regime also stems from the institutionalization of human rights with the major European powers. As the EU has continued to grow, it has also continued to make human rights integral to its very identity. Longstanding members of the EU have both domestic and international commitments to human rights, and new or prospective members must exhibit a commitment to human rights in order to join. The case of

Turkey's admittance into the EU provides an excellent example. Although Turkey has been a candidate for EU membership, human rights concerns, particularly its treatment of ethnic Kurds, remain a significant impediment to ascension. The norm of human rights is so entrenched in Europe that Donnelly (2003) argues that European states voluntarily accept the human rights regime, reflecting a fundamental commitment to the norm.

CONCLUSION

The history of the human rights regime suggests that once institutions are created, they take on a life of their own. In the case of the human rights regime, it is hard to imagine such regime being created absent hegemonic support (particularly given that it directly conflicts with the idea of sovereignty). Since the regime was created it has continued to institutionalize international standards of human rights, even when the hegemon's support has been unenthused. The strength and resiliency of the international human rights regime, while theoretically surprising, suggests that it can indeed persist even when directly attacked by the hegemon. The September 11th attacks can be viewed as an exogenous shock that has had a serious but not necessarily terminal effect on international human rights. While this affected the domestic resolve of the United States in support of international human rights, it appears that the institutionalization of human rights norms in Europe, as well as widespread acceptance of human rights, thus far has been sufficient to uphold the regime absent the hegemon. Certainly, states that were repressing their citizens prior to 9/11 have used the war on terror and subsequent human rights violations by the United States as justification for continued repression. Nonetheless, other major powers remain strongly committed to human rights, and more importantly, continue to expand the regime today.

Our relatively optimistic assessment of the human rights regime should not be interpreted to mean that the regime is indestructible. As noted above, neoliberal institutionalism suggests that international regimes can survive hegemonic decline if other major powers possess shared interests in the regime. To the extent that the US rejection of human rights is translated into rejection by other major powers, particularly European powers where the commitment to the regime is the strongest, the regime could be in danger. It is worth noting that the two major powers that are the closest allies in the war on terror, Australia and the United Kingdom, have both passed anti-terror legislation which represents a weakening of their commitment to human rights. Another terrorist attack or increased hegemonic attacks on the regime in general has the potential to weaken the international human rights regime. Constructivist theory might further suggest the conditions under which the regime would be threatened in the long term. The extent to which the United States is able to successfully redefine what it means to be a member of the international community in terms of the war on terror could pose the greatest threat to international human rights. If liberal democracy gives way to support for the war on terror as the key characteristic to acceptance in the community of states, the human rights regime could face greater challenges in the future. However, the recent election of President Barack Obama may signal a reprieve for the assault on the human rights regime, if the United States is able to reverse the Bush policies regarding torture. While Obama's election may signal a readiness to return to longstanding values of individual liberty and respect for personal integrity, support for torture during the war on terror has grown and may well persist.

NOTES

[…]

10. It should be noted that the United States was also at the forefront of promoting human rights internationally prior to World War II. In his "Fourteen Points," President Woodrow Wilson advocated self-determination as part of his plan to make the "world safe for democracy." His idea of an international body designed to promote peace came to fruition in the League of Nations, albeit without American participation. Nonetheless, human rights were addressed in the League of Nations as the organization sought to protect marginalized groups in the form of minority rights and those living in mandated territories as well as labor rights (Forsythe 1989).

11. The United States met with its allies at Dumbarton Oaks in 1944, Yalta in 1945, and finally in San Francisco in 1945 for the purpose of creating what would become the UN.

12. Forsythe (2000) argues that this period represents a regime without hegemonic leadership due to increasing domestic opposition to human rights. We contend that US leadership, though weakened, remained due to its strong ideological bond to human rights, and its continued rhetorical support for many of the values of the regime.

13. The US ratified the Convention against Torture in 1994.

14. This evidence is based on a study conducted by the Detainee Abuse and Accountability Project (Mertus and Tanzreena 2007).

15. We accessed the Washington Post article online on the Common Dreams News Center available at: www.commondreams.org/headlines02/1226-03.htm.

16. The Washington Post posted a 2002 memo from Assistant Attorney General Jay Bybee on its website at www.washingtonpost.com/wpsrv/politics/documents/cheney/torture_memo_aug2002 .pdf. A March 2003 memo entitled "Detainee Interrogations in the Global War on Terrorism: Assessment of Legal, Historical, Policy, and Operational Considerations" can be found at: news.findlaw.com/wp/docs/torture/30603wgrpt2. html. The New York Times reported additional memos in 2005.

17. The Krauthammer article "The Truth about Torture" is available at: www.weeklystandard.com/ Content/Public/Articles/000/000/006/400rhqav.asp?pg=1.

18. The Democracy Now interview of Louise Arbour is available at: www.democracynow .org/2007/9/7/un_high_commissioner_for_human_rights.

19. For further elaboration of constructivism see Adler (1991), Checkel (1998), Katzenstein (1996a, b).

REFERENCES

Adler, Emanuel. 1991. "Cognitive Evolution: A Dynamic Approach for the Study of International Relations and their Progress." In Progress in Postwar International Relations, ed. Emanuel Adler. New York: Columbia University Press.

Amnesty International. 2009. Figures on the Death Penalty. (www.amnesty.org/en/death-penalty/numbers).

Arbour, Louise. 2007. Interview with Democracy Now on September 7, 2007. (www.democracynow.org/2007/9/7/un_high_commissioner_for_human_rights).

Brown, Seyom. 2000. Human Rights in World Politics. New York: Addison Wesley Longman.

Brysk, Alison. 1993. "From Above and Below: Social Movements, the International System, and Human Rights in Argentina." Comparative Political Studies 26:259–285.

Brzoska, Michael. 1992. "Is the Nuclear Non-Proliferation System a Regime? A Comment on Trevor McMorris Tate." Journal of Peace Research 29:215–220.

Checkel, Jeffrey T. 1998. "The Constructivists Turn in International Relations Theory." World Politics 50:324–348.

Czempiel, Ernst-Otto. 1981. Internationale Politik: Ein Konfliktmodell. Paderborn: Schöningh. Dershowitz, Alan M. 2002. "Want to torture? Get a warrant." San Francisco Chronicle 22 January. (www.sfgate.com/cgi-bin/article.cgi?file=/chronicle/archive/2002/01/22/ED5329.DTL).

Donnelly, Jack. 1986. "International Human Rights: A Regime Analysis." International Organization 40:599–642.

Donnelly, Jack. 2003. Universal Human Rights in Theory and Practice. Ithaca: Cornell University Press. Dorsey, Ellen. 2000. "U.S. Foreign Policy and the Human Rights Movement." In The United States and Human Rights, ed. David P. Forsythe. Lincoln and London: University of Nebraska Press.

Efinger, Mandred and Michael Zürn. 1990. "Explaining Conflict Management in East-West Relations: A Quantitative Test of Problem-Structural Typologies." In International Regimes in East-West Politics, ed. Volker Rittberger. London: Pinter.

Evans, Tony. 1996. US Hegemony and the Project of Universal Human Rights. New York: St. Martin's Press. Farer, Tom J. 1992. "The United Nations and Human Rights: More than a Whimper, Less than a Roar." In Human Rights in the World Community: Issues and Actions, ed. Richard P. Claude and Burns H. Weston. Philadelphia: University of Pennsylvania Press.

Forsythe, David P. 1989. Human Rights and World Politics. Lincoln: University of Nebraska Press. Forsythe, David P. 2000. Human Rights in International Relations. Cambridge: Cambridge University Press. Gilpin, Robert. 1981. War and Change in World Politics. Princeton: Princeton University Press.

Gilpin, Robert. 1987. The Political Economy of International Relations. Princeton: Princeton University Press. Harrelson-Stephens, Julie and C.F. Abel. 2006. "Bureaucratizing Torture." Paper presented at Public Administration and Theory Network, Olympia.

Hasenclever, Andreas, Peter Mayer, and Volker Rittberger. 1996. "Interests, Power, Knowledge: The Study of International Regimes." International Studies Review 40:177–228.

Hasenclever, Andreas, Peter Mayer, and Volker Rittberger. 1997. Theories of International Regimes. Cambridge: Cambridge University Press.

Howard-Hassmann, Rhoda E. 2005. "The Second Great Transformation: Human Rights Leap-Frogging in the Era of Globalization Pursuing Global Justice." Human Rights Quarterly 27:1–40.

Human Rights Watch 2004. "The Road to Abu Graib." 8 June. (www.hrw.org/en/node/12123/section/1). Katzenstein, Peter J. 1996a. The Culture of National Security: Norms and Identity in World Politics. New York: Columbia University Press.

Katzenstein, Peter J. 1996b. Cultural Norms and National Security: Police and Military in Postwar Japan. Ithaca: Cornell University Press.

Keck, Margaret and Kathryn Sikkink. 1998. Activists Beyond Borders: Advocacy Networks in International Politics. Cornell: Cornell University Press.

Keohane, Robert O. 1983. "The Demand for International Regimes." In International Regimes, ed. S. D. Krasner. Ithaca: Cornell University Press.

Keohane, Robert O. 1984. After Hegemony: Cooperation and Discord in the World Political Economy. Princeton: Princeton University Press.

Keohane, Robert O. 1998. "International Institutions: Can Interdependence Work?" Foreign Policy 110:82–96.

Keohane, Robert O., and Joseph S. Nye, Jr. 1977. Power and Interdependence: World Politics in Transition. Boston: Little, Brown.

Keohane, Robert O., and Lisa L. Martin. 1995. "The Promise of Institutionalist Theory." International Security 20:39–51.

Kindleberger, Charles. 1981. "Dominance and Leadership in the International Economy: Exploitation, Public Goods, and Free Rides." International Studies Quarterly 25:242–254.

Krasner, Stephen D. 1982. "Structural Causes and Regime Consequences: Regimes as Intervening Variables." International Organization 36:185–205.

Krasner, Stephen D., ed. 1983. International Regimes. Ithaca: Cornell University Press.

Kratochwil, Friedrich. 1989. Rules, Norms, and Decisions. Cambridge: Cambridge University Press. Kratochwil, Friedrich., and John Gerard Ruggie. 1986. "International Organization: The State of the Art." International Organization 40:753–775.

Krauthammer, Charles. 2005. "The Truth about Torture: It's Time to be Honest about Doing Terrible Things." The Weekly Standard 5 December. (www.weeklystandard.com/Content/Public/Articles/000/000/006/400rhqav.asp?pg=1).

Massimino, Elisa. 2004. "Leading by Example." Criminal Justice Ethics, Winter/Spring.

McKeown, Timothy. 1983. "Hegemonic Stability Theory and 19th Century Tariff Levels in Europe." International Organization 37:73–91.

Mertus, Julie, and Tazreena Tanzreena. 2007. "Human Rights Post-September 11." In Exploring International Human Rights: Essential Readings, ed. Rhonda L. Callaway and Julie Harrelson-Stephens. Boulder: Lynne Rienner Press.

Nye, Joseph. 1990. Bound to Lead: The Changing Nature of American Power. New York: Basic Books. Pease, Kelly-Kate. 2003. International Organizations: Perspectives on Governance in the Twenty-First Century. New Jersey: Prentice Hall.

Priest, Dana, and Barton Gellman. 2002. "'Stress and Duress' Tactics used on Terrorism Suspects Held in Secret Overseas Facilities." Washington Post 26 December.

Puchala, Donald J., and Raymond F. Hopkins. 1982. "International Regimes: Lessons from Inductive Analysis." International Organization 26:245–275.

Putnam, Robert. 1988. "Diplomacy and Domestic Politics: the Logic of Two-Level Games." International Organization 42:427–61.

Risse, Thomas, and Kathryn Sikkink. 1999. "The Socialization of International Human Rights Norms into Domestic Practices: An Introduction." In The Power of Human Rights: International Norms and Domestic Change, ed. Thomas Risse, Stephen C. Ropp, and Kathryn Sikkink. Cambridge: Cambridge University Press.

Risse, Thomas, Stephen C. Ropp, and Kathryn Sikkink. 1999. The Power of Human Rights: International Norms and Domestic Change. Cambridge: Cambridge University Press.

Rochester, J. Martin. 1986. "The Rise and Fall of International Organizations as a Field of Study." International Organization 40:777–813.

Roth, Kenneth. 2004. "Time to Stop 'Stress and Duress'." The Washington Post Page A29. (www.washingtonpost.com/wp-dyn/articles/A22623-2004May12.html).

Roosevelt, Franklin D. 1941. "Annual Message to Congress" June 6. (www.fdrlibrary.marist.edu/4free .html). Ruggie, John Gerard. 1975. "International Responses to Technology: Concepts and Trends." International Organization 29:557–583.

Sikkink, Kathryn. 1993. "The Power of Principled Ideas: Human Rights Policies in the United States and Western Europe." In Ideas and Foreign Policy: Beliefs, Institutions, and Political Change, ed. Judith Goldstein and Robert O. Keohane. Ithaca and London: Cornell University Press.

Snidal, Duncan. 1985. "The Limits of Hegemonic Stability Theory," International Organization 39:579–614. Strange, Susan. 1983. "Cave! Hic Dragones: A Critique of Regime Analysis." In International Regimes, ed. Stephen Krasner. Ithaca: Cornell University Press.

Tate, Trevor McMorris. 1990. "Regime-building in the Non-Proliferation Regime." Journal of Peace Research 27:399–414.

Young, Oran. 1980. "International Regimes: Problems of Concept Formation." World Politics 32:331–356. Young, Oran. 1986. "International Regimes: Toward a New Theory of Institutions." World Politics 39:104–122. Young, Oran. 1989. "The Politics of International Regime Formation: Managing Natural Resources and the Environment." International Organization 43:349–376.

Wendt, Alexander.1992. "Anarchy is What States Make of It: The Social Construction of Power Politics." International Organization 46:391–425.

Wendt, Alexander.1995. "Constructing International Politics." International Security 20:71–81. WorldPublicOpinion.org. 2008. "World Public Opinion on Torture: Country by Country Results."(www. worldpublicopinion.org/pipa/pdf/jun08/WPO_Torture_Jun08_countries.pdf).

*Julie Harrelson-Stephens is an associate professor of political science at Stephen F. Austin State University.

Rhonda L. Callaway is an associate professor in and department chair of political science at Sam Houston State University in Texas.

Harrelson-Stephens, Julie, and Rhonda L. Callaway. "'The Empire Strikes Back': The US Assault on the International Human Rights Regime." *Human Rights Review* 10 (2009): 431–452.

Part 4:
Human Rights and International Organizations

In the post-9/11 era, the question of individual security and the protection of human rights has maintained precedence on the agenda of nongovernmental and humanitarian organizations (NGOs) such as Amnesty International, Human Rights Watch, and international organizations (IGOs) like the United Nations. The fatal events of 9/11 and the subsequent invasions of Iraq and Afghanistan by the United States have had a profound effect on the way that both NGOs and IGOs attempt to advance humanitarian goals. The question that dominated the political arena after 9/11 and has consistently resurfaced in the work of the UN Security Council is the primacy of protecting state security and implementing counterterrorist action even at the risk of infringing on human rights. The global response to terrorism has, in practice, led to significant setbacks in equality, political freedom, social equity, and individual liberties.

Being constantly destabilized by national governments, subnational political forces and the War on Terror, these international organizations have tried to simultaneously promote and protect human rights while maintaining political impartiality and independence. While the UN attempted to use the endorsement of human rights as a diplomatic tool against terrorism, the immediate politics of counterterrorism appears to seldom be compatible with the long-term goals of peace, equality, and political liberty.

Rosemary Foot ("The United Nations, Counter Terrorism, and Human Rights: Institutional Adaptation and Embedded Ideas") examines the actions of the UN Security Council Counter-Terrorist Committees and analyzes the political duality of implementing antiterrorist measures for the sake of preserving national security while, at the same time, undermining a key norm of a democratic civil society—the rights of the individual. Hans Peter Schmitz ("Transnational NGOs and Human Rights in a Post-9/11") discusses the evolution of the activist human rights movement and addresses the impact of 9/11 on the human rights advocacy campaign led by different international NGOs. Both Foot and Schmitz argue that amid the ever-present challenges of advocating for the protection of civil liberties during a War on Terror, the consistent work of these international organizations has managed to reinforce the necessity for continuing discussion about human rights as a global priority.

As you read the articles in this section, consider the following:

1. What effects have the U.S. deviation from human rights norms had on the processes of key UN committees? In your opinion, have these effects made the UN more effective or less so? Why?

2. What components of the global War on Terror have been most challenging for the NGO community? Which have offered the NGO community new opportunities? Taking into account the regime changes in Iraq and Afghanistan as well as the other changes documented by Schmitz, do you believe the overall international context in which human rights NGOs work today is more conducive to achieving their aims than before, or less?

3. Based on the differing strategies Schmitz presents, how well would you say NGOs have adapted to the post-9/11 context, and how, in your opinion, could they better adapt?

The United Nations, Counter Terrorism, and Human Rights: Institutional Adaptation and Embedded Ideas

by Rosemary Foot*

I. INTRODUCTION

A significant casualty of the struggle against terrorism has been respect for human rights. [...]

This attack on rights raises a number of important questions. How robust are commitments to the protection of human rights turning out to be as the struggle against terrorism unfolds? Has the concept of human security shown any staying power in an era when the security of the state has apparently become of more central concern? Has the steady embodiment of human rights ideas in treaties, and in state and non-state domestic, regional, and global institutions over the post-1945 period been able to impose any constraints on behavior in the twenty-first century?

This article investigates these questions by focusing on the counter-terrorist activities of the UN Security Council. Particular attention is given to the actions of the Council's Al Qaeda/Taliban Sanctions Committee and the Counter-Terrorism Committee, established under Resolutions 1267 and 1373 respectively.

[...]

II. COUNTER-TERRORIST RESOLUTIONS AND THE WORK OF THE COMMITTEES

The Security Council's attention to terrorist threats increased markedly in the post Cold War era. [...] On several occasions, the United States was the primary target of terrorist strikes. [...] [This] moved terrorism up the US security agenda and Washington's response incorporated an operational role for the UN.[6] Security Council Resolution 1267, passed in October 1999 under Chapter VII of the Charter, imposed mandatory financial and aviation sanctions on members of the Taliban regime in Afghanistan as a result of the sanctuary they offered to Osama bin Laden and his associates. It also established a committee of the Security Council made up of all fifteen members to oversee state efforts to implement these sanctions. Later, the scope of the sanctions were made global in their effects since they involved financial, arms, and travel embargoes on the Taliban, bin Laden, Al Qaeda and all those in association with that organization wherever they might be located.[7]

The primary tasks of the 1267 Committee have been to target "individuals, groups, undertakings or entities associated with Al-Qaeda or the Taliban, or those controlled by their associates."[8] Names appear on a consolidated list as a result of information provided by one or more member states. Current members of the Security Council have sole power to review the justification for adding a name. Once a name is on the sanctions list, all states are expected to report on the steps they have taken to comply with Resolution 1267, as well as with subsequent related resolutions. Should individuals or entities assert that they have been wrongly listed, the aggrieved party has to request its state of residence or citizenship to petition on its behalf. This request can be denied.[9]

The terrorist assaults on US territory in September 2001 led to a sudden increase in the numbers of names on the 1267 list, some 466 as at the end of 2005 and most provided by the US authorities.[10] The increased workload and desire to enhance the levels of implementation of 1267 measures led eventually to an enhancement in the Committee's resources, most significantly in the establishment of an expert Analytical Support and Sanctions Monitoring Team (hereafter Monitoring Team) under Resolution 1526 of 30 January 2004. It replaced the five-person monitoring group previously established via Resolution 1363 of 30 July 2001, a group whose working practices had come under considerable criticism.[11] The new Monitoring Team, based in New York and charged with the task, *inter alia*, of reviewing state implementation of 1267 requirements, was also invited to draw up "concrete recommendations for improved implementation of the measures and possible new measures."[12] The reasons for the team's decision to make several recommendations that relate to an absence of due process are discussed below.

The 9/11 terrorist attacks resulted in the passage of Security Council Resolution 1373 on 28 September 2001 under Chapter VII provisions, like 1267. This significant resolution "imposed sweeping legal obligations on UN member states. It created an unprecedented campaign of nonmilitary, cooperative law enforcement measures to combat global terrorist threats."[13] Whether or not states were parties to other anti-terrorism conventions, they were required not only to freeze assets and deny terrorists safe haven, but also to "update laws and to bring terrorists to justice, improve border security and control traffic in arms, cooperate and exchange information with other states concerning terrorists, and provide judicial assistance to other states in criminal proceedings related to terrorism."[14]

The Counter-Terrorism Committee (CTC) is also a committee of all fifteen members of the Security Council and was set up to monitor state implementation of these obligations, primarily through state provision of reports on the legislative and executive actions they were undertaking. All 191 member states produced one report in the first round, and many have provided reports in additional rounds. [. . .]

Over time, the CTC has also had its resources enhanced. Originally deemed, by its first Chair, the body that obtained funding only after all other UN needs had been satisfied,[16] the CTC was revitalized by Security Council Resolution 1535 of March 2004 when it established a Counter-Terrorism Committee Executive Directorate (CTED). CTED was tasked to deal with the backlog of state reports and to act as a "broker" by putting states facing implementation difficulties in contact with those able to offer assistance. Resolution 1535 also authorized the CTC, through CTED, to make site-visits [. . .]

[. . .] Whereas 1267 seeks to identify and impose constraints on named terrorists, 1373 seeks to institute a set of global standards with the objectives of preventing and deterring terrorism, as well as finding and prosecuting terrorists. The approach adopted in the two resolutions is also different. Resolution 1267 involves coercive measures that seek to punish or compel changes in the behavior of the groups or individuals listed. Resolution 1373 does not list targets but concentrates primarily on enabling activities by acting, as the first Chair of the Committee Sir Jeremy Greenstock put it, as a "switchboard" in order to put states in touch with those organizations and states which can provide training, information, and practical advice.[20] The first Chair of the CTC was adamant that, unlike the 1267 Committee, his Committee was neither a condemnatory body nor a sanctioning committee, a message that subsequent chairs have continued to send. Predominantly, CTC came to be seen as a technical body, working with, rather than against, states and international, regional, and sub-regional bodies to enhance capacities in the fight against terrorism. Experts suggest that this may be one key reason why states have been more willing to submit reports to the 1373 Committee than to 1267.[21]

[. . .]

A. Institutional Signaling

Early on, observers noted the absence of concern with the human rights consequences of the Committees' actions and many believed this absence had added to a sense of impunity when it came to fighting terrorism. Immediately after 9/11, human rights professionals realized that the nomenclature of a "war on terrorism" would make it more difficult to protect rights in the course of that struggle.[24] Robert K. Goldman, appointed as the UN independent expert on the protection of human rights and fundamental freedoms while countering terrorism, summarized in 2005 many of the points that were made after 9/11: "That resolution [1373], regrettably, contained no comprehensive reference to the duty of States to respect human rights in the design and implementation of such counter-terrorism measures."[25] He went on: "[T]his omission may have given currency to the notion that the price of winning the global struggle against terrorism might require sacrificing fundamental rights and freedoms."[26] In reference to the individual listing of terrorist suspects under bodies such as the 1267 Committee, Goldman noted that while the identification and freezing of assets of persons and groups involved in terrorism were "appropriate and necessary measures to combat terrorism," they entailed "severe consequences" [...]

The NGO Human Rights Watch (HRW) produced a report in 2004 which highlighted similar omissions. It pieced together information from the public record and concluded, *inter alia*, that "when governments describe new draft anti-terror or security laws containing provisions that rights-trained experts would readily recognize as inviting abuse, the CTC says nothing... when governments describe actions with major rights implications, the CTC does not even raise the issue."[28] HRW investigated the state reports of Egypt, Uzbekistan, Malaysia, Morocco, and Sweden and noted the Committee's failure to take up rights-related matters. The HRW publication also provided evidence of Committee questioning that may have reinforced a sense that the successful countering of terrorism required a trade-off to be made between human rights and security.[29] These findings were in tune with those of other UN human rights experts, especially when it came to consideration of the anti-terrorist legislation that states around the world were busy drafting or revising. Less than three months after passage of Resolution 1373, on Human Rights Day in December 2001, 17 UN Special Rapporteurs and independent experts of the UN Commission on Human Rights (UNCHR) voiced their alarm over both the scope of the anti-terrorist laws that governments were adopting and the alacrity with which they were targeting groups such as "human rights defenders, migrants, asylum-seekers and refugees, religious and ethnic minorities, political activists and the media."[30]

B. The Failure to Address Rights

How can we best explain this failure to consider the wider consequences of counter-terrorist action when designing the procedures of these Committees, or in the case of 1373, when framing the original resolution? Timing seems to have had something to do with it. True, challenges were launched against individual targeting even prior to September 2001. However, when the 1267 Committee first began its work in 1999, the sanctions were directed only at the known quantity of the Taliban regime, a government recognized by three states, which had few assets officially outside the country, operated mainly through the black market in illicit narcotics, and was already "awash with weapons" thus obviating the impact of any arms embargo.[31] Within a few weeks of 9/11, the US put about 200 extra names on the consolidated list, and these were immediately accepted because of the sympathy felt towards the US at that time.[32]

However, concerns soon began to quicken. This was especially so when some of these individuals and groups sought legal redress and initiated the appeals' processes in a number of predominantly European countries.[33] [...]

CTC's failure to address human rights in the early years may have been partially due to the circumstances in which Resolution 1373 was pushed through. The apparently global reach and deadly aims of Al Qaeda was a threat for which most governments seemed ill-prepared and the impulse was to counter-attack, not to think about wider consequences. [...] However, previous resolutions dealing with terrorist acts (for example, one passed in 1996 by the UN General Assembly, and another in 1999 passed by the Security Council) managed to combine attention both to victims' rights and to the need to advance anti-terrorist measures in strict conformity with human rights standards.[35] Indeed, Security Council Resolution 1269 adopted on 19 October 1999 shares a number of similarities with Resolution 1373 but not when it comes to making reference to human rights.

Thus, it seems likely that Resolution 1373—largely framed by the United States and promoted as an act of solidarity with Washington—may have been deliberately designed to reflect the US preference for fighting the global war on terror unhindered by what it saw as inapplicable or outdated humanitarian laws. [...] The Bush Administration left no room for the idea that terrorist suspects might have rights and instead concluded that unfortunately and unavoidably innocents would be swept up in a general move against alleged terrorist populations. [...]

Moreover, the first Chair of the CTC, in striving to depoliticize the UN approach to terrorism, stated unequivocally that, while human rights matters were of concern to his Committee, other parts of the UN system held the expertise in this area and it should be their role to test whether states were operating in conformity with human rights standards.[39] Broadly, UN Secretary General Kofi Annan at first appeared to agree, but still intimated that the distancing of the CTC from wider consequences had perhaps gone too far. [...]

These kinds of arguments, and others that will be discussed in the next section, slowly began to take effect, resulting in both Committees retreating from their original stances and embracing some concern with the human rights, or due process, implications of their work. The UN Security Council passed Resolution 1456 in January 2003. Resolution 1456 not only called on the CTC to intensify its efforts to obtain state compliance with Resolution 1373, but added that states had to ensure that the measures they were taking to combat terrorism were in compliance with international law, "in particular international human rights, refugee, and humanitarian law."[41] That resolution was a significant turning point since the phrasing on rights was repeated in subsequent counter-terrorism resolutions, including 1566 passed after the Beslan massacre, and 1624, passed after the bombings in London.[42] With the decision in 2004 to revitalize the CTC, came the appointment within CTED of an expert on human rights, humanitarian, and refugee law, who liaises with the OHCHR and nongovernmental human rights organizations and provides expert advice in reference to state reports. In the 1267 process, the Monitoring Team devised and recommended a number of improvements in the listing and de-listing procedures for individuals and groups, including better definition of the phrase "associated with Al Qaeda" [...] So far, the Monitoring Team has had more success in winning acceptance of improved procedures for listing than for de-listing.

III. REESTABLISHING A CONCERN FOR RIGHTS

Annan's 2002 remarks were an early attempt to ensure that human rights concerns would begin to be reflected in the procedures of these two influential Committees. The Secretary General's credibility in the area of human rights promotion was high. [...] [Among other things, i]n October 2001, he had set up a "Policy Working Group on the United Nations and Terrorism" which had a sub-group devoted to human rights consequences. Partly as a result of this, the final report of the Group, issued in August 2002, attempted to place human rights firmly at the centre of the UN role in countering terrorism. As it stated:

> The United Nations must ensure that the protection of human rights is conceived as an essential concern. Terrorism often thrives where human rights are violated, which adds to the need to strengthen action to combat violations of human rights. Terrorism itself should also be understood as an assault on basic rights. In all cases, the fight against terrorism must be respectful of international human rights obligations.[45]

It cautioned against the UN offering "blanket or automatic endorsement of all measures taken in the name of counter-terrorism."[46] Specifically [...] it advocated a change in tone: states should be encouraged to view the implementation procedures as ways of improving democratic governance (and thus, by implication, not as opportunities to undermine it). It also successfully recommended that the OHCHR should publish a digest of the core jurisprudence of international and regional human rights bodies on protecting human rights in the struggle against terrorism and that the OHCHR convene a gathering of international, regional, and subregional organizations, as well as NGOs, on the topic. It suggested regular dialogue between the CTC and the OHCHR. The UN, it added, needed to send a "consistent, clear, principled message" at this time of difficulty, not only that "targeting of unarmed civilians is wrong in all circumstances," but also that "security cannot be achieved by sacrificing human rights."[47]

These were messages that were being reinforced elsewhere in the UN. [...] Robinson's successor [...] reminded the Committee that the best and only way to defeat terrorism was by respecting human rights, promoting social justice and democracy, and upholding the rule of law.[49] The Vice-Chair of the Human Rights Committee of the International Covenant on Civil and Political Rights (ICCPR), Sir Nigel Rodley, in June 2003, made one of the most potent and direct statements to the CTC. In response to the earlier CTC argument that it would leave the human rights components to other bodies within the UN system, Rodley noted that this was insufficient. UN human rights bodies—notably the UN Commission on Human Rights (UNCHR)—were simply too subject to political manipulation. Thus, any monitoring the UNCHR might undertake would be unreliable, he stated.[50] From a legal perspective, the findings of that and other UN human rights bodies would not carry the weight of Security Council decisions adopted under Chapter VII provisions. Neither was his Human Rights Committee, a body set up under the ICCPR, able to monitor compliance. [...] Perhaps more importantly, the human rights expert's presence would avoid sending the signal that the CTC was "expecting measures to be taken that could be at odds with a State's human rights obligations."[52]

Other regional organizations were as active as the UN-appointed experts. [...]

The CTED chair's own recommendation in mid 2004 that a human rights expert be appointed to his team,[56] and then the April 2005 decision by the UNCHR to appoint a UN Special Rapporteur on human rights and counter-terrorism, reflected this accumulating pressure. The extent to which this evolution in approach to counter-terrorism had become accepted policy was spelled out in the CTC's first report on CTED given to the Security Council in December 2005 just three months after CTED had become fully staffed. [...]

The 1267 Committee came under similar pressure and from several directions. [...]

However, as with the 1373 Committee, criticism of 1267 procedures came from states well outside the European region. [. . .] [For example, f]ifteen lawsuits were filed in five states and before the European Court of Justice. These suits, if decided against the UN, could directly challenge the compatibility between the sanctions regime and the protection of fundamental rights. The team argued that state criticism of the 1267 Committee risked the tainting of its entire work, undermining global support for its objectives. [. . .]

The Monitoring Team made its arguments for improving procedures on the grounds that this would enhance the effectiveness of and participation levels in the sanctions procedure: it would mean that some states would be less leery of taking action against those listed. Other governments emphasized the need for change in order to retain support for the idea of targeted rather than comprehensive sanctions. They saw the former as a more humanitarian and focused alternative to the latter and as a welcome alternative to armed humanitarian intervention.[61] But there was also a broader, more philosophical debate at work that affected the workings of both Committees. The debate comprised ideas about the enhancement of overall levels of security, the determination of the causes of terrorism, and the relationship between counter-terrorist action and democratic governance.

UN officials were particularly active in exploring these ideas, especially in their attempts to recapture a notion of security that reflected UN formulations first advanced in the 1990s.[62] [. . .]

These sentiments were reinforced and repeated in several different venues. [. . .]

These kinds of arguments merged with those made in the human rights community, within regional organizations, and in certain state capitals. As functionary bodies, the Al-Qaeda/Taliban Committee and the CTC evolved in response.

IV. STATE POWER AND INSTITUTIONAL ADAPTATION

The idea that powerful states were behind these adjustments in the procedures of the 1267 and 1373 Committees, or were the source of the revised phrasing of anti-terrorist resolutions from the time of the passage of Resolution 1456, is unsupported by evidence. Mexico, in fact, played a crucial role. Under Foreign Minister Castenada, the government made the decision to open up its own human rights practices to international scrutiny and to promote human rights protections overseas. In spring 2002, Mexico tried unsuccessfully to get the UNCHR to pass a resolution that referred to the need to counter terrorism within a human rights framework. However, it successfully promoted the same resolution in the General Assembly in the autumn, and this became the basis for Resolution 1456 of January 2003.[68]

I have described this Resolution as a signal moment for the move from counter-terrorist measures to measures that consider what Annan described at the high-level Security Council debate of that resolution as the "'collateral damage' of the war on terrorism: damage to the presumption of innocence, to precious human rights, to the rule of law and to the very fabric of democratic governance."[69] At that 2003 foreign-ministerial level meeting, Germany, Mexico, and Chile supported the thrust of the Secretary-General's remarks, noting that counter-terrorist action had to respect human rights law. China and Russia, however, both stated that the fight against terrorism needed to be based on the UN Charter and on international law—code words for a more traditional reading of the Charter and of Article 2(7) with its stress on non-interference in domestic affairs. The US Secretary of State, Colin Powell, made no reference—direct or indirect—to that portion of Annan's statement quoted above.[70] Yet, Resolution 1456 passed unanimously, and included the new paragraph that made reference to the need to take action in compliance with human rights, refugee, and humanitarian law.[71]

Middle-range states kept up the pressure. [...]

US statements at both meetings, however, stressed disappointment at state failure to comply with 1267 requirements, which warranted further committee investigation of the culprits and quite possibly, Council action. [...]

Briefings from the Chair of the CTC to the Security Council, and then comments on those briefings by participating states, reveal a similar pattern. [...] These statements suggested that the US government believed human rights concerns to be unhelpful diversions and intimated a desire to turn the CTC into a more condemnatory body.

A number of factors explain why the human rights arguments had become difficult to resist: "discursive entrapment" coupled with the influence of identity; domestic political considerations; and the political nature of the UN Security Council.[77] Past Security Council commitments to protecting human rights and human security, as well as individual states' acceptance of this, were now difficult to disavow. Undoubtedly, there was discomfort among states that projected themselves as supportive of rights and democratic freedoms, a feature that was of particular importance to the European Union as it sought to impose such conditions on new candidates for membership.[78] Moreover, within European states in particular, legal challenges and revelations of abusive practices had stirred up considerable debate. Other states, such as Chile and Mexico, appeared keen to reinforce the sense that they had turned away from their authoritarian pasts.[79] Indonesia's actions reflected similar concerns and also were prompted by the government's desire to maintain good relations with Islamic groups within the wider society.

A number of states, as well as the UN Secretariat, wanted to retain a role for the UN in the struggle against terrorism. This goal encouraged a search for consensus. More cynically, there might have been the belief that the addition of this paragraph in Resolution 1456 and in subsequent Security Council counter-terrorism resolutions, together with the appointment of a human rights expert, would make no real difference to proceedings anyway. [. . .]

V. Too Little, Too Late?

This article has shown how quickly states responded to the US call to participate in the "global war on terror" and noted how swiftly evidence accumulated at the UN and within NGOs that governments had picked up a signal that rights protections could more openly be sacrificed. Undoubtedly, the human rights regime was damaged as a result, perhaps to such a degree that the small changes noted above in 1267 and 1373 procedures and in the wording of Security Council resolutions have come too late. These adjustments are too inconsequential, especially when compared with a US administration that signaled by its behavior and in the shaping of Resolution 1373 that it had accepted that the struggle against terrorism unavoidably would involve damage to human rights.

This is a powerful negative argument, but it is still too early to conclude that damage to the rights regime is fatal. The process of change in both Committees has been slow. Bureaucratic inertia (for which the UN is infamous), big power resistance, and the different priorities and working methods of Committee chairs[80] have probably been responsible for this. However, the moves that have taken place, as well as the arguments formulated, have provided openings for a deepening of procedures that are attentive to human rights. Over time, the new human rights official appointed to CTED might be able to pose rights-related questions directly to states, and participate in state visits at which recommendations can be made for better protection of rights while countering terrorism.[81] These potential developments may appear modest, but are typical of the way that human rights are promoted within the UN framework. Similarly, the incremental changes introduced into 1267 procedures could result in an independent appeals process for those seeking removal from the list.

Moreover, steadily increasing UN attention to human rights consequences seems likely because it would be extremely damaging to that body if it is not seen as upholding human rights: hence the danger associated with any European Court decision that found the organization to be in breach of fundamental rights. Human rights now influence the work of virtually all of the UN bodies and specialized agencies.[82] In the post Cold War era, the UN—including the Security Council—has emphasized that international peace and security requires attention to the protection of human rights. According to the High-Level Panel, contemporary readings of the Charter reflect the intentions of its founders who recognized the "indivisibility of security, economic development and human freedom."[83] The Charter's opening words claim that the United Nations was created "to reaffirm faith in fundamental human rights" and "to promote social progress and better standards of life in larger freedom."[84] This understanding has made it difficult for Security Council Committees to ignore the persistent criticisms of their failure fully to protect human rights in an anti-terrorist era. In a more political vein, at a time of overwhelming US material power and a perceived preference for acting unilaterally, both Russia and China are determined to maintain a role for the UN Security Council in addressing international threats to peace and security. Many other states agree with this (though sometimes for different reasons), and this determination reinforces a search for basic consensus. This particular search for agreement has created a focal point around the idea of the UN Security Council playing its part in the struggle against terrorism but within a rights-based framework.

With respect to the US administration, however, the position is troubling. What is plain from the evidence presented above is that the United States has distanced itself from many of its core allies in its willingness to continue both the verbal and actual down-grading of concern about human rights in an anti-terrorist era. This isolation obviously is not helpful to sustaining global cooperation. A failure further to improve human rights protections will not help to engender compliance with anti-terrorist measures among those states which, in general, are better able both, to carry out such measures, as well as to offer support to those with less state capacity. But as Edward Luck notes, the isolation reflects an ambivalence that is well-established.[85] The US accords the UN an important but not a central role in anti-terrorist activities. If it finds that its particular approach to this struggle is being disregarded, the US could attempt to make the UN less prominent in the conduct of a campaign, which as Kofi Annan has said challenges the "core values the United Nations stands for: the rule of law; the protection of civilians; mutual respect between people of different faiths and cultures; and peaceful resolution of conflicts."[86]

VI. CONCLUSION

This study of evolutionary change in two of the United Nations most important committees dealing with terrorism shows the embedded nature of the idea of human rights within certain states, regional institutions, as well as in the UN itself. The changes to Committee workings, as well as the return to discussion of rights and human security have come about for three main reasons: the persuasiveness of the argument; role-playing and self-identification; and strategic calculation. Some officials expressed support for a rights-based framework in terms of the rightness of the idea. Underlying this was the notion that it represented appropriate behavior for certain democratic or democratizing states and organizations. For others, voicing support offered a way to ensure that those states troubled about dimensions of the Committees' work would remain willing to sustain their counter-terrorist efforts. This would also help to strengthen the position of the Security Council as a core actor when it came to dealing with terrorism. Others still chose to argue that human rights abuse increased the numbers of terrorist recruits, and thus measures that took no account of the consequences were counter-productive. No state spoke against the notion of developing counter-terrorist efforts that were more respectful of human rights; and the signal that came from silence could be countered by others willing to use the UN as an institutional platform from which to express this need for greater levels of respect.

Those that regularly decided to make the argument in support of a human rights framework (apart from the human rights NGOs, of course) were Secretariat officials, UN experts, certain middle-range states, and European and Latin American regional organizations. Although the United Kingdom and France, in their individual statements and as members of the Permanent-5, chose less often than other EU members to make the case, they did always associate themselves with an EU statement that invariably took a strong stand on the issue. The powerful states of China, Russia, and especially the United States decided either to keep quiet on the matter or to use ambiguous phrasing. The US overtly signaled its priority as being compliance with measures against terrorists. Meanwhile, it remained silent about collateral damage, even though this resulted in distancing from its natural allies.

Institutional procedures helped to facilitate the evolution in the Committees' approaches, described above. Over the course of the post Cold War era, the Security Council has been operating on the basis of consensus decision-making, and this model was explicitly chosen for the work of the 1267 and 1373 Committees. Perhaps more significant to the outcome is the agreement that Committee business would be somewhat more transparent than was usual. This meant that a number of Security Council meetings were open, any member state that wished to contribute to the debate could do so, and many reports were made public. In addition, both Committees had specialist teams appointed to them and those appointed at later stages have begun to use their expertise and professionalism to bolster the authority of team recommendations.

The power of the human rights norm has, then, been demonstrated within the setting of the UN; but in the wider international system its power is not so clear. Severe damage has been inflicted, and the process of repair is complex and not helped by a US failure strongly to support international humanitarian and human rights law during the anti-terrorist campaign. Nevertheless, some recovery is a realistic expectation given the apparent embeddedness of the human rights idea in certain domestic, regional, and international institutions. If studies that support a correlation between the experience of severe human rights abuse and the recruitment to a terrorist cause are accurate, then this gives us another reason to welcome this initial finding.

NOTES

[…]

6. The range of reasons for Security Council activism in this era is covered well in Edward C. Luck, *The Uninvited Challenge: Terrorism Targets the United Nations, in* MULTILATERAL-ISM UNDER CHALLENGE: POWER, INTERNATIONAL ORDER AND STRUCTURAL CHANGE, 340–1 (Edward Newman, Ramesh Thakur, & John Tirman eds., 2006).

7. Eric Rosand, *The Security Council's Efforts to Monitor the Implementation of Al-Qaeda/Taliban Sanctions,* 98 AM. J. INT'L L. 746 (2004)

8. *Id.*

9. Rosand, *Security Council's Efforts* 747–48; Chantal de Jonge Oudraat, *The Role of the Security Council, in* TERRORISM AND THE UN, *supra* note 4, at 157. *See also* Watson Institute for International Studies, Brown University, Strengthening Targeted Sanctions Through Fair and Clear Procedures, at Tbl. 1, 27, Tbl. 3, 35 (Mar. 2006) (hereinafter Watson Report), *available at* http://watsoninstitute.org/pub/Strengthening_Targeted_Sanctions.pdf. This report was sponsored by the governments of Switzerland, Germany, and Sweden. The author was fortunate in being able to take part in a workshop in New York, January 2006 organized by the Permanent Mission of Germany to the UN to discuss the first draft of this report.

10. Watson Report, supra note 9, at 27, Table 1.

11. Rosand, *Security Council's Efforts, supra* note 7, at 753–55.

12. S.C. Res. 1526, ¶8, U.N. Doc. S/RES/1526 (30 Jan. 2004).

13. DAVID CORTRIGHT, GEORGE A. LOPE Z, ALISTAIR MILLAR, LINDA GERBER, AN ACTION AGENDA FOR ENHANCING THE UNITED NATIONS PROGRAM ON COUNTER TERRORISM 3 (Sept. 2004), *available at* http://www. fourthfreedom.org/pdf/Action_Agenda.pdf.

14. Eric Rosand, *Security Council Resolution 1373, the Counter-terrorism Committee and the Fight Against Terrorism,* 94 AM. J. INT'L L. 334 (Apr. 2003) [hereinafter Rosand, *Security Council Resolution 1373*]. *See also* the CTC website, *available at* http://www. un.org/Docs/sc/committees/1373/cted.html; Eric Rosand, *Resolution 1373 and the CTC: The Security Council's Capacity Building, in* INTERNATIONAL COOPERATION IN COUNTERTERRORISM: THE UNITED

NATIONS AND REGIONAL ORGANIZATIONS IN THE FIGHT AGAINST TERRORISM (Giuseppe Nesi ed., 2006).

[…]

16. U.N. SCOR, 4512th mtg., at 4, U.N.Doc. S/PV.4512 (15 Apr. 2002).

[…]

20. Thierry Tardy, *The Inherent Difficulties of Inter-Institutional Cooperation in Fighting Terrorism, supra* note 4, at 125.

21. Rosand, *Security Council's Efforts, supra* note 7, at 758–59.

[…]

24. Interviews at the Office of the High Commissioner for Human Rights, Geneva (Oct. 2005), New York (May–June 2006)(on file with author), confirm this early apprehensiveness. Names withheld to protect confidentiality.

25. *Promotion and Protection of Human Rights: Protection of human rights and fundamental freedoms while countering terrorism,* U.N. ESCOR, Comm'n on Hum. Rts., U.N. Doc. E/CN.4/2005/103 at 6, 21 (7 Feb. 2005)(*prepared by* Robert K. Goldman).

26. *Id.* at 6.

[…]

28. *See Hear No Evil, supra* note 15, at 3.

29. *Id.* at 8.

30. *Quoted in* Digest of Jurisprudence of the UN and Regional Organizations on the Protection of Human Rights While Countering Terrorism, 8, *available at* http://www.ohchr. org/English/issues/terrorism/.

31. Chantal de Jonge Oudraat, *The Role of the Security Council, supra* note 9, at 157.

32. Rosand, *The Security Council's Efforts, supra* note 7, at 749.

33. The Monitoring Team's report submitted to the Security Council on 11 July 2005 refers to fifteen lawsuits filed in five member states challenging implementation of sanctions. U.N. Doc. S/2005/761, at 15 (6 Dec. 2005). Some five countries are involved, only two outside Europe.

[…]

35. U.N. G.A. Res. 186, U.N. Doc. A/RES/50/186 (6 Mar. 1996). It records serious concern "at the gross violations of human rights perpetrated by terrorist groups," and reaffirms that "all measures to counter terrorism must be in strict conformity with international human rights standards." S.C. Res. 1269, U.N. Doc. S/Res/1269, ¶2 (19 Oct. 1999), adopted by the Security Council called for "international cooperation … on the basis of the principles of the Charter of the United Nations and norms of international law, including respect for international humanitarian law and human rights."

[…]

39. U.N. SCOR, 4453d mtg. at 5, U.N. Doc. S/PV.4453 (18 Jan. 2002).

[…]

41. S.C. Res. 1456, ¶6, U.N. Doc. S/RES/1456 (20 Jan. 2003).

42. *Id.* ¶6; S.C. Res. 1566, U.N. Doc. S/RES/1566 (8 Oct. 2004); S.C. Res. 1624, U.N. Doc. S/RES/1624 (14 Sept. 2005).

[…]

45. Report of the Policy Working Group on the United Nations and Terrorism, U.N. G.A. 57th Sess., Item 162, Provisional Agenda, at 2, U.N. Doc. A/57/273-S/2002/875 (2002).

46. *Id.* ¶14.

47. *Id.* at 12.

[…]

49. Speech by Sergio Vieira de Mello, The High Commissioner for Human Rights To the Counter-Terrorism Committee of the Security Council (21 Oct. 2002), *available at* http://www.un.org/Docs/sc/committees/1373/HC.htm.

50. Security Council Counter-Terrorism Committee UN Headquarters, briefing by Sir Nigel Rodley, Vice-chairperson Human Rights Committee, ¶5 (19 June 2003), *available at* http://www.unhchr/ch/huricane/huricane.nsf.

[…]

52. *Id.*

[…]

56. The vacancy for this post was put on the UN website on 23 November 2004. The organizational plan drawn up by the first head of CTED was endorsed by the CTC on 29 July 2004 and by the Security Council on 12 August. *See* U.N. Doc. S/2004/642. The plan stated that the team would have "expertise in every area covered by resolution 1373 (2001) and other relevant provisions of the declarations annexed to resolutions 1377 (2001) and 1456 (2003)." at 7. *See also* the discussion of the plan in U.N. Doc. S/PV/5059 (19 Oct. 2004); S.C. Res. 1526, ¶8, U.N. Doc. S/RES/1526 (30 Jan. 2004).

[…]

61. Biersteker, et al, *Consensus from the bottom up? Assessing the influence of the sanctions reform processes, in* INTERNATIONAL SANCTIONS, *supra* note 22, at 15–30.

62. UNITED NATIONS DEVELOPMENT PROGRAMME (UNDP), NEW DIMENSIONS OF HUMAN SECURITY (1994). This is not to suggest that the UN was the only source of ideas about how to conceive security.

[…]

68. U.N. Doc. A/RES/57/219 (4 Dec. 2002).

69. *Threats to International Peace and Security caused by terrorist acts,* S.C. Agenda, U.N. Doc. S/PV.4688, at 3, (20 Jan. 2003).

70. *Id.* at 1–27. Some of my 2006 interviewees in New York, knowledgeable about this process, commented on Chinese and Russian reservations about making reference to humanitarian and human rights law; others suggested that the United States was the major conservative force, with China and Russia content to let the US take the lead in attempting to stop change. When the "incitement to terrorism" Resolution, 1624, was passed unanimously on 14 Sept. 2005 during the Summit Meeting of the Security Council, the debate followed similar lines. President Bush, for example, failed to refer to the need to ensure anti-terrorist measures were in accordance with human rights standards, unlike the statements of a number of other delegations: for example, the Philippines, Argentina, Benin, Brazil, and Greece. *See* U.N. Doc. S/PV.5261 (14 Sept. 2005).

71. U.N. Doc. S/RES/1456/2003, ¶6. (20 Jan. 2003).

[…]

77. Interviews, personal and via e-mail, have been helpful to the development of these arguments.

78. For discussion of this process, including the teaching of new norms, see INTERNATIONAL INSTITUTIONS AND SOCIALIZATION IN EUROPE: INTRODUCTION AND FRAMEWORK (Jeffery T. Checkeled, 2007); see special issue 59 INT'L ORG. (2005).

79. For one, ultimately pessimistic, discussion of Mexico's attempts to promote human rights internally and externally, see HUMAN RIGHTS WATCH, LOST IN TRANSITION: BOLD AMBITIONS, LIMITED RESULTS FOR HUMAN RIGHTS UNDER FOX (May 2006), *available at* http://hrw.org/reports/2006/mexico0506/.

80. Cortright has described the first four chairs of the CTC as follows:

> The first chair … established a record of political evenhandedness, fully in keeping with U.S. interests, and pushed the organizational agenda vigorously. The second chair, Inocencio Arias of Spain, was less energetic. In the view of many UN officials, CTC

momentum lagged. In 2004 the chair went to Russia and its young UN ambassador Andrey Denisov, who tried to energize the Security Council program. Danish ambassador Ellen Loj took the chair in April 2005 with an ambitious agenda to enhance technical assistance and link it to expanded development assistance efforts. Cortright, *supra* note 3 at 4.

81. Some members of UN delegations interviewed in New York in 2006 expressed support for these future developments. Confidential interviews (on file with author).

82. JULIE MERTUS, THE UNITED NATIONS AND HUMAN RIGHTS: A GUIDE FOR A NEW ERA (2005), convincingly demonstrates this.

83. UNITED NATIONS, A MORE SECURE WORLD, supra note 2, at 1, *available at* http://www .un.org/secureworld/report2.pdf.

84. *Id.*

85. Luck, *supra* note 6, at 350.

86. *Id.* at 351; *Secretary-General Offers Global Strategy*, U.N. Doc. SG/SM/9757 (10 Mar. 2005).

*Rosemary Foot is professor of international relations and Swire Senior Research Fellow in the International Relations of East Asia, St Antony's College, University of Oxford.

Foot, Rosemary. "The United Nations, Counter Terrorism and Human Rights: Institutional Adaptation and Embedded Ideas." *Human Rights Quarterly* 29, no.2 (2007): 489–514. © 2007 by The Johns Hopkins University Press. Reprinted with permission of The Johns Hopkins University Press.

Transnational NGOs and Human Rights in a Post-9/11 World

by Hans Peter Schmitz*

[…]

[…]Well before 9/11, NGOs across different sectors of transnational activism had begun to develop more proactive and preventative strategies […] Despite facing different kinds of challenges in the post-9/11 world, many development, human rights and humanitarian groups were joined in a focus on improving the legitimacy and accountability of Northern-based advocacy, a desire move beyond defending a narrow set of civil and political rights, and a need to adopt new networking and mobilization strategies […]

[…]

In a post-9/11 world, human rights NGOs mobilized effectively against efforts to limit basic civil and political rights, while activists in other sectors implemented lessons learned during the 1990s and earlier. For humanitarian organizations, the Rwandan genocide and other humanitarian crises of the 1990s led to a fundamental questioning of the norms of impartiality and independence (Anderson 1999). An increased focus on the consequences and effectiveness of humanitarian aid as well as greater accountability to those receiving aid became central to reform efforts expressed in the adoption of codes of conduct. After 9/11, when aid groups faced efforts by the US military to take over humanitarian aid in Afghanistan and Iraq, individual organizations already had experience in dealing with the inevitable politicization of the humanitarian model (de Torrente 2004; O'Brien 2004). In the development sector, a profound sense of crisis also preceded 9/11 and focused primarily on the failures of development aid and the "charity" model. During the 1990s, development NGOs increasingly looked towards human rights ideas as a key to regaining legitimacy. A rights-based approach (RBA) to development (Uvin 2004) emerged as NGOs explored more sustainable ways of supporting economic development. Finally, human rights groups began well before 9/11 to question the success of *ex post* "shaming" strategies and develop more sustainable efforts to prevent abuses. Post-9/11, the already established focus on violence committed by non-state armed groups aligned with new concerns about terrorism and sectarian violence.

Initiated in the 1990s, the significant strategic shifts within sectors of transnational activism were accompanied by increased collaboration among transnational activist groups. The rights-based development agenda, the broad support for the International Criminal Court (ICC) the landmines ban, and the INGO Accountability Charter of 2006 represent a few examples of joint efforts to increase the effectiveness and accountability of transnational activist groups. The events following 9/11 offered nothing more than a reminder about the inadequacies of a reactive and ameliorative activist model which had been in crisis for some time and had failed to effectively address fundamental injustices causing poverty, ethnic divisions, and discrimination [...]

[...]

During the 1960s and 1970s, human rights groups established their moral authority based on strategies of "bearing witness" and "shaming" the perpetrators through meticulous research and publication of violations (Hopgood 2006, 14). This particular strategy was first developed by AI in the 1960s and 1970s and later modified by a new crop of advocacy groups such as HRW (founded in 1978) which further professionalized the campaign-style approach with an expanded focus on mass media and lobbying efforts.

As a coalition of authoritarian states began in the 1960s to target NGOs within the United Nations-(Korey 1998, chapter 3), activists concluded that their "principal efforts would need to be focused for a long time *outside* the UN" (Sidney Liskofsky, cited in Korey 1998, 139). With a predominant focus on civil and political rights as well as state agents perpetrating violations, those activists developed a distinct nonpartisan and transnational human rights movement. Unlike their predecessors, represented by the generation of Eleanor Roosevelt, the type of activism strove to establish a more independent and transnational network dedicated to the collection and dissemination of human rights-related information. Combining the power of new communication technologies, reliable information, and the sacred symbolism created by an organization such as AI (Hopgood 2006), popular support for the idea of human rights as a universal value spread primarily in Western Europe and North America.

The 1977 Nobel Peace Prize awarded to AI and the creation of Helsinki Watch in 1978 marked the early success of this new type of transnational human rights organization. While AI had already become a global player during the 1970s, the emergence of Helsinki Watch and Americas Watch (in 1981) represented a crucial step "to subject the State Department's annual country reports [on human rights] to close and critical scrutiny" (Korey 1998, 342). From the 1980s onward, AI and HRW would dominate the human rights discourse with their "shaming" strategies, developing a largely reactive model of exposing human rights violations after they took place. This model became increasingly outmoded with the end of the Cold War and the realization that it had little appeal among citizens in the Global South and failed to address many of the root causes of persistent patterns of violations.

Amnesty International's membership base, its parallel structures of professional and volunteer organization, and its refusal to solicit any funding sources other than membership dues, represent an outlier in the NGO world. HRW is a more typical example of an NGO without an individual membership base which relies more heavily on larger donations by foundations. The trade-offs between the two types of transnational organizing became apparent when HRW quickly rose during the 1980s to become the main competitor of AI and was able to respond more quickly to new human rights issues favored by large donors (e.g. child soldiers). The broader support and legitimacy AI enjoyed as a result of representing close to 2 million members organized in close to 50 national sections also represented a core limitation making the organization less nimble and driven by tensions between the professionals (International Secretariat) and the volunteers organized in the national sections. During the 1990s, AI moved only very slowly in convincing its membership and supporters that fundamental change was inevitable and required a more overtly political approach leaving behind the singular focus on principles and symbolic "idolatry" (Ignatieff 2001). By 2001, AI embarked on a trial period of abandoning its mandate in favor of broader campaign themes, including the promotion of social and economic rights.

The emergence of HRW and its success in challenging AI created a more competitive environment among human rights groups and led to some innovation, but it did not prevent the profound crisis of the movement during the 1990s. This crisis was largely the result of a failure to take seriously the human rights issues of the Global South as well as a blindly principled view[1] that was ill-prepared for developing more sophisticated analyses of the social and political root causes of many human rights violations. The professionalization of human rights activism also created growing complacency on the part of (liberal) states and the general public. As the visibility and mass media efforts of human rights groups increased, the general public became content with delegating these tasks to an elite group of activists. The membership of AI peaked in the late 1980s, indicating a crisis in popular support well before the post-Cold War challenges to the transnational "shaming" model of human rights activism.

With the end of communism in 1989/90 human rights groups not only lost one of the cornerstones of their principled, nonpartisan strategy, but also realized that traditional state-sponsored repression became less important in accounting for global patterns of violations. As patterns of ethnic and communal violence as well as global economic inequality became more prominent, the limits of a reactive "shaming" model came into sharp relief since human rights groups largely lacked political strategies designed to address the structural causes of these violations. Efforts to address poverty or ethnic divisions as root causes for many human rights violations force human rights groups to become more overtly political, join alliances with like-minded groups, and debate the relative merits of different conflict resolution and poverty reduction programs.

Transnational human rights activism has evolved since the end of the Second World War from a limited lobbying effort by committed individuals to a transnational movement led by professionals, heavily reliant on campaigns and media attention. AI's system of adopted political prisoners created a powerful link between victims and their defenders abroad, while HRW was at the forefront of developing campaign-style mass media strategies. The very success of this emphasis on exposing violations left the human rights movement unprepared for the challenges of the post-Cold War period. As human rights NGOs became more prominent and successful, the attention of the general public waned and its Northern bias solidified. The "shaming" strategy born in the 1970s and aided by advances in technology and communication was less effective in preventing violations in the first place, failed to move perpetrators immune to reputational costs associated with committing atrocities, and could not effectively be used to address structural causes of violations which defied the model of linking a specific perpetrator and action to a violation.

THE POST-COLD WAR PERIOD: CRISIS AND INNOVATION

Transnational activists witnessed in the early 1990s the disappearance of many authoritarian regimes as familiar sources of human rights violations while facing new challenges emerging as a result of ethnic conflict, the increasing prominence of violent non-state actors, and the failures of the state community to respond effectively to humanitarian crises in Rwanda, the former Yugoslavia, Zaire/Democratic Republic of Congo, Sudan, and elsewhere. A profound experience of crisis not only affected human rights groups, but also other areas of transnational activism where an expressed apolitical, neutral approach to improving people's lives was dominant. Humanitarian organizations faced the paradox of well-intentioned aid contributing to more violence (Terry 2002) and development groups began to understand how their increasing role "to fill the vacuum left by nation states" (Lindenberg and Bryant 2001, 1) slowed democratization and the emergence of domestic accountability patterns between rulers and ruled.

The post-Cold War period is marked by a growing realization that effective responses to persistent abuse patterns required a shift away from a primarily reactive activism towards prevention and addressing root causes of violations. As a result, human rights activism has moved well beyond the state as the main target and has also challenged the sectoral separation between advocacy and service groups. As early adopters within the development sector began in the mid-1990s to develop a RBA to their work (Uvin 2004), the human rights discourse now expanded into the humanitarian, development, and environmental sectors of transnational activism.

Three notable developments set the post-Cold War period apart and can *be* understood as a response to new challenges and the crisis of the particular model of principled activism emerging in the 1960s and 1970s. First, humanitarian and development NGOs primarily focused on service delivery began to expand their advocacy role (Lindenberg and Bryant 2001) and adopted human rights frameworks in their activities. Second, new types of advocacy groups emerged which sought to move beyond the focus on civil and political rights to address structural causes of abuses, including resource conflicts and ethnic divisions. At the same time, traditional human rights organizations began in the early 1990s to shift attention away from state governments and explicitly address violations committed by non-state actors (Andreopoulos et al. 2006). Third, the same groups played a significant role in the accelerated establishment of international institutions designed to address human rights issues (e.g. the International Criminal Court, the International Convention to Ban Landmines, or the Kimberley Agreement on Conflict Diamonds).

HUMANITARIAN AID AND RIGHTS-BASED APPROACHES TO DEVELOPMENT

Growing cooperation across the advocacy/service divide, primarily in the humanitarian, development, and human rights sectors, represents a distinct response to the limitations of activism within each of these sectors. Following an increased awareness of the failures of foreign aid and humanitarian/development efforts, service-oriented organizations became more aware of the political consequences of their work and developed greater advocacy capacities (Lindenberg and Bryant 2001; Rugendyke 2007) designed to support local development interventions by targeting national level and international causes of inequality and stunted development[2]. These shifts were most pronounced in the humanitarian and development sectors.

For humanitarian aid groups, the core value of neutrality and nondiscrimination (Leebaw 2007, 227) was fundamentally challenged during their operations in refugee camps following the Rwandan genocide in 1994. As some Hutus "genocidaires" used the aid to reorganize in the camps and sustain the violence, humanitarian groups faced accusations that their aid "strengthened the power of the very people who had caused the tragedy" (Terry 2002, 2). Beyond the cases of possibly doing harm by enabling continued violence, humanitarian aid frequently violated the dignity of those receiving aid as increased professionalization and technical capabilities to deliver aid were not matched by adequate concerns for the basic rights of those affected by natural or human-made disasters. As humanitarian groups faced increasing criticisms, fundamental norms of neutrality, impartiality, and independence were weighted against the possible negative consequences of short-term aid (Barnett and Weiss 2008). In response, aid groups developed a number of codes of conduct (Hilhorst 2005) specifically designed to regulate humanitarian relief activities and increase the legitimacy of organizations previously only focused on the moral imperative to aid the suffering.

After 9/11, those codes played a significant role in helping many humanitarian groups to formulate a common response to efforts by the United States and allied military forces blurring the lines between combat and humanitarian aid in Afghanistan and Iraq (O'Brien 2004). In Iraq shortly after the US invasion, humanitarian NGOs faced the dilemma of maintaining independence and neutrality while at the same time receiving funding from Western governments as well as relying on US-led coalition forces for their security. In this situation, the bombing of the ICRC headquarters on October 27, 2003 and the murder of Margaret Hassan, the director of CARE (Iraq) in October 2004 caused many humanitarian groups to leave Iraq (Sunga 2007, 114). As neutrality and independence as core elements of humanitarian legitimacy were severely undercut by coalition forces and terrorist attacks, debates about the future of humanitarianism proliferated (de Torrente 2004; O'Brien 2004). But NGOs were already familiar with the basic contours of this conundrum and Iraq presented a case where humanitarian principles had to be married with a more pronounced effort of political advocacy challenging the behavior of belligerents. These debates had emerged long before 9/11 and have ultimately been resolved by strengthening human rights as core principles for legitimate action.

The dignity of those receiving aid has also become a greater concern in the area of more long-term development aid. Here, the main cause pushing the shift away from neutrality and charity was precipitated by a widespread perception of failure of development aid overall. Human rights ideas became central to closing the gap between organizations working in traditional development areas of education or health care and advocacy NGOs primarily focused on "shaming" strategies. Many of the major development NGOs, including CARE, Oxfam, and ActionAid, adopted some version of a rights-based approach to development and supplemented their service activities with expanded advocacy efforts. A similar, if slower movement in the opposite direction emerged among traditional human rights groups. As aid groups moved into advocacy, organizations such as AI experimented with campaigns on social and economic rights and began to develop tentative ideas about how to broaden their legitimacy and take seriously the challenge of how a "more acutely political, as opposed to moral activism might be more attentive to the question of whom activists represent" (Ignatieff 2002, 10).

Addressing Root Causes of Human Rights Violations

Based on growing awareness of the limits of apolitical, professionalized activism across the humanitarian, development, and human rights sectors, transnational NGOs also began in the 1990s to devote more resources to understanding better the causes of poverty, systematic abuses, and their own frequent failures to contribute to a sustainable improvement of the conditions motivating their interventions in the first place. In many cases, a better understanding of what causes atrocities led to the creation of new types of transnational NGOs, including the International Crisis Group (founded in 1995) and Global Witness (founded in 1998) whose focus include competition for resources (e.g. diamonds, timber, oil) and/or an emphasis on predicting imminent crises and alerting the global public. More traditional human rights NGOs, such as AI or HRW, have also increased their efforts to address complex and varied sources of human rights violations, for example by supporting stricter controls of arms sales and UN efforts to limit the availability of small arms.

Addressing root causes of gross violations and seeking new alliances with humanitarian and development NGOs reflect efforts by traditional human rights groups to move from a reactive to a preventive human rights strategy. For decades, AI sustained an explicit policy of only holding governments accountable for human rights violations committed on the territory of a state. The core strategy of letter-writing campaigns mobilized AI members and targeted government officials in defense of individuals deemed worthy of the designation "prisoner of conscience." With HRW emerging during the final years of the Cold War as a key challenger to AI's global leadership on human rights issues (Korey 1998, 340), both organizations experienced periods of crises before 1989, but faced even more competition from new groups in an increasingly crowded field of transnational activism. With the end of the Cold War, both organizations' original purpose of primarily targeting state repression within the context of super polver competition had lost relevance.

One of the first significant changes to the methodology of transnational human rights activism after the end of the Cold War was to explicitly target violent and nonviolent non-state actors implicated in gross violations. In 1991, AI adopted its new policy of targeting non-state actors primarily within the context of failed states, ethnic violence, and atrocities committed by warlords. The human rights violations were familiar to its traditional mandate (extrajudicial killings, torture, disappearances), but required different strategic and tactical responses. Multinational corporations also became targets of human rights groups either because of their explicit or implicit support of state repression (e.g. Royal Dutch/Shell in Nigeria or UNOCAL in Burma/Myanmar) or because of their direct control over workers in their own or their suppliers' factories. By shifting the target of mobilization away from states, human rights groups not only abandoned the fiction of state sovereignty over a given territory and population, but also moved into new issue areas, including conflict resolution, social and economic rights, and economic development.

STRENGTHENING INTERNATIONAL INSTITUTIONS

The participation of advocacy networks in the creation and evolution of global human rights institutions has become a major focus of scholarly research (Martens 2005). During the 1970s, a coalition of states across ideological divides tried (and failed) to revoke the consultative status of many human rights organizations and inadvertently confirmed the rising power of nongovernmental participation (Shestack 1978, 91). The expansion of UN human rights institutions offered new opportunities for human rights groups (1) to use the proceedings of the UN human rights institutions for their shaming efforts exposing state violations (Korey 1998: ch. 11; Martens 2006); (2) to further strengthen international human rights institutions (Clark 2001; Khagram et al. 2002; Joachim 2007); and (3) to lobby for mandate changes in international institutions lacking an explicit focus on human rights (Nelson 2000; Oestreich 2007).

After much internal debate, AI decided in the early 1970s to launch its first single-issue campaign focused on torture and to lobby the United Nations for a separate convention to ban the practice under any circumstances. Although the AI Secretariat ultimately rejected the 1984 UN torture convention, the organization played a central role in establishing strengthened international agreements on core mandate issues, including torture, disappearances, and capital punishment. Transnational groups also played prominent roles in the creation and adoption of the UN anti-landmines treaty (Price 1998), the establishment of the ICC (Glasius 2002), the inclusion of sexual violence in the definition of war crimes (Spees 2003), the adoption of the Kimberley Agreement to end the sale of conflict diamonds, and more generally, in giving human rights a more prominent position in global governance (signified in the creation of the UN High Commissioner for Human Rights in 1993). Despite the formal limits on the participation of NGOs in intergovernmental institutions (Friedman et al. 2005), transnational activists have used the post-Cold War period to establish human rights concerns across mandates of international institutions, reflecting a belief that strengthened international institutions are central to sustainable human rights change.

AFTER 9/11: INTERVIEWS WITH US-BASED HUMAN RIGHTS GROUPS

The events following the attacks of September 11, 2001 have had a profound effect on transnational NGOs, but those effects are best understood in the context of changes taking place during the 1990s. This history can be written as a smashing success measured in organizational growth as well as increased influence and power, but it also reveals episodes of profound crisis of the professionalized model across all sectors of activism. Success and crisis created during the 1990s conditions facilitating fundamental organizational reforms and strategic reorientation within many organizations, but also across the main sectors of humanitarian relief, human rights, development, and environmental protection. These reforms helped the global NGO community, and in particular US-based groups, to respond in a more concerted fashion to the events following the attacks of 9/11 and specifically the policies of the Bush Administration. This section presents evidence from 12 interviews with the leadership of selected US-based human rights conducted between 2005 and 2008. While the semi-structured interviews covered issues of governance, effectiveness, accountability, networking, and leadership, the primary focus here is on evidence speaking to the NGOs' responses to the events of and subsequent to 9/11.

The broader study[3] included interviews with 152 leaders of transnational NGOs based in the United States (Hermann et al. 2010). A basic population of transnational NGOs was determined based on organizations rated for financial health by Charity Navigator (www.charitynavigator.com). The sample for the study was then determined based on criteria of size, financial efficiency, and main area of activity, including organizations active in conflict resolution (13 organizations), human rights (21), humanitarian relief (32), environmental activism (22), and sustainable development (64). The interviewers typically travelled to the headquarters of the organization and the interviews took between 90 and 120 minutes. Confidentiality was promised to all organizations included in this study.

The events of 9/11 and the subsequent military response by the Bush Administration had significant repercussions for US-based and international NGOs. Organizations relying on funding from the United States Agency of International Aid (USAID) faced increased pressures to align themselves with US foreign policy goals (Sunga 2007, 107) and to refrain from any advocacy critical of US policies. Naomi Klein summarized the Bush Administration's views in 2003, writing: "NGOs should be nothing more than the good hearted charity wing of the military, silently mopping up after wars and famines. Their job is not to ask how these tragedies could have been averted or to advocate for policy solutions" (Klein 2003). Following the 9/11 attacks, counterterrorism laws were broadened in many developed nations, affecting overseas funding for development and civil society support (Sidel 2008). While this "disciplining" of civil society (Howell et al. 2008, 92) across the world should not be underestimated, the interviews with TNGO leaders show little evidence that 9/11 was a major watershed for transnational activism.

The interviews reveal that NGOs active in the development, humanitarian, and human rights sectors consistently focused on how to address shortcomings in their own effectiveness and accountability. While there is evidence that issues of terrorism-related state repression as well as specific US policies (e.g. renditions, Guantanamo) garnered greater attention relative to other advocacy topics, NGOs have not changed their missions as a result of any material pressure that may have been applied. Shifts in funding opportunities implemented by the newly incoming administration prior to 9/11 as well as the wars in Afghanistan and Iraq shaped the focus of US-based NGOs, especially for humanitarian and development organizations with substantial US government contracts.[4] But many of these organizations also took this opportunity as a challenge to diversify funding sources and ease their dependency on USAID or other governmental donors.

For the advocacy sector, the interviews reveal consistent evidence suggesting a continued strong role of transnational human rights groups in the US policy process. In one example of early 2005, NGOs lobbied successfully against a US veto in the United Nations Security Council referring the situation in Darfur/Sudan to the ICC. In this case, NGOs effectively challenged the Bush Administration's initial argument for an "African solution" by pointing to the strong support of African nations for the ICC and by using statements from African leaders in support of a referral to the ICC.[5] Human rights groups did not change their views on the inviolability of human dignity even after the attacks on US soil, and much of their internal debates reflect a desire to overcome the limits of the reactive model of transnational mobilizing which had become apparent during the 1990s.

For the service delivery sector, the interviews with humanitarian organizations offer additional evidence about how current thinking about strategic and organizational change is primarily driven by experiences dating back to the 1990s. While 9/11 and its consequences, in particular the wars in Afghanistan and Iraq, had a major impact on humanitarian groups, the concomitant challenges to the traditional humanitarian model of impartiality had emerged well before 2001 and most prominently during the 1990s. Following the Rwandan genocide, humanitarian organizations had already developed codes of conduct and addressed some of the political consequences of their interventions. The US policies after 9/11, and particularly the challenge of operating alongside belligerents, reignited a debate between those activists advocating for a return to the principles of neutrality and impartiality, and others claiming that such an option no longer existed and would do more harm than good.

A representative of one humanitarian organization interviewed for our study pointed out that in a post-9/11 world "independent, neutral, impartial organizations are being marginalized" and governments are now looking for organizations to "help them implement their political goals."[6] This development is particularly pronounced in the US-led post-9/11 wars, but the interviewee identified a larger trend that began with the end of the Cold War. "But that kind of the West going in as to solve crisis and having a military, political, and aid presence, that's something that we see not just in Afghanistan and Iraq." In response, some humanitarian activists see a return to impartiality and neutrality as the best option for the future. This view reflects a desire to return to the original mission of humanitarianism which focuses primarily on short-term survival and does not concern itself with long-term questions of conflict resolution or development (Rieff 2002).

Others within the humanitarian community have challenged this perspective and argued that humanitarian aid has always been political and should explicitly address "not only the tragic symptoms of conflict, but also its root causes. Not all wars are inevitable. Nor is global poverty inevitable" (O'Brien 2004, 38). To some degree, the two positions are not necessarily incompatible, since capabilities vary across individual organizations and those responding immediately following a disaster *may* find that the traditional humanitarian creed provides sufficient guidance for their efforts. The wars in Afghanistan and Iraq presented a new context for the debate on the consequences of humanitarian activism, but the basic issues had arisen well before 9/11.

Finally, in the sustainable development sector, the interviews confirm an ongoing shift away from the traditional donor model of transferring resources from rich to poor nations. An increasing number of development organizations are using a rights-based understanding of poverty to justify their increased efforts in advocacy and a relative decline of providing direct aid which may only create and sustain dependencies. These trends emerged well before 9/11 and show strong similarities to debates with the humanitarian and human rights sectors. As is the case elsewhere, there are development organizations which have moved much more quickly in embracing a RBA as well as more extensive advocacy strategies, while others express skepticism about such changes and fear that donors or members will punish such profound changes in mandate and strategy. Just as AI struggled with abandoning its letter-writing model and shifting towards broader campaigns, child sponsorship organizations in the United States and elsewhere face a tension between developing broader strategies empowering local communities and maintaining the traditional focus on transferring funds to a child and family in need. In both cases, the singular link between an individual or a group of sponsors in the North and someone in need in the Global South proved to be a successful business model, but its limitations became increasingly visible in the 1990s.

[...] This profound shift currently taking place in the development sector creates unique challenges and tensions. While barriers between different sectors of transnational activism are disappearing, individual organizations struggle with developing the appropriate organizational structures and capabilities to accomplish much more complex tasks and mandates. Across all three sectors discussed here, acknowledging the fact that neutral and impartial activism has always been a fiction creates extensive challenges not only in maintaining donor support but also for recruitment and training of staff. The interviews show across all sectors that NGO leaders see organizational learning and increasing their own impact as the key challenge.

CONCLUSION

The 9/11 attacks and the subsequent reassertion of state power in nations around the world has profoundly shaped the environment within which US-based NGOs with human rights mandates operate. But those effects need to be placed in the context of a broader understanding of the evolution of transnational human rights activism as well as the developments in the post-Cold War period of the 1990s. A significant number of NGOs across major areas of transnational activism were for some time engaged in a fundamental review of their activities and focused on increasing their impact as individual organizations and in cooperation with other civil society groups. Looking beyond the traditional human rights sector dominated by organizations such as AI or HRW, it is particularly instructive to observe that human rights ideas became central to this reform process within the humanitarian and development sectors.

A key paradox emerging from this analysis is the simultaneous strengthening of the global human rights discourse occurring alongside the profound crisis and weakness of transnational activism overall. During the past decades, humanitarian, human rights, and development NGOs have perfected addressing symptoms rather than root causes. Violations are reported and aid is handed down to victims of disasters and poverty, but only rarely are the root causes of these conditions addressed. While many organizations across these three sectors began in the 1990s to explore what a more proactive, preventive (and effective) strategy would look like, 9/11 highlighted the limitations of the reactive model and increased the urgency to create more effective strategies and coalitions with the ability to address structural conditions of discrimination, poverty, and exclusion. In this context, the US-led military response represented a more challenging global environment since many NGOs were at the same time experimenting with new and more overtly political strategies while also facing increased pressures from governments using security arguments as an excuse for increased repression. While the majority of transnational NGOs interviewed for this study were capable of mitigating such pressures, smaller and local NGOs were more likely to respond by avoiding controversial issues.

Human rights groups based in the United States (or elsewhere) were largely unable to prevent or end any of the policies implemented by the Bush Administration in response to the terrorist attacks. Governmental secrecy combined with a lack of public attention and support severely undercut the effectiveness of NGOs relying primarily on information dissemination through mass media and shaming efforts. But this research also shows that human rights groups were not powerless during the Bush years. After 9/11, US-based NGOs continued to lobby successfully on many human rights-related topics, for example on the ICC referral of the Darfur situation. The creation of the offshore detention facility Guantánamo Bay and the extraordinary efforts to manipulate the definition of torture certainly exposed the weaknesses of law and transnational activism, but those efforts also confirm that the presence and vigilance of human rights groups limits the range of options available to governments.

In the humanitarian sector, the debate about the future of impartiality and neutrality began well before 9/11. The military interventions in Afghanistan and Iraq added the challenge of a military taking over humanitarian tasks in order to "win the hearts and minds" of those occupied. Unlike the human rights area, there is no clear-cut case for all organizations to shift away traditional, principled behavior, in this case impartial and neutral aid to those suffering. As the presence of aid agencies becomes more permanent, the fiction of being neutral disappears and organizations need to weigh the long-term consequences of their presence. A more permanent transnational presence usually distinguishes the activities of sustainable development organizations from humanitarian or human rights groups. Here, the widespread adoption of a rights-based approach is unrelated to 9/11 and represents the most remarkable transformation of a transnational sector. Yet, the motives for this shift are very similar to other sectors, where organizations have also been primarily driven by an increased awareness of their own limitations and a desire to effect sustainable impact that relies less and less on their presence.

The analysis of transnational human rights activism today can no longer be limited to the activities of organizations such as AI and HRW. The continued diffusion of the human rights discourse has not only contributed to lowering barriers between different types of transnational NGOs, but has also led to the articulation of profound challenges to traditional practices within various sectors of NGO activism. Human rights may not be the only promising basis for facilitating social and political change, but they are increasingly seen by many as a framework broadly conducive to local empowerment and government accountability. While 9/11 exposed once again the weaknesses of a reactive model of transnational activism, many organizations have begun well before 2001 to reflect on their mandates and strategies and a few have implemented extensive reforms designed to overcome long-standing challenges such as the gap in capacity between Northern and Southern organizations or the lack of strategies designed to address the actual causes of the conditions transnational NGOs have sought to address for decades. It is a whole different issue to evaluate whether those changes in transnational organizing and strategy are effectively implemented and actually make the difference suggested by their proponents.

NOTES

1. The failure of AI to adequately address the South African apartheid regime and its refusal to adopt Nelson Mandela as a prisoner of conscience are *an* example for the limitations of a principled view that failed to recognize structural patterns of abuse.

2. Examples include more explicit efforts to lobby national governments to support neglected regions and local communities as well as campaigns against agricultural subsidies in Europe and the United States.

3. This research was partly supported by National Science Foundation Grant No. SES-0527679 (Agents of Change: Transnational NGOs as Agents of Change: Toward Understanding Their Governance, Leadership, and Effectiveness) and the TNGO Initiative at the Moynihan Institute of Global Affairs at Syracuse University. For more information on the methodology and results, please visit www.maxwell.syr.edu/moynihan_tngo.aspx.

4. Broadly in line with the general argument of this chapter, the organization CARE had begun well before 9/11 to adopt a rights-based approach and to expand its advocacy activities. As a result of 9/11, a prior advocacy focus on "countries in conflict" became largely reduced to Afghanistan, partially reflecting funding priorities of USAID, a major donor of CARE.

5. Interview 1 with a representative of a human rights organization.

6. All quotes in this section from Interview 2 with a representative of a humanitarian organization.

REFERENCES

Anderson, M.B. (1999). *Do No Harm. How Aid Can Support Peace-or War* (Boulder, CO: Lynne Rienner).

Andreopoulos, G., Kabasakal Arat, Z.F., and Juviler, P. (2006). *Non-State Actors in the Human Rights Universe* (Bloomfield, CT: Kumarian Press).

Barnett, M. and Weiss, T.G. (2008). *Humanitarianism in Question: Politics, Power, Ethics* (Ithaca, NY: Cornell University Press).

Clark, A.M. (2001). *Diplomacy of Conscience. Amnesty International and Changing Human Rights Norms* (Princeton, NJ: Princeton University Press).

Friedman, E. J., Hochstetler, K., and Clark, A.M. (2005). *Sovereignty, Democracy, and Global Civil Society. State-Society Relations at UN World Conferences* (Albany: State University of New York Press).

Glasius, M. (2002). "Expertise in the Cause of Justice. Global Civil Society Influence on the Statute for an International Criminal Court," in Glasius, M., Kaldor, M., and Anheier, H. (eds), *Global Civil Society* 137–68, http://www.lse.ac.uk/Depts/global/Publications/Yearbooks/2002/2002chapter6.pdf.

Hilhorst, D. (2005). "Dead Letter or Living Document? Ten Years of the Code of Conduct for Disaster Relief," *Disasters*, 29/4, 351–69.

Hirono, M. (2008). *Civilizing Missions. International Religious Agencies in China* (Houndmills: Palgrave Macmillan).

Hopgood, S. (2006). *Keepers of the Flame. Understanding Amnesty International* (Ithaca, NY: Cornell University Press).

Howell, J., Ishkanian, A., Obadare, E., Seckinelgin, H., and Glasius, M. (2008). "The Backlash against Civil Society in the Wake of the Long War on Terror," *Development in Practice*, 18/1, 82–93.

Ignatieff, M. (2001). *Human Rights as Politics and Idolatry* (Princeton, NJ: Princeton University Press).

Ignatieff, M. (2002a). "Is the Human Rights Era Ending?" *New York Times*, February 5, 2002, A25.

Ignatieff, M. (2002b). "No Exceptions? The United States' Pick-and-Choose Approach to Human Rights is Hypocritical. But That's Not a Good Reason to Condemn It," *Legal Affairs*.

Joachim, J. (2007). *Agenda Setting, the UN, and NGOs. Gender Violence and Reproductive Rights* (Washington, DC: Georgetown University Press).

Jordan, L., and Tuijl, P. van (2000). "Political Responsibility in Transnational NGO Advocacy," *World Development* 28/12, 2051–65.

Keck, M. E. and Sikkink, K. (1998). *Activists beyond Borders: Advocacy Networks in International Politics* (Ithaca, NY: Cornell University Press).

Kennedy, D. (2004). *The Dark Sides of Virtue. Reassessing International Humanitarianism* (Princeton, NJ: Princeton University Press).

Khagram, S., Riker, J. V., and Sikkink, K. (2002). *Restructuring World Politics: Transnational Social Movements. Networks and Norms* (Minneapolis, MN: University of Minnesota Press).

Klein, N. (2003). "Bush to Ngos: Watch Your Mouths," *Globe and Mail*, June 24, 2003.

Korey, W. (1998). *NGOs and the Universal Declaration of Human Rights. A Curious Grapevine* (Houndmills/Basingstoke: Macmillan).

Leebaw, B. (2007). "The Politics of Impartial Activism. Humanitarianism and Human Rights," *Perspectives on Politics*, 5/2, 223-39.

Lindenberg, M., and Bryant, C. (2001). *Going Global: Transforming Relief and Development NGOs* (Bloomfield, CT: Kumarian Press).

Martens, K. (2005). *NGOs and the United Nations: Institutionalization, Professionalization and Adaptation* (Houndmills/Basingstoke: Palgrave Macmillan).

Nelson, P. J. (2000). "Heroism and Ambiguity. NGO Advocacy in International Policy," *Development in Practice*, 10/3-4, 478-90.

O'Brien, P. (2004). "Politicized Humanitarianism: A Response to Nicholas de Torrente," *Harvard Human Rights Journal*, 17, 31-40.

Oestreich, J. E. (2007). *Power and Principle. Human Rights Programming in International Organizations* (Washington, DC: Georgetown University Press).

Price, R. (1998). "Reversing the Gun Sights: Transnational Civil Society Targets Land Mines," *International Organization*, 52/3, 613-44.

Rieff, D. (1999). "The Precarious Triumph of Human Rights," *New York Times*, August 8, 1999. 36-41.

Rieff, D. (2002). *A Bed for the Night. Humanitarianism in Crisis* (New York: Simon and Schuster).

Rodio, E. B. and Schmitz, H. P. (2010). "Beyond Norms and Interests: Understanding the Evolution of Transnational Human Rights Activism," *The International Journal of Human Rights*, 14/3, 442-59.

Rugendyke, B. (2007). *NGOs as Advocates for Development in a Globalizing World* (New York: Routledge).

Shestack, J. J. (1978). "Sisyphus Endures: The International Human Rights NGO," *New York Law School Law Review*, 24/1, 89-123.

Sidel, M. (2008). "Counter-terrorism and the Enabling Legal and Political Environment for Civil Society: A Comparative Analysis of 'War on Terror' States," *The International Journal of Not-for-Profit Law*, 10/3, 7-49.

Simmons, B. A. (2009). *Mobilizing for Human Rights. International Law and Domestic Politics* (Cambridge: Cambridge University Press).

Spees, P. (2003). "Women's Advocacy in the Creation of the International Criminal Court: Changing the Landscapes of Justice and Power," *Signs: Journal of Women in Culture and Society*, 28/4, 1233-54.

Sunga, L. S. (2007). "Dilemmas Facing NGOs in Coalition-Occupied Iraq," in Bell, D.A. and Coicaud, J. M. (eds), *Ethics in Action. The Ethical Challenges of International Human Rights Non-Governmental Organizations* (Cambridge: Cambridge University Press), 99-116.

Tarrow, S. (2005). *The New Transnational Activism* (Cambridge: Cambridge University Press).

Terry, F. (2002). *Condemned to Repeat? The Paradox of Humanitarian Action* (Ithaca, NY: Cornell University Press).

*Hans Peter Schmitz is associate professor of political science and co-director of the Syracuse University's Transnational NGO Initiative.

APPENDIXES

Appendix 1:

Key Anti-Terror Laws and Cases Affecting Human Rights

USA-PATRIOT ACT (2001)

An act expanding government jurisdiction in an effort to impede, prevent, and punish any subsequent terrorist activity. Later, the Patriot Act redefined the meaning of domestic terrorism and reinstated new penalties for entities in violation of U.S. criminal law addressing terrorism. The act extended the use of security measures for combating terrorist attacks by providing for more stringent law enforcement and increased funding for FBI agencies involved in intelligence investigations. The act permitted heightened surveillance procedures, including wiretapping, searches, seizure of communications systems, interception of voice mails, and "sneak and peak" warrants; it also allowed government agencies to exercise full authority in obtaining information from U.S. and non-U.S. citizens suspected of terrorism and fraudulent action. The act provided amendments to the Money Laundering Control Act of 1986 by proposing subsequent measures for the exposure, elimination, and legal prosecution of monetary transactions, money laundering, or international financing of any activity threatening the stability of the nation. Some of the other measures introduced by the Patriot Act included an increase in border patrol security and enforcement of obligatory detention and deportation laws for immigrants and non-U.S. citizens.

TIPS (TERRORIST INFORMATION AND PREVENTION SYSTEM) (2002)

A type of surveillance or information-gathering network—to be a part of the U.S. War on Terror measures—designed to recruit domestic citizens and workers with access to civilians' homes or employed in local businesses to gather information and report any type of suspicious or fraudulent activity. This intelligence program was intended to utilize individuals (usually cable repair, mail services personnel, or truck drivers) as informants to detect any irregular behavior that might be linked to coercive actions or terrorism threatening the nation's stability.

THE BYBEE MEMO (2002)

One of the three legal memorandums (also known as the Torture Memos) that established the framework for the use of torture techniques by the U.S. government with prisoners in Afghanistan, Iraq, and Guantanamo Bay; these memorandums raised the legal standards for employing severe interrogation procedures during the War on Terror. The Bybee Memo (signed by Assistant Attorney General Jay S. Bybee, Head of the Office of Legal Counsel in the U.S. Department of Justice) asserted that torture techniques such as waterboarding, sleep deprivation, hypothermia, and other physical and mental coercion of prisoners might be lawfully permitted in the War on Terror under the discretion and authority of the U.S. president.

HOMELAND SECURITY ACT (2002)

An act establishing the Department of Homeland Security and the subsequent position of Secretary of Homeland Security in a direct response to the terrorist attacks of 9/11. The act set the groundwork for the Department of Homeland Security to protect the stability and integrity of the nation from possible terrorist threats and to take preemptive measures to preserve the safety of the American people.

DOMESTIC SECURITY ENHANCEMENT ACT (PROPOSED 2003)

Anti-terrorism draft legislation (also known as the Patriot Act II) proposed by the U.S. Department of Justice; it expanded government powers to conduct extensive surveillance, searches, and wiretapping of U.S. citizens while suspending some aspects of the checks and balances system. The Act increased government secrecy, reduced personal privacy, and dismissed government accountability in the name of fighting terrorism. The draft did not reach a congressional debate.

RASUL VS BUSH (2004)

A case in which the Supreme Court held that U.S. courts possess the authority to consider and decide on the legal petitions of foreign citizens held in Guantanamo Bay since the United States exercises full command and jurisdiction of the military base. This case established that the right to habeas corpus is not dependent on citizenship status and that any detainee, regardless of nationality or citizenship, has the right to a legal appeal and contestation of his imprisonment.

Hamdi vs Rumsfeld (2004)

A case in which the Supreme Court held that U.S. citizens who are detained by the U.S. government have the right to a due process trial and must be granted the opportunity to contest their confinement and "enemy combatant" status in front of an impartial jury.

Hamdan vs Rumsfeld (2006)

A case in which the Supreme Court established that the military tribunal that originally tried Salim Ahmed Hamdan, a citizen of Yemen who worked as a bodyguard and chauffeur for Osama bin Laden, had not been granted by an act of Congress the authority to conduct that trial; it also established that the military tribunal was in direct violation of U.S. domestic laws and international laws of war, including the Geneva Conventions and the Uniform Code of Military Justice. Hamdan's trial by the military tribunal was deemed to be illegitimate and automatically dismissed.

Military Commissions Act (2006)

An act that handed over absolute power to the U.S. president to bypass the Constitution, declare individuals to be "enemy combatants," determine the period of detention for these specific prisoners, and redefine torture techniques at his discretion. Notably, the act allowed individuals to be found to be enemy combatants with no right to hear the evidence against them. The act undermined the principle of habeas corpus in federal courts and established the form of military commissions that would conduct trials for detainees in Guantanamo Bay. The Supreme Court would subsequently find the act unconstitutional (see *Boumediene vs Bush*, below) because of its extreme restrictions of detainee rights.

Boumediene vs Bush (2008)

A case in which the Supreme Court held that all detainees, including foreign citizens, declared as "enemy combatants" and detained at Guantanamo Bay, have the constitutional right to seek habeas corpus reprieves and challenge their confinement. The Court ruled that detainees are protected under the Geneva Conventions, have the right to invoke the Suspension Clause, and are entitled to exercise their Fifth Amendment right of due process in federal courts.

EXECUTIVE ORDER 13491—ENSURING LAWFUL INTERROGATIONS (2009)

An Order issued by Pres. Barack Obama reaffirming the U.S. government's compliance with international treaties such as the Geneva Conventions and faithful implementation of U.S. domestic laws in the interrogation and detention of prisoners. The Order emphasized humane treatment of all detainees held in U.S. custody and assured the safe and legitimate gathering of intelligence information from prisoners.

HOLDER VS HUMANITARIAN LAW PROJECT (2010)

A case in which the Supreme Court held that the U.S. government possesses the authority to prohibit the provision of nonviolent material and support for terrorist groups—including legal services and counsel—without violating the free speech clause of the First Amendment.

Appendix 2:
Universal Declaration of Human Rights

PREAMBLE

Whereas recognition of the inherent dignity and of the equal and inalienable rights of all members of the human family is the foundation of freedom, justice and peace in the world,

Whereas disregard and contempt for human rights have resulted in barbarous acts which have outraged the conscience of mankind, and the advent of a world in which human beings shall enjoy freedom of speech and belief and freedom from fear and want has been proclaimed as the highest aspiration of the common people,

Whereas it is essential, if man is not to be compelled to have recourse, as a last resort, to rebellion against tyranny and oppression, that human rights should be protected by the rule of law,

Whereas it is essential to promote the development of friendly relations between nations,

Whereas the peoples of the United Nations have in the Charter reaffirmed their faith in fundamental human rights, in the dignity and worth of the human person and in the equal rights of men and women and have determined to promote social progress and better standards of life in larger freedom,

Whereas Member States have pledged themselves to achieve, in co-operation with the United Nations, the promotion of universal respect for and observance of human rights and fundamental freedoms,

Whereas a common understanding of these rights and freedoms is of the greatest importance for the full realization of this pledge,

Now, Therefore THE GENERAL ASSEMBLY proclaims THIS UNIVERSAL DECLARATION OF HUMAN RIGHTS as a common standard of achievement for all peoples and all nations, to the end that every individual and every organ of society, keeping this Declaration constantly in mind, shall strive by teaching and education to promote respect for these rights and freedoms and by progressive measures, national and international, to secure their universal and effective recognition and observance, both among the peoples of Member States themselves and among the peoples of territories under their jurisdiction.

Article 1.

All human beings are born free and equal in dignity and rights. They are endowed with reason and conscience and should act towards one another in a spirit of brotherhood.

Article 2.

Everyone is entitled to all the rights and freedoms set forth in this Declaration, without distinction of any kind, such as race, colour, sex, language, religion, political or other opinion, national or social origin, property, birth or other status. Furthermore, no distinction shall be made on the basis of the political, jurisdictional or international status of the country or territory to which a person belongs, whether it be independent, trust, non-self-governing or under any other limitation of sovereignty.

Article 3.

Everyone has the right to life, liberty and security of person.

Article 4.

No one shall be held in slavery or servitude; slavery and the slave trade shall be prohibited in all their forms.

Article 5.

No one shall be subjected to torture or to cruel, inhuman or degrading treatment or punishment.

Article 6.

Everyone has the right to recognition everywhere as a person before the law.

Article 7.

All are equal before the law and are entitled without any discrimination to equal protection of the law. All are entitled to equal protection against any discrimination in violation of this Declaration and against any incitement to such discrimination.

Article 8.

Everyone has the right to an effective remedy by the competent national tribunals for acts violating the fundamental rights granted him by the constitution or by law.

Article 9.

No one shall be subjected to arbitrary arrest, detention or exile.

Article 10.

Everyone is entitled in full equality to a fair and public hearing by an independent and impartial tribunal, in the determination of his rights and obligations and of any criminal charge against him.

Article 11.

(1) Everyone charged with a penal offence has the right to be presumed innocent until proved guilty according to law in a public trial at which he has had all the guarantees necessary for his defence.

(2) No one shall be held guilty of any penal offence on account of any act or omission which did not constitute a penal offence, under national or international law, at the time when it was committed. Nor shall a heavier penalty be imposed than the one that was applicable at the time the penal offence was committed.

Article 12.

No one shall be subjected to arbitrary interference with his privacy, family, home or correspondence, nor to attacks upon his honour and reputation. Everyone has the right to the protection of the law against such interference or attacks.

Article 13.

(1) Everyone has the right to freedom of movement and residence within the borders of each state.

(2) Everyone has the right to leave any country, including his own, and to return to his country.

Article 14.

(1) Everyone has the right to seek and to enjoy in other countries asylum from persecution.

(2) This right may not be invoked in the case of prosecutions genuinely arising from non-political crimes or from acts contrary to the purposes and principles of the United Nations.

Article 15.

(1) Everyone has the right to a nationality.

(2) No one shall be arbitrarily deprived of his nationality nor denied the right to change his nationality.

Article 16.

(1) Men and women of full age, without any limitation due to race, nationality or religion, have the right to marry and to found a family. They are entitled to equal rights as to marriage, during marriage and at its dissolution.

(2) Marriage shall be entered into only with the free and full consent of the intending spouses.

(3) The family is the natural and fundamental group unit of society and is entitled to protection by society and the State.

Article 17.

(1) Everyone has the right to own property alone as well as in association with others.

(2) No one shall be arbitrarily deprived of his property.

Article 18.

Everyone has the right to freedom of thought, conscience and religion; this right includes freedom to change his religion or belief, and freedom, either alone or in community with others and in public or private, to manifest his religion or belief in teaching, practice, worship and observance.

Article 19.

Everyone has the right to freedom of opinion and expression; this right includes freedom to hold opinions without interference and to seek, receive and impart information and ideas through any media and regardless of frontiers.

Article 20.

(1) Everyone has the right to freedom of peaceful assembly and association.

(2) No one may be compelled to belong to an association.

Article 21.

(1) Everyone has the right to take part in the government of his country, directly or through freely chosen representatives.

(2) Everyone has the right of equal access to public service in his country.

(3) The will of the people shall be the basis of the authority of government; this will shall be expressed in periodic and genuine elections which shall be by universal and equal suffrage and shall be held by secret vote or by equivalent free voting procedures.

Article 22.

Everyone, as a member of society, has the right to social security and is entitled to realization, through national effort and international co-operation and in accordance with the organization and resources of each State, of the economic, social and cultural rights indispensable for his dignity and the free development of his personality.

Article 23.

(1) Everyone has the right to work, to free choice of employment, to just and favourable conditions of work and to protection against unemployment.

(2) Everyone, without any discrimination, has the right to equal pay for equal work.

(3) Everyone who works has the right to just and favourable remuneration ensuring for himself and his family an existence worthy of human dignity, and supplemented, if necessary, by other means of social protection.

(4) Everyone has the right to form and to join trade unions for the protection of his interests.

Article 24.

Everyone has the right to rest and leisure, including reasonable limitation of working hours and periodic holidays with pay.

Article 25.

(1) Everyone has the right to a standard of living adequate for the health and well-being of himself and of his family, including food, clothing, housing and medical care and necessary social services, and the right to security in the event of unemployment, sickness, disability, widowhood, old age or other lack of livelihood in circumstances beyond his control.

(2) Motherhood and childhood are entitled to special care and assistance. All children, whether born in or out of wedlock, shall enjoy the same social protection.

Article 26.

(1) Everyone has the right to education. Education shall be free, at least in the elementary and fundamental stages. Elementary education shall be compulsory. Technical and professional education shall be made generally available and higher education shall be equally accessible to all on the basis of merit.

(2) Education shall be directed to the full development of the human personality and to the strengthening of respect for human rights and fundamental freedoms. It shall promote understanding, tolerance and friendship among all nations, racial or religious groups, and shall further the activities of the United Nations for the maintenance of peace.

(3) Parents have a prior right to choose the kind of education that shall be given to their children.

Article 27.

(1) Everyone has the right freely to participate in the cultural life of the community, to enjoy the arts and to share in scientific advancement and its benefits.

(2) Everyone has the right to the protection of the moral and material interests resulting from any scientific, literary or artistic production of which he is the author.

Article 28.

Everyone is entitled to a social and international order in which the rights and freedoms set forth in this Declaration can be fully realized.

Article 29.

(1) Everyone has duties to the community in which alone the free and full development of his personality is possible.

(2) In the exercise of his rights and freedoms, everyone shall be subject only to such limitations as are determined by law solely for the purpose of securing due recognition and respect for the rights and freedoms of others and of meeting the just requirements of morality, public order and the general welfare in a democratic society.

(3) These rights and freedoms may in no case be exercised contrary to the purposes and principles of the United Nations.

Article 30.

Nothing in this Declaration may be interpreted as implying for any State, group or person any right to engage in any activity or to perform any act aimed at the destruction of any of the rights and freedoms set forth herein.

Source: available at http://www.ohchr.org/EN/UDHR/Documents/UDHR_Translations/eng.pdf.

Appendix 3:

Report of The Constitution Project's Task Force on Detainee Treatment

Statement of the Task Force

April 2013

This report of The Constitution Project's Task Force on Detainee Treatment is the result of almost two years of intensive study, investigation and deliberation.

The project was undertaken with the belief that it was important to provide an accurate and authoritative account of how the United States treated people its forces held in custody as the nation mobilized to deal with a global terrorist threat.

The events examined in this report are unprecedented in U.S. history. In the course of the nation's many previous conflicts, there is little doubt that some U.S. personnel committed brutal acts against captives, as have armies and governments throughout history.

But there is no evidence there had ever before been the kind of considered and detailed discussions that occurred after September 11, directly involving a president and his top advisers on the wisdom, propriety and legality of inflicting pain and torment on some detainees in our custody.

Despite this extraordinary aspect, the Obama administration declined, as a matter of policy, to undertake or commission an official study of what happened, saying it was unproductive to "look backwards" rather than forward.

In Congress, Sen. Patrick J. Leahy of Vermont introduced legislation to establish a "Truth Commission" to look into the U.S. behavior in the years following the September 11 attacks. The concept, successful in South Africa, Guatemala and several other countries, is predicated on recognizing the paramount value to a nation of an accurate accounting of its history, especially in the aftermath of an extraordinary episode or period of crisis. But as at the White House, Congress showed little appetite for delving into the past.

These responses were dismaying to the many people who believed it was important for a great democracy like the United States to help its citizens understand, albeit with appropriate limits for legitimate security concerns, what had been done in their name.

Our report rests, in part, on the belief that all societies behave differently under stress; at those times, they may even take actions that conflict with their essential character and values. American history has its share of such episodes, like the internment of Japanese-Americans during World War II, that may have seemed widely acceptable at the time they occurred, but years later are viewed in a starkly different light. What was once generally taken to be understandable and justifiable behavior can later become a case of historical regret.

Task Force members believe that having as thorough as possible an understanding of what occurred during this period of serious threat—and a willingness to acknowledge any shortcomings—strengthens the nation, and equips us to better cope with the next crisis and ones after that. Moving on without such a reckoning weakens our ability to claim our place as an exemplary practitioner of the rule of law.

In the absence of government action or initiative, The Constitution Project, a nonpartisan public-interest organization devoted to the rule of law principle, set out to address this situation. It gathered a Task Force of experienced former officials who had worked at the highest levels of the judiciary, Congress, the diplomatic service, law enforcement, the military, and parts of the executive branch. Recognized experts in law, medicine and ethical behavior were added to the group to help ensure a serious and fair examination of how detention policies came to be made and implemented.

The Task Force members include Democrats and Republicans; those who are thought to be conservatives and those thought to be liberals; people with experience in and sensitivity to national security issues and those who have an understanding that the government's reach and authority is subject to both tradition and law to appropriate limits. The Task Force members also were able to bring to the project a keen collective understanding of how government decisions are made.

Although the report covers actions taken during three different administrations beginning with that of President Bill Clinton and ending with that of President Barack Obama, most of the activity studied here occurred during the administration of President George W. Bush. This is unavoidable as Bush was president when the horrific attacks on U.S. soil occurred on September 11, 2001, and thus had the burden of responding quickly and decisively to the situation.

While the report deals largely with the period of the Bush administration's response to the attacks, the investigation was neither a partisan undertaking nor should its conclusions be taken as anything other than an effort to understand what happened at many levels of U.S. policymaking.

There is no way of knowing how the government would have responded if a Democratic administration were in power at the time of the September 11 attacks and had to bear the same responsibilities. Indeed, one of the controversial methods examined here—capture and rendition of terror suspects to foreign governments known to abuse people in their custody—had its first significant use during the Clinton administration, well before September 11.

Any effort to understand how extraordinary decisions were reached on approving harsh treatment of detainees must begin with a recognition of the extraordinary anxiety that enveloped the nation after September 11. The greatest fears of Americans and their leaders in that period were of further attacks from those who had demonstrated that they were capable of wreaking havoc in New York and Washington. The abstract problems that might come with unchecked executive power were not a priority or an immediate concern for most Americans inside and outside of government.

Those already-intense anxieties were further stoked by the anthrax scares that played out in the following months.

Philip D. Zelikow, a historian at the University of Virginia who served as counselor in the State Department during the Bush administration and as executive director of the 9/11 Commission, said that following the collective national trauma of the attacks, "Officials tried to do everything they could think of, improvising frantically, making many mistakes while getting some things right."

These officials were guided by a simple and compelling mandate from the president that was, by itself, worthy—but may have affected the way some decisions were made. President Bush's order was to do whatever was necessary to prevent another such attack.

Task Force members generally understand that those officials whose decisions and actions may have contributed to charges of abuse, with harmful consequences for the United States' standing in the world, undertook those measures as their best efforts to protect their fellow citizens.

Task Force members also believe, however, that those good intentions did not relieve them of their obligations to comply with existing treaties and laws. The need to respect legal and moral codes designed to maintain minimum standards of human rights is especially great in times of crisis.

It is encouraging to note that when misguided policies were implemented in an excess of zeal or emotion, there was sometimes a cadre of officials who raised their voices in dissent, however unavailing those efforts.

Perhaps the most important or notable finding of this panel is that it is indisputable that the United States engaged in the practice of torture.

This finding, offered without reservation, is not based on any impressionistic approach to the issue. No member of the Task Force made this decision because the techniques "seemed like torture to me," or "I would regard that as torture."

Instead, this conclusion is grounded in a thorough and detailed examination of what constitutes torture in many contexts, notably historical and legal. The Task Force examined court cases in which torture was deemed to have occurred both inside and outside the country and, tellingly, in instances in which the United States has leveled the charge of torture against other governments. The United States may not declare a nation guilty of engaging in torture and then exempt itself from being so labeled for similar if not identical conduct.

The extensive research that led to the conclusion that the United States engaged in torture is contained in a detailed legal memorandum attached to this report. It should be noted that the conclusion that torture was used means it occurred in many instances and across a wide range of theaters. This judgment is not restricted to or dependent on the three cases in which detainees of the CIA were subjected to waterboarding, which had been approved at the highest levels.

The question as to whether U.S. forces and agents engaged in torture has been complicated by the existence of two vocal camps in the public debate. This has been particularly vexing for traditional journalists who are trained and accustomed to recording the arguments of both sides in a dispute without declaring one right and the other wrong. The public may simply perceive that there is no right side, as there are two equally fervent views held on a subject, with substantially credentialed people on both sides. In this case, the problem is exacerbated by the fact that among those who insist that the United States did not engage in torture are figures who served at the highest levels of government, including Vice President Dick Cheney.

But this Task Force is not bound by this convention.

The members, coming from a wide political spectrum, believe that arguments that the nation did not engage in torture and that much of what occurred should be defined as something less than torture are not credible.

The second notable conclusion of the Task Force is that the nation's highest officials bear some responsibility for allowing and contributing to the spread of torture.

The evidence for this finding about responsibility is contained throughout the report, but it is distilled in a detailed memo showing the widespread responsibility for torture among civilian and military leaders. [See Appendix 2] The most important element may have been to declare that the Geneva Conventions, a venerable instrument for ensuring humane treatment in time of war, did not apply to Al Qaeda and Taliban captives in Afghanistan or Guantánamo. The administration never specified what rules would apply instead.

The other major factor was President Bush's authorization of brutal techniques by the CIA for selected detainees.

The CIA also created its own detention and interrogation facilities—at several locations in Afghanistan, and even more secretive "black sites" in Thailand, Poland, Romania and Lithuania, where the highest value captives were interrogated.

The consequence of these official actions and statements are now clear: many lower-level troops said they believed that "the gloves were off" regarding treatment of prisoners. By the end of 2002, at Bagram Air Base in Afghanistan, interrogators began routinely depriving detainees of sleep by means of shackling them to the ceiling. Secretary of Defense Donald Rumsfeld later approved interrogation techniques in Guantánamo that included sleep deprivation, stress positions, nudity, sensory deprivation and threatening detainees with dogs. Many of the same techniques were later used in Iraq.

Much of the torture that occurred in Guantánamo, Afghanistan and Iraq was never explicitly authorized. But the authorization of the CIA's techniques depended on setting aside the traditional legal rules that protected captives. And as retired Marine generals Charles Krulak and Joseph Hoar have said, "any degree of 'flexibility' about torture at the top drops down the chain of command like a stone—the rare exception fast becoming the rule."

The scope of this study encompasses a vast amount of information, analysis and events; geographically speaking, much of the activity studied occurred in three locations outside the continental United States, two of them war zones. Fact-finding was conducted on the ground in all three places—Iraq, Afghanistan, and Guantánamo Bay, Cuba—by Task Force staff. Task Force members were directly involved in some of the information-gathering phase of the investigation, traveling abroad to meet former detainees and foreign officials to discuss the U.S. program of rendition.

As the Task Force is a nongovernmental body with no authority in law, the investigation proceeded without the advantages of subpoena power or the obligation of the government to provide access to classified information.

Nonetheless, there is an enormous amount of information already developed and Task Force staff and members have interviewed dozens of people over the course of the past few months; the passage of time seems to have made some people more willing to speak candidly about events.

The Task Force and its staff have surveyed the vast number of reports on the subject generated by the government, news media, independent writers and nongovernmental organizations, some more credible than others. The Task Force has attempted to assess the credibility of the many assertions of brutal treatment as far as possible. For example, accounts by former detainees, either previously reported or in interviews with Task Force staff, may be measured against the accounts of interrogators and guards who now speak more openly than they did at the time—or against such credible reports as those provided by the International Committee of the Red Cross (ICRC) and the Senate Armed Services Committee, both of which had access to confidential information not available to the public.

The architects of the detention and interrogation regimes sought and were given crucial support from people in the medical and legal fields. This implicated profound ethical questions for both professions and this report attempts to address those issues.

Apart from the ethical aspects, there were significant, even crucial mistakes made by both legal and medical advisers at the highest levels.

On the medical side, policymakers eagerly accepted a proposal presented by a small group of behavioral psychologists to use the Survival, Evasion, Resistance and Escape program (SERE) as the basis to fashion a harsh interrogation regime for people captured in the new war against terrorism.

The use of the SERE program was a single example of flawed decision-making at many levels—with serious consequences. The SERE program was developed to help U.S. troops resist interrogation techniques that had been used to extract false confessions from downed U.S. airmen during the Korean War. Its promoters had no experience in interrogation, the ability to extract truthful and usable information from captives.

Lawyers in the Justice Department provided legal guidance, in the aftermath of the attacks, that seemed to go to great lengths to allow treatment that amounted to torture. To deal with the regime of laws and treaties designed to prohibit and prevent torture, the lawyers provided novel, if not acrobatic interpretations to allow the mistreatment of prisoners.

Those early memoranda that defined torture narrowly would engender widespread and withering criticism once they became public. The successors of those government lawyers would eventually move to overturn those legal memoranda. Even though the initial memoranda were disowned, the memorable language—limiting the definition of torture to those acts that might implicate organ failure—remain a stain on the image of the United States, and the memos are a potential aid to repressive regimes elsewhere when they seek approval or justification for their own acts.

The early legal opinions had something in common with the advice from psychologists about how to manipulate detainees during interrogation: they both seemed to be aimed primarily at giving the client—in this case, administration officials—what they wanted to hear. Information or arguments that contravened the advice were ignored, minimized or suppressed.

The Task Force report also includes important new details of the astonishing account—first uncovered by Human Rights Watch—of how some U.S. authorities used the machinery of the "war on terror" to abuse a handful of Libyan Islamists involved in a national struggle against Libyan dictator Muammar el-Gaddafi, in an effort to win favor with el-Gaddafi's regime. The same Libyans suddenly became allies as they fought with NATO to topple el-Gaddafi a few short years later.

Task Force staff also learned that procedures in place in Afghanistan to evaluate prisoners for release are not as independent as they have been presented. Decisions of review boards, in some cases, are subject to review by a Pentagon agency that often consults with members of Congress as to whether to release prisoners from Bagram.

Stepping back from the close-quarters study of detention policies, some significant, historical themes may be discerned. The first is a striking example of the interplay of checks and balances in our system, in which the three branches of government can be seen, understandably, to move at different speeds in responding to a crisis. Following the September 11 attacks, the immediate responsibility for action fell appropriately on the executive branch, which has direct control of the vast machinery of the government. It encompasses not only the nation's military might but the president himself as the embodiment of the nation's leadership and thus the individual best positioned to articulate the nation's anger, grief and considered response.

The other branches of government had little impact in the early years on the policies put in place by the Bush administration. The judiciary, the "least-dangerous branch" as noted by Alexander Hamilton in the Federalist Papers, is designed to be more deliberate in its involvement; courts cannot constitutionally pronounce on policies until they are presented with a "case or controversy" on which they may render judgments. Thus, in those first few years, the executive branch was essentially unimpeded in its actions in regard to treatment of detainees.

That would change. When cases involving U.S. detention policies slowly made their way into the judicial system, a handful of judges began to push back against administration actions. Decisions ultimately handed down by the Supreme Court overturned some of the basic premises of the administration in establishing its detention regime. Officials had counted on courts accepting that the U.S. Naval base at Guantánamo, Cuba, was outside the legal jurisdiction of the United States. As such, the officials also reasoned that detainees there would have no access to the right of *habeas corpus*, that is, the ability to petition courts to investigate and judge the sufficiency of reasons for detention.

The Supreme Court upset both assumptions.

But the limits of judicial authority soon became evident. As various judges issued rulings based on the Supreme Court pronouncements, both the courts and the administration engaged warily. While often in direct disagreement, both judges and executive branch officials seemed to be always sensitive to the potential for constitutional confrontation and sought to avoid outright conflict. Courts, ever anxious about the possibility of defiance undermining their authority, generally allowed the administration to delay action. The administration, for its part, often worked to make cases moot, sometimes even freeing prisoners who were the subject of litigation, even though officials had once described those very detainees as highly dangerous.

Congress proved even slower than the courts to take any action that would create a confrontation with the White House. That would change, however, with the election of President Obama.

Another evident trend is that the detention policies of the Bush administration may be, in a loose sense, divided into two different periods. The aggressive "forward-leaning" approach in the early years changed, notably beginning in the period for 2005 to 2006. There were, no doubt, many reasons for this, probably including the limited pushback of the courts.

A full explanation of how the aggressiveness of the detention policies was altered in this period would involve an examination of the apparent changes in the thinking of President Bush, a difficult task and generally beyond the scope of this report. One factor, however, was certainly the disclosure of the atrocities at Abu Ghraib in 2004 and the ensuing condemnation both at home and abroad accompanied by feelings of—and there is no better word for it—shame among Americans, who rightly hold higher expectations of the men and women we send to war.

Over the course of this study, it became ever more apparent that the disclosures about Abu Ghraib had an enormous impact on policy. The public revulsion as to those disclosures contributed to a change in direction on many fronts; those in the government who had argued there was a need for extraordinary measures to protect the nation soon saw the initiative shift to those who objected to harsh tactics. Task Force investigators and members believe it is difficult to overstate the effect of the Abu Ghraib disclosures on the direction of U.S. policies on detainee treatment.

The Task Force also believes there may have been another opportunity to effect a shift in momentum that was lost. That involved an internal debate at the highest levels of the ICRC as to how aggressive the Geneva-based group should be with U.S. policymakers. The ICRC, by tradition, does not speak publicly about what its people learn about detention situations. But some officials were so offended by their discoveries at Guantánamo that they argued the group had to be more forceful in confronting the Defense Department. This report details for the first time some of the debate inside the ICRC over that issue.

In the end, the top leadership of the ICRC decided against confrontation and a valuable opportunity may have been missed.

Another observation is that President Obama came to quickly discover that his promised sweeping reform of the detention regime could not be so easily implemented. A major reason for this was that Congress, when finally engaged in the issue, resisted. The opposition to President Obama's plans was sometimes bipartisan, notably to those proposals to close Guantánamo and bring some of the detainees onto U.S. soil for trial. Many believe President Obama and his aides did not move swiftly enough, thus allowing opposition to build in Congress.

This report is aimed, in part, at learning from errors and improving detention and interrogation policies in the future. At the time of this writing, the United States is still detaining people it regards as dangerous. But in some instances the treatment of supposed high-value foes has been transformed in significant ways.

The U.S. military, learning from its experience, has vastly improved its procedures for screening captives and no longer engages in large-scale coercive interrogation techniques. Just as importantly, the regime of capture and detention has been overtaken by technology and supplanted in large measure by the use of drones. If presumed enemy leaders—high-value targets—are killed outright by drones, the troublesome issues of how to conduct detention and interrogation operations are minimized and may even become moot.

The appropriateness of the United States using drones, however, will continue to be the subject of significant debate—indeed, it was recently the subject of the ninth-longest filibuster in U.S. history—and will probably not completely eliminate traditional combat methods in counter- terror and counter-insurgency operations in the foreseeable future. As we have seen, any combat situation can generate prisoners and the problems associated with their detention and interrogation. As 2012 ended, the U.S. military was believed to still be taking in about 100 new prisoners each month at the Bagram detention facility in Afghanistan, most of them seized in night raids around the country. But interviews by Task Force staff with recent prisoners appear to show a stark change in their treatment from the harsh methods used in the early years of U.S. involvement in Afghanistan.

While authoritative as far as it goes, this report should not be the final word on how events played out in the detention and interrogation arena.

The members of the Task Force believe there may be more to be learned, perhaps from renewed interest in the executive or legislative branches of our government, which can bring to bear tools unavailable to this investigation— namely subpoena power to compel testimony and the capability to review classified materials.

Even though the story might not yet be complete, the Task Force has developed a number of recommendations to change how the nation goes about the business of detaining people in a national-security context, and they are included in this report. We hope the executive and legislative branches give them careful consideration.

Source: The Constitution Project. *The Report of The Constitution Project's Task Force on Detainee Treatment.* Washington, DC: The Constitution Project, 2012: 1–8.